A Faith Expressed

Helene R. Hill

Celo Valley Books
Burnsville, North Carolina

Published by:
Celo Valley Books
160 Ohle Road
Burnsville, North Carolina 28714

Books may be ordered by sending
$20.00 plus $5.00 tax/shipping to:
Ms. Helene R. Hill
266 Merrimon Avenue
Asheville, NC 28801

All illustrations are courtesy of Naomi Ruth Gleason Wray.

ISBN 0-923687-69-6
978-0-923687-69-4
Library of Congress Catalog Card Number 2006921806

Illustration copyright © 2006 by Naomi Ruth Gleason Wray
Text copyright © 2006 by Helene R. Hill
All rights reserved.
Printed in the United States of America

No part of this book may be reproduced or transmitted in any form or by any means, electronic or mechanical, including photo-copying, recording, or by any information storage and retrieval system, without the written permission of the publisher, except where permitted by law. Reviewers may quote if they give the title, author, and publisher of this work in the article or review.

*Dedicated to many wonderful women
—and many good men!—
who often, in unknown ways, have helped to shape my life
and give me help along the journey to a beautiful life with God,
as I have moved through the years.
I cannot begin to name them all.*

*Also dedicated posthumously to
Dr. Ruth E. Decker,
mentor and teacher,
who loved God incredibly,
and pointed me in the right direction
to do the same.*

Contents

Preface	xi
Abbreviations	xix
Aspects of Faith	1
You Are an Image of God	3
Can We Not Trust God?	5
Joy in People	8
How Similar Are Islam and Christianity?	11
Abundant Grapes	13
Unconditional Love	15
Do You Believe?	17
The Prophet Amos	19
The Bible as Midrash	23
Risk Taking	27
We Can Kill Giants	30
Eve	33
What's in a Cracked Pot?	36
The Return of Tears	38
Notes	41
Thoughts About God	43
When You Say "God," What Do You Mean?	45
God Is Love—No Matter What!	49
The Holy	51
How Big Is Your God?	53
God's Surprises	56
God Is a Spendthrift	59
An Amazingly Creative and Changing God	63

God Will Never Wear Out	66
Is God Monarch or Lover?	69
God Is a Verb	72
Nonsexist Names, Titles, Phrases, Applied to God	75
Notes	79

God's Reflection in Our Natural World 81

Heaven Is Under Our Feet	83
Epiphany	85
Recent Trip to the North	87
Honoring Trees	90
Lawns	94
Wonderful Sand	97
Christmas Mail	100
Notes	102

Reflecting God to Others 103

I Am Who I Am	105
You Are Loved	109
Jubilee! Community Church	111
We're All in This Boat Together!	113
Different, Yet One!	116
There Is Only One You	119
Put the Big Rocks in First!	121
Connections	123
Let Us Honor Our Bodies	126
Keep the Main Thing the Main Thing	129
Life Is Give and Take	131
Dancing Sarah's Circle	134
A Moment of Grace	137
Being Present to the Moment	140
Giving	143
Diversity	147
Racism	150
Notes	152

Outreach in Our World 155
  God So Loved the World—Then and Now 157
  Bumper Stickers 161
  Soup – Soup – Soup – Soup 164
  Salt Shakers? 168
  Compassion 170
  Is This the Home for Unwed Mothers? 174
  O World, I Cannot Hold Thee Close Enough . . . 177
  Human Needs and Mission Projects 181
  Hospital Visit 185
  Neighborhood Center 188
  Our Christian Faith Means Doing Justice 192
  Visit to Neighborhood Center 195
  God Bless! 198
  Be Grateful to Everyone 201
  Thank You, Deaconesses, for Your Good Work . . 204
  Housing Is Basic to Decent Life 207
  Life-giving Center 211
  A Place to Live 213
  Elderly Irish in Boston 216
  Missions in Nepal 219
  Nicaragua 222
  Nicaragua Experiences 225
  Hurricane Mitch 229
  Who Remembers the Poor? 232
  Missionary Letter 235
  Child Labor in Southeast Asia 239
  Arise, Shine, for Your Light Has Come 242
  We're All God's Children 247
  Prison Visit 250
  The Death Penalty 254
  Notes 256

About Getting Older 259
  Gratefully Aging 261

Getting Old	264
Facing Death	266
Notes	267

Praise and Thank You 269
   Praise God 271
   Several Prayers 274
   Saying Thank You 277
   Thank You, God! 279
   Thank You, Thank You, Thank You! 281
   Notes 284

Bibliography and Recommended Reading 285
About the Author 289
About the Illustrator 291

Preface

The way this book came about is that I am part of a sometimes fairly small cadre of residents who volunteer for Morning Devotions, a brief meditation each day for the Brooks-Howell community, the retirement community where I live.

The first thing I must say is that this book did not originate from an intention to write a book. The brief pieces that have found their way into these pages were delivered orally at Brooks-Howell. I retained them in a folder just because I am often a "saver." It is important to note, however, that I am often a "disorganized saver." Thus, in many cases, I did not save the "backups" for the quotes from other sources, nor the newsletters from which they came. So, when I decided to collect these oral talks into this book, I found that I had made myself extra work; I needed to seek source information as well as permissions for quoted pieces. This collection of my talks, then, is far from complete. Some pieces are simply not here because there was no backup available; I had cleared my desk and thrown them out. Some others are here but in rewritten (and properly credited) form, to meet space or copyright requirements.

Brooks-Howell Home is a specialized retirement community. It was created particularly for retired deaconesses of the United Methodist Church. The women of our church realized that they (the deaconesses) had traditionally been paid very little for their good work, and would need financial help in retirement. The community was later broadened to include missionaries from overseas (as the church itself reorganized!), and then later, "outreach patients," local people who come into the nursing units at full cost. It is a community of over a hundred residents at any one time. It meets the requirements for nursing homes in the state of North Carolina. A majority of our residents are women, as is the case with older groups everywhere.

These meditations are brief oral pieces, usually using a Scripture passage, a brief message, and a prayer. The criticism has sometimes been made by my listeners that my pieces are too long. Well, when I wrote these thoughts, I was living in an independent apartment at the far end of our complex, probably the farthest away from the central building where we hold our Morning Devotions—and I wanted to make it worth my while to get up early enough to walk that far to deliver these thoughts! Then too, I need to say that I like to talk, and it seems I always have something to say! (The only person who ever told me I have a small mouth is my dentist!)

As I formulated these pieces, I found myself often thinking through my Christian faith as I decided on something to share. I tried to make the connection with the events/activities that seemed to express that faith or that absorbed my concern and prayer at that time. I find it important to make connections between my faith and the world I live in, and my daily involvements. In the process, I found that these brief pieces were unconsciously expressing the faith by which I live. In that sense, this book is a testament of faith—it states where I am in my faith at this time.

Not long ago, a resident friend, Laura Wells, also a deaconess, phoned to express her appreciation for a meditation I had shared, as she sometimes does. Then she suggested that I publish them. My response to her was simply, "Huh!?!?" I finally got the courage to run them by an editor/publisher, a wonderful woman, Diana Donovan. Her response was positive. So I said, "Well, let's do it!" I never realized, when I said yes, what work it would take!

A Bit About the Deaconess

In the year 2000, I received my fifty-year United Methodist Deaconess pin. A deaconess is in some ways like a missionary, but there are differences. A deaconess is always a woman, and always a layperson, not ordained. (She is not, as some mistakenly think "the wife of a deacon.") Deacons relate only to their Annual Conference, but deaconesses relate directly to the national body of the United Methodist Church. She is commissioned by a bishop at the national level of our church body, to work under the appointment of a bishop in the local conference. She can work throughout the United States or its possessions in any church-related vocation. In more recent years, that scope has been widened to include generally, any socially aware ministries, any "helping human ministry." Some of these tasks are on the cutting edge of our church's ministry, or in tasks such as school social work, teaching, (all kinds of teaching!!), health and healing ministries, and a wide variety of ecumenical human concerns. Among our active deaconesses today, one works in a small, isolated, indigenous Alaskan village, another is a college professor for nursing students, another a professor in a small Catholic college, a kindergarten teacher, an editor, an administrator at the national level of our church, a skilled midwife/professor. These are intelligent women, with good educations and widely varying experience, who bear a concern for the health of our church in its ongoing ministry to people in need.

Our latest brochure speaks of our "alleviating suffering, eradicating causes of injustice and all that robs life of dignity and worth, making possible the development of human potential, and sharing in building the global community through the church universal." Deaconesses generally accept the mandate of the Women's Division of the church, which means they work essentially with women and children. That's a wide scope and a big job!

There is an impression in some areas of our church life that deaconesses are a "thing of the past." Some will tell you that since it is now possible for women to be ordained, deaconesses no longer exist because this lay ministry is no longer needed. That seems often to be the perception of the ordained ministry, but it is not so! The ordained ministry is only one part of the church's ministry, not the whole! The deaconess relationship is a lay ministry. Each deaconess seeks her own professional preparation. This is often underwritten by the church in some way. A deaconess is not ordained; she is commissioned by a bishop and appointed yearly, but not as an ordained person. Yes, some serve as pastors. They have sometimes done that in the past, as well as the present, to fill the need for that service. Being a pastor, however, is not the normal service of a deaconess. There were 24 deaconesses commissioned by our church, in April 2004.

My Background

My background is that of a social worker, ACSW (Association of Certified Social Workers) with my master's degree in social welfare from Boston University. I worked for thirty years with the Community Centers Department of what was then the Board of Missions of our church. This body was reorganized some years ago, and is now called the Board of Global Ministries. I worked in six different centers, starting as the Girls' Worker, and moving on to become director (of another agency), and then a consultant. I have lived and worked in fifteen cities, and with many immigrant groups, for it is usually the poor from other countries or minorities who live in what we know as inner cities, where our community centers are located. I have worked with Puerto Ricans, Italians, Cubans, Greek, Syrian, Lebanese, African Americans, Hispanics, and groups of people who are sometimes commonly known as "poor whites." For eleven years before retirement, I worked as a school social worker in a large, rural, consolidated school in southwestern Michigan—primarily a Dutch (and Christian Reformed) community. In this setting I became acquainted with rural poverty, in contrast to the urban poverty settings in which I had previously worked.

As I approached retirement, I realized that I would still have several "good years" physically. I read widely, and did some personal thinking, to see where my interests lay! Two years before retirement, I was fortunate to attend a pre-retirement seminar sponsored by our Deaconess Office. It was one of the finest "conferences" I have ever been a part of. Here I made the decision that I would concentrate on peace issues in retirement. At that time I was reading Helen Caldecott's book *Missile Envy*, and thought that probably I would work in the area of nuclear disarmament. As I read more and listened to the current news, I had the clearest "calling," or sense of direction for my life work that I had ever had. I knew that I must go to Nicaragua to help with their revolution, which had taken place in 1979. I retired in 1986. My experience in Nicaragua, in retirement, opened a vast new aspect of life for me. A new career was born for me, that of peace advocate—a calling with which I continue. It was with my experience in Nicaragua that I made connections on a worldwide basis, and began to see some of the insidious empire-building and newly created colonization (and untimely deaths of the indigenous peoples of our world) that are now seen by so many. Yes, I still must write a book about Nicaragua and my experience there, and since.

I applied to go to Nicaragua as a missionary through my church body. Of course! Why not? I learned that those who choose and/or sanction missionaries are simply not interested in retired people, deaconess or no! I finally understood that retired people are not a good financial investment. There is good support for missionaries, but that was not available to me. So I found a way to live with families, and go anyway. (I lived with three different families, fortunately all in the same barrio in Managua, so that I could continue relationships with all of them.)

I had no transportation, and struggled, with little support from others. I had enough money from my Social Security, but had no other built-in financial or personal support. Soon, however, I became acquainted with the missionaries from our church who were working in the area, as well as with missionaries from other denominations. I depended on them for moral support, and gave them support in return. I grew as a result of this ecumenical experience; it broadened my understanding, and began to shape my life in much wider terms.

When I returned to the United States, I taught again in what the women's body of our church (United Methodist Women) calls our Schools of Mission. I had taught early in my career, and then work became too heavy for me to continue. The Schools of Mission are a summer experience for the women of our church. The program keeps us educated and "on target" with current problems and issues of our world, and provides the scriptural base for same.

At the time of this writing, my church relationship is as follows. I continue to belong to First United Methodist Church in Grand Rapids, Michigan, (West Michigan Conference), but I regularly attend Jubilee! Community Church in Asheville, North Carolina, where I live, here at Brooks-Howell Home. I made the decision, early after my move to Brooks-Howell, not to formally leave West Michigan Conference because I have been so grateful for that relationship. West Michigan Conference has produced two women bishops for leadership in our church. The first was Marjorie Matthews, now deceased, who was a good friend and the first woman bishop in our church body. The second is Sharon Rader, who is also a friend. I continue to value highly my relationship with First United Methodist Church.

I have also found Jubilee! to be a great help in continuing life and witness. While the church itself is not a part of the "connectional ministry" of the United Methodist Church, it is pastored by a very creative man, a United Methodist pastor who is on what is called "extension ministry" from his conference relationship in another region. He too has retained his relationship and connection to the United Methodist Church. Jubilee! attracts people from a wide variety of religious faiths, including many "church drop-outs," many of whom are people who want to find a "more relevant connection between faith and life" than they sometimes find in their more traditional worship bodies.

Jubilee! has a unique way of handling its outreach giving and mission work. It does not give to buildings or to the construction of such, but rather to people. It has its own way of handling requests, and it gives primarily to requests that come to it from the local community. Groups who seek funds make application. Only 501-C-3 agencies are considered. The Outreach Team handles all requests. The application comes before this group, who assign one of our members to "Check it out!" and bring a report about the concern—with a recommendation for funding, or not, or for more or less funding, as the case may be—to the next meeting of the group. The committee takes all approved requests to the board, where they are usually approved for the requested funding. The funds are then given by check as a part of one or another of the three regular Sunday celebrations (services). I find it fascinating, and a good use of my social work/community organization understandings, to serve on this committee or team.

For pleasure and for my own continuing learning, I read widely, and enjoy a variety of books and experiences. One way I have found to be useful is to read and evaluate books for the women of our UMC church. We have a church-wide reading program that keeps us women educated and constantly expanding our understandings of our faith. This reading also builds awareness of our political, economic, and social world, and of the UMC's responses to problems through its widely flung mission program.

After my experience in Nicaragua, where I had found and worked in a Christian base community, I came back to the States wanting—more than anything!—"the book backup" on liberation theology. I was privileged to spend six months as the Georgia Harkness Scholar in Residence at Garrett Evangelical Theological Seminary. I might have spent the entire year, but was already committed to teaching, and so could not spend more than that. At Garrett, I found not only liberation theology, but its sister, feminist theology. The sisterhood of this group of gutsy women is not acknowledged by the Latin American liberal theologians, of course! But it is surely seen as related by women. Feminist theology again sent me off into a continuing lifetime venture with the amazingly insightful women theologians among us. I have come to see, and feel, a growing appreciation and companionship with these good sisters.

For thirty years, until recently, I lived with an informally adopted daughter, a younger woman who was a worker at one of our community centers. Together, we have sheltered a number of young people, many students, having decided early on that we could take students who came to these shores to study. We have thus enriched our own lives with good people from Zimbabwe and Nepal, young Afro-American theologians, and young people from our church body who work on short-term bases in various work projects. What fun!!

A Bit About My Faith

When I was in college, our church history professor, Dr. Ruth Decker, spoke one day, as she understood it, of the basic difference between the Catholic and Protestant faiths. In the

Catholic faith, she said, one works throughout one's lifetime for salvation, through experiences of Mass and other understandings of the faith. In Protestantism, one accepts the salvation of Christ, and moves on from there to put faith into practice in the world in which one lives. That is a very encapsulated, simplified explanation of our differences, but for a lifetime it has satisfied me, and I have sought to put my faith into practice in the situations in which I have lived. It has certainly been a growing experience.

At first, faith did not mean too much. I can remember times when I was not a regular churchgoer, nor have I ever been an avid Bible scholar. I value the Bible very much, but I have been turned off by the misuse of the Bible to "beat people over the head with their sins." That does not send me—nor do I find it helpful for my own growth and well-being. Gradually, I began to see the relevance of faith to life, as I found myself living that faith. I love people, and have learned to care about them in an everyday way. I always seemed to know that I needed more than my own understandings of what life is all about and so I sought whatever help I could find, to nourish that caring and love for others. Interestingly, after several years in the public school situation, where one could not speak directly of God in any way, of one's personal faith, I found myself saying that my faith had grown amazingly—I had to put into practice what I believed about God and his/her relationship to our world without speaking directly of my faith. In other words, conveying to children the love of God without making that connection directly is an amazing way to make one's faith known!

This book is another way I can make my experience of faith known. And so I offer you an aspect of this experience of mine—*A Faith Expressed*.

Abbreviations

ABCCM	Asheville-Buncombe Community Christian Ministry
CDCA	Center for Development in Central America
CEPAD	Council of Evangelical Churches of Nicaragua.
DS	district superintendent
ESV	English Standard Version (of the Bible)
MFSA	Methodist Federation for Social Action, not formally a part of the UMC, but very important in the church, nonetheless. There are chapters in many of the conferences. MFSA keeps our church aware of many social issues. It usually works on a shoestring, money-wise.
MSG	*The Message* (contemporary translation of the Bible by Eugene Peterson)
ND	National Division: National Division of the Board of Global Ministries of the United Methodist Church
NGOs	nongovernmental organizations
NIV	New International Version (of the Bible)
NRSV	New Revised Standard Version (of the Bible)
UMC	United Methodist Church
UMW	United Methodist Women
UNCA	University of North Carolina at Asheville
WD	Women's Division: Women's Division of the Board of Global Ministries of the United Methodist Church

Aspects of Faith

You Are an Image of God

You are a child of God. I am a child of God. How wonderful it is to know that! Each one of us bears the imprint of the wonderful, creative God who made us, who values and respects us, loves and protects and challenges us daily.

During the last several weeks, I have had a very interesting experience. I have been working to put together a program to take place in April, honoring several women for their wonderful work in peace and justice. In the process I have tried to corral bibliographical material about each one of them. To start, I asked each one to write two or three pages on what she had done in peace and justice work. You would not believe how many phone calls I have made, how many pleadings I have issued, how many individual contacts I have made, just to get these essential basic materials from the women themselves.

I have learned again that it is embarrassing to us to brag about ourselves, or to tell others what we have done in good works. Again I recalled the delightful *despedida*—the "going-away party" that was held for me when I left Grand Rapids, Michigan, eight years ago. My pastor and a couple of others pulled together a number of speakers who told about various parts of my life there, and I was roasted and toasted to a fare-thee-well! The evening was full of fun and laughter, with some very embarrassing moments, and some very heartwarming moments as different ones told about parts of my life there that they remembered. Overall, it was a great time for all involved. We really did have a wonderful party. Between each speaker, this good pastor presented me with various awards and trophies, and two or three of these still stand in my home—cherished reminders of a long-to-be-remembered evening. But *yes*, I found it very difficult, as a friend said, "to play that role." I was often embarrassed, to say the least!

But I learned one other thing as I have worked on this upcoming program: It is important for all of us to write down what we have done, to remember it well and to acknowledge it as ours—in order to help others. For many of us, especially those of us whose families have not been the strong supports and "fans," if you will, that we should like for them to be about our work—it is important for ourselves as well. In my own family, because we were widely separated when our mother died, my family has not shared my life. My brother who just died seemed to have no idea, no comprehension, of what was involved in the work I did. That may well be the case for some of you as well. I know that a number of you have already been honored for good work that you have done—and you are the better for that recognition. But, acknowledged by others or not, it gives you an ego boost to note what you have done. We all need to know who we are in all of our creativity and goodness. We need to acknowledge openly that we have done good! And it doesn't hurt to leave notes about it so that others may be encouraged.

We were raised in an era when church doctrine was mostly based on our sense of guilt. That doctrine says that we are never quite good enough, but that every day we have sinned and come short of the glory of God. Yes, we acknowledge that no one is perfect and so we forgive ourselves and others and move on in life. But we need to ask where this doctrine of sin came from, or who it came from, and look closely at how it got so deep into our church's heart and life. We need to look at the damage it has done to our sense of worth and goodness about ourselves, and at how many have left the church because of it. We were raised also with the sense that no one should be proud about what she or he has done in life; we should be humble always.

But . . . if we are children of God—and we are—then we also know that we are creative images of God. We are made in God's image. God has put within us the joys of life itself, and that includes the ability to create, an amazing and awesome joy. . . . Amen.

—given at Brooks-Howell Home, March 26, 2003

Can We Not Trust God?

Our Scripture is from Matthew 21:43, Peterson translation:
"This is the way it is with you. God's kingdom will be taken back from you and handed over to a people who will live out a kingdom life."[1]

Jubilee! Community Church is a rich source of understandings for me! This last Sunday, our celebration was centered on guilt—the guilt that we often carry around with us. For whatever reason, we seem to see the fact that we cannot live in perfection every moment as all our fault. We tell ourselves we're just bad, bad sinners, and what we've done in our lives is so bad that it cannot be forgiven. Thus, we beat ourselves over the head with our sins and shortcomings. I am reminded of the depiction of a young Jesuit in the movie *The Mission*, which was made in 1986 and which you may have seen. It was nominated for several Academy Awards, and received one for photography.

Set in the mid-1800s, this young priest carried with him a heavy load wherever he went, in penance for his previous sinful life. Yes, he had come to be a priest in some South American country, but felt that his sins had been so great that he had assigned himself this penance: He carried a heavy bag on his back wherever he went. The bag was a strong one, full of tin cans, trash, and heavy items, and he tied it tightly and carried it across his shoulders, hanging down his back, wherever he went. In the film, he was with a group of priests heading up a mountain to a mesa area, where they intended to found a wonderful community. It was a sheer cliff they were climbing, and every step was difficult as they slowly made their way almost straight up the mountain, with raging waters below. The heavy bag, full of trash of all kinds, eventually fell to the roaring waters below. It was impossible to rescue it. The shock on the penitent man's face was terrible to behold. What should he

Aspects of Faith 5

do, now that he had lost his bag of penance, his heavy burden of guilt? The leader of the group of priests reached out to help this well-meaning man to understand that he had obviously done enough penance, and that it was time to release it and move onward. The man finished his climb, free of his burden. When they arrived, there on the top, on the mesa, they found the flat land they sought and the native people they intended to live with. The priest who no longer carried his sack began to move through life as a free man.

Do we carry such a burden? If so, why? We are so great at beating up on ourselves. Is it that we do not understand the love of God?

Some of us here at Brooks-Howell cried this past week over the cutting down of one more big maple tree, among others. Think of that maple.

I once had several big, mature maple trees in my yard in Grand Rapids. Each year they produced enough seeds to start a forest. Once I asked a tree man to come and look at my trees, and I asked him why my trees made so many seeds. He told me that the trees were dying—and the overproduction of seeds was God's way of ensuring that new life, more maple trees, would continue. What an abundance of life!

And in Michigan, we were always aware of the snow. Have you thought about the fact that each snowflake is different? Although each one is based on the same hexagonal pattern, each design is different from the others. And there are so many, it would be impossible to count them. With a creative God like this, how can we doubt that God's love and grace are sufficient for us?

I was struck on Monday morning by the theme of what Reverend Steve Terrell told us when speaking to us here at Brooks-Howell. He said bluntly, "How can we be so audacious as to not love ourselves? We are God's image; we are made in the likeness of God." And again on Sunday, our pastor at Jubilee! reminded us that it is great arrogance to carry our guilt around, as though God's grace were not sufficient. Do you really think your sin is so great that God cannot deal with it? If so, ask yourself, Who do you think you are? And remind yourself that focusing on guilt is simply a lack of trust in the love of our God and in the forgiveness of God or the grace of God. Would we not be better off focusing on God's love and grace?

Be like the name of the dog of one of our Jubilants—Amazing Grace. She once was lost and now is found! God's grace is indeed amazing! It is sufficient! No matter who we are or how we goof up, day after day, God's grace is sufficient for you and for me. God's love is so great and so abundant that it is unbelievable.

I share with you the community prayer we used on Sunday October 18, 1998.

Let us pray.

> *Why is it, Holy River, that we insist on trucking around a Dumpster full of guilt on our backs?*
> *Why is it, Holy Forgiveness, that we cannot accept you?*
> *Cannot accept the possibility that you love us—goofs and all.*
> *Cannot accept the truth that your name is Love, not condemnation.*
> *Why can we not acknowledge that we messed up and move on?*
> *What is it about guilt that we like so much that we cannot let it go?*
> *Or what is it about ourselves that we dislike so much that we cling so tightly to our guilt?*
> *Holy, cleansing, life-giving River,*
> > *shake us loose in your rapids,*
> > *bounce us around in your rocks,*
> *so that we loosen our death-grip on our guilt and*
> *open our lives to your forgiving flow.*
> *Grant us the great and good sense to remember*
> *that guilt is not god,*
> > *that hate is not holy,*
> > *and that blame never healed. Amen.*
>
> —*given at Brooks-Howell Home, October 22, 1998*

Joy in People

The theme for this quarter at Jubilee! is called "Ticket to Ride." The questions that are being asked are:

What is it that makes life worth the living for you?
What is it that makes you happy and joyful in your journey?
Where do you find your creative self?

Members have been asked to share their joys during our celebrations. Some of the answers so far have included a woman's bout with cancer, which continues. An older man's informal adoption of two delightful younger women from Jubilee!—the three have become supportive family for each other. One young woman has found her joy in dancing. Another, Glenis Redmond, in poetry.

I find my joy—my Ticket to Ride—in people, just plain ordinary people who are not so ordinary. It should be remembered that, truly, none of us is ordinary. We are all very special, because we are each one an image of God. That is an understanding that comes with maturity.

Many different people and various groups of people have blessed my life through the years. I've worked with Greek, Syrian, and Lebanese people, with Puerto Ricans, Cubans, and Italians, with African-Americans and southern "poor-whites." In a school setting, as a social worker, I worked with a Dutch community. In retirement, I taught English to Salvadoran adults and to Nicaraguan junior and senior high school young people.

It's very clear that it's not a matter of what ethnic group a person comes from. I find that friends sustain me and give me life, no matter what language they speak or how we have met or what experiences we have shared. I rejoice in calling people "friend," in the connections we make, and in the communication that develops between us.

What triggered my sharing this was reading a quote in our

church newsletter. The quote said, "My father said that if a man has five friends when he dies, he has lived a good life." I commented to a friend at Jubilee!, "Well, I think I have five friends. If I were to talk about my Ticket to Ride, it would be about people, and about friends." The friend picked it up and asked me to share this Sunday. I agreed to do so.

Putting this together has not been easy, not because there is nothing to say but because there is too much to say. I decided to tell about one good friend who is now deceased. Her name was Minnie Holley Barnes, of Tazewell, Virginia. She was one of thirteen children, the granddaughter of an Indian chief and a mixture of Native American and African-American.

Holley, living in Virginia, saw my ad in the *Methodist Woman*[2] for a volunteer summer worker. I was director of the community center in Harrisburg, Pennsylvania, then, and she applied for the position. She worked with us for three summers as a wonderful volunteer. During those three summers we shared a small, three-room apartment and had a wonderful day camp for our youngsters. Holley had had wide experience, both in an interracial camp in Cincinnati and in Girl Scouting, although her life career had been as a teacher in the West Virginia School for the Blind and Deaf. She brought to birth and led the only blind and deaf troop of Girl Scouts in the country.

Just before she left that last summer she was with us, she told me that she would be married in two weeks to an old childhood sweetheart. She was sixty-three years old that summer! Holley had five years or so of a good marriage, and then her husband died. We remained friends until her death.

The sequel to this story is that this spring, Lois Marquart, whom some of you know, a deaconess from Wisconsin, came to visit. One thing she wanted to do while here was to go to Virginia and look up the small rural parish area that had been her very first appointment as a church and community worker, fifty years before. I agreed to be her transportation, and we drove and found Oakwood, Virginia, even though the American Automobile Association could not find it on their maps. There, over lunch, I met a wonderful United Methodist woman who is ninety-one years old and still physically active. In the course of our lunch I asked if, by any chance, she had

Aspects of Faith 9

heard of Minnie Holley. Her eyes got big and round and she said, "Oh yeah! Everyone knew Holley. She was great." Holley was one of my good friends.

People are my Ticket to Ride. Just this past Sunday, I was feeling really down in the dumps. I had an eyelash in my eye from early morning that would not settle down—enough of an annoyance that my church experience had been miserable, and I was feeling really rotten. And then the phone rang, and my former pastor from Michigan and his good wife said they were on their way to visit. I perked up in a hurry. People will do it for me every time. Of course we had a wonderful and too-brief visit, and my evil spirits vanished! People, especially old friends, or any friends, are my joy in life. What is your Ticket to Ride?

Let us pray.

Gracious God, we thank you that you have made us for communion with you and with each other, and that we are not happy in isolation. Thank you for your love for us and for our love for you. Thank you that you have taught us to love, and that we can see and recognize your image in each one of your children. And now we thank you for the abundance of this food, another expression of your love, and for the people who are here with us to care for us in this community. Amen.

—given at Brooks-Howell Home, July 19, 2001

How Similar Are Islam and Christianity?

Romans 8:26–27: "Likewise the Spirit helps us in our weaknesses; for we do not know how to pray as we ought, but that very Spirit intercedes with sighs too deep for words" (NRSV).

For many of us, these are days of uncertainty. They are days when we wonder how to pray. They are days when we are terribly disappointed that our country seems to think it necessary to bomb a country already desperately poor and needy, with no government, no infrastructure left, no normal social services for people in need, and more land mines than any country in the world. Most of those land mines are made by our own country and placed there sometime ago by our own people, acting under our own foreign policy. How is it possible to maintain a sense of order in our lives in these days?

Reading the last newsletter from the Asheville Friends meetinghouse, I came upon an item that may help in our understanding of these our brothers and sisters. The article is entitled "Five Pillars of Islam—How Similar to our Quaker Beliefs." The article says the five pillars of Islam are faith, prayer, charity, fasting, and pilgrimage, and tells a bit about each area. Sounds already like our Christian faith, does it not? The areas are spoken of in the newsletter:

Faith: "There is no God except God." [Sometimes we are tempted to put other things in the place of God—wealth, power, and the like.]

Prayer: "There is no hierarchical authority in Islam, and no priests, so communal prayers are led by a learned person who knows the Quran, chosen by the congregation. Although it is preferable to worship together in a mosque, a Muslim may pray almost anywhere—fields, offices, factories, universities [and private homes, like my neighbors Ameen and Jamel].

Visitors to the Muslim world are struck by the centrality of prayers in daily life."

Charity: "One of the most important principles of Islam is that all things belong to God, and that wealth is therefore held by human beings in trust. Our possessions are purified by setting aside a portion for those in need, and, like the pruning of plants, this cutting back balances and encourages new growth."

Fasting: "Every year in the month of Ramadan, all Muslims fast from first light until sundown, abstaining from food, drink, and sexual relations. Those who are sick, elderly, or on a journey, and women who are pregnant or nursing, are permitted to break the fast and make up an equal number of days later in the year. Besides providing spiritual growth, fasting facilitates true sympathy with those who go hungry."

Pilgrimage: "The annual pilgrimage to Makkah (Mecca) is an obligation only for those who are physically and financially able to perform it. Nevertheless, about two million people go to Makkah each year from every corner of the globe providing a unique opportunity for those of different nations to meet one another. Pilgrims wear special clothes: simple garments which strip away distinctions of class and culture, so that all stand equal before God."[3]

I was struck, as I am sure you are, with the similarities to our own Christian faith. Perhaps this helps us to understand a bit more about our brothers and sisters.

Let us pray.

O Joyful and Abundant One, we find ourselves sick at heart at our country's bombing of our brothers and sisters. It makes no difference to us that they are far from us physically, and we do not feel the bombing and see the destruction of life that it brings. Nor does it make a difference that some of them may be evil people. We, too, have known our own share of evil against others, and we are hardly in a position to condemn the evil-doing of others. We know that they, as we, are still part of the divine family, and of our families, too. They, like us, are capable of the good deeds we know to be part of your kingdom. We need to send to them our love and our caring. Help us all to learn to forgive, and to learn how to spread your love and peace to all of our family. Amen.

—*given at Brooks-Howell Home, October 17, 2001*

Abundant Grapes

In *The Message*, Eugene Peterson quotes Jesus:

"I am the real vine and my father is the Farmer. He cuts off every branch that doesn't bear grapes. And every branch that is grape-bearing he prunes back so it will bear even more.

"Live in me. Make your home in me just as I do in you. In the same way that a branch can't bear grapes by itself but only by being joined to the vine, you can't bear fruit unless you are joined with me.

"I am the Vine; you are the branches. When you're joined with me and I with you, the relation intimate and organic, the harvest is sure to be abundant. Separated, you can't produce a thing. Anyone who separates from me is deadwood, gathered up and thrown on the bonfire. But if you make yourselves at home with me and my words are at home in you, you can be sure that whatever you ask will be listened to and acted upon. This is how my Father shows who he is—when you produce grapes, when you mature as my disciples.

"I've loved you the way my Father has loved me. Make yourselves at home in my love. If you keep my commands you'll remain intimately at home in my love" (John 15:1–10).[4]

Once, our world lived in a vital connection with the earth. We worked the ground, cared for the soil, nurtured growth, and supported the vocation of farming. We could see the vital connection between what grows and blossoms from the earth, and what feeds us daily. Nowadays we simply fill our carts with prepackaged foods and meats and canned goods, and find it hard to see the connection between the foods we eat and the connection to the good earth of even the fresh fruits and vegetables.

I am reminded of an incident in my former home. Behind our garage grew a big and beautiful and wonderfully fruitful grapevine. When we first moved to that neighborhood, there were grapevines in the backyards of most of the homes. But later, ours was the only grapevine left. Each fall we enjoyed the grapes and shared them with friends. A new family moved in next door, and as the grapes began to form and get big enough to look like grapes, the youngster came over and asked for some grapes. I told him the grapes were not ripe and he would need to wait several months. He looked at me, put his hands on his hips, and demanded to know, "Why ain't they ripe?" There was no connection to nature in this young soul, no understanding of the slow process foods go through, to mature, so that we can enjoy their sweet ripeness. With no such connection, how could this child later understand the kind of interdependence Jesus was trying to explain?

The grapevine nourishes the branches and is essential to the growth and maturing of the grapes. The connection is vital. Just so, our relationship with Christ is at the very heart of our lives, giving the nourishment our souls need and the dynamic growth that is necessary to our spiritual lives.

I have found Jubilee! the church I attend regularly here, a fascinating community that encourages us to depend on Christ in ever-new ways. Our solid spiritual grounding is in Christ, and we are weak and useless without that solid grounding.

Let us pray.

Gracious God, thank you for our solid grounding in the life and ministry of Jesus Christ. Keep us close to this solid vine which nourishes and feeds us daily. Amen.

—*given at Brooks-Howell Home, May 16, 2003*

Unconditional Love

Lately, my life seems to be moving too fast. Even with the recent several days in my sister's quiet monastery, I returned immediately to a very heavy schedule. The few days were a blessing for their quiet and the lack of telephone, TV, radio, appointments, and all the things that just must be done *now!* Yesterday I talked with two much younger people, in separate conversations, who also seemed to feel that the days are moving too swiftly, and that there is simply not enough time to do what needs to be done in their lives and to savor the doing.

The other piece for me, in all honesty, is that—Yes, I have begun to slow down. So it takes me longer to do things. I can no longer manage forty-eight-hour days, as it seems I used to be able to do!

Perhaps you have the same feelings sometimes. And then I know that some of you have come to terms with these changes, and now *do not try* to do more than you are able.

In the midst of all of these thoughts on handling the time we are given, I find that I am loving life more and more. I find life very good, and I love it dearly! It is not just that I love my apartment, that I am in decent health, and that there are good friends around, and wonderful connections with many who are not here with me—through phone and e-mail and letters, and a lot of wonderful hugs on Sundays. It is not just that. There is a wonderful peace that has settled in at the heart and soul of my life, and for that I am very grateful!

Even with the dilemma of this terrible presidential election, I find myself rejoicing in the life I am living and loving. In a meeting the other night, we were each one asked to share what it is that we really love about life. I wish I had taken notes on what different people love, because I found myself saying "*Amen!*" over and over and over. At my turn, I shared that what I really love about life is connecting with people, and also connecting people with God's love. And God's love is found in people, of course.

This past Sunday, our pastor gave a meditation on unconditional love. I think I want to repeat those words over and over and over and over and over! *Unconditional love.* It is so amazing! Unconditional love is, of course, the love of God. A few quotes that appeared in our bulletin will help us to concentrate on this kind of love.

"Love and compassion are necessities, not luxuries. Without them, humanity cannot survive."

—Dalai Lama

"I have found the paradox that, if I love until it hurts, then there is no hurt, but only more love."

—Mother Teresa

"Most individuals have found God more clearly in and through others. The love of others is the love of God experienced in this life." —Wendy Wright

"Love alone is capable of uniting living beings in such a way as to complete and fulfill them, for it alone takes them and joins them by what is deepest in themselves."

—Teilhard de Chardin

In closing, I should like to share a portion of our Jubilee! Community prayer about unconditional love. I quote:

Pry the lid off our hearts, Holy Freedom.
Wrest the cover from our minds.
Pull the cork from our souls so that we may give and receive love
   without looking for cultural expectations or approval . . . without
   simply trying to appease our loins instead of pleasing our hearts.

Free us to find love in waterfalls and sunrises,
   in fresh breezes and booming thunderstorms,
   in simple acts of kindness,
   in belly laughs and shared tears.
And then free us to give love in the same way.
Open our lives to the joy of unfettered, unconditional love,
   the only kind You know. Amen.

—*given at Brooks-Howell Home, November 9, 2001*

16   A Faith Expressed

Do You Believe?

Today's meditation is a reminder that faith and trust are a strong part of your life and mine. Trust makes for a healthy life, while a lack of trust spells paranoia and mental illness.

The theme of faith and trust are strong parts of our biblical and Christian heritage. There are numerous hymns with this theme, and faith is an essential part of our Christian life. At the present time, the outgoing message on my answering machine suggests that if you believe in goodness, you will see it all around you. It has surprised me that I have had a number of comments of appreciation for this reminder. People seem to need to be reminded of the importance of believing in goodness. Perhaps it is because there is so much garbage in our world these days. We seem to forget that the goodness of people can be trusted.

Perhaps you have heard of Peace Pilgrim, the woman who walked 25,000 miles to witness for peace. She walked with only the clothes on her back and an apron with pockets for carrying essentials. She trusted others for food and for lodging. She accepted rides as they were offered, food as offered, and lodging as offered. Otherwise, she walked. She was occasionally hungry and occasionally spent a night sleeping on the ground. This good woman has written her story. In it, she tells of several times when others would have molested her, but were stopped by an understanding of her faith and fearlessness and the trust that was an essential part of her life. We marvel at her faith in others, and at the single-mindedness of her journey.

Howard Hanger, my pastor, reminded us Sunday that one cannot take a walk or go to sleep or drink a cup of water without trust in the goodness of others.

Thank God that the goodness of human beings seems to be built into our very lives. I think of Anne Frank, who after months in hiding during the years of the Holocaust could still write in her diary, "In spite of all, I still believe that people are good at heart."

Every one of us who plants seeds in the soil in the springtime trusts that the sun and rain and the good earth will bring them to fruition. All of us have known great faith as we stepped out on our life journeys. For some of us, if we had known what difficulties we would encounter, we might have closed the door on our great adventures. And yet, I find myself saying of most of my journeys, "I wouldn't have missed that for the world!"

Faith and trust require both curiosity and chutzpah, that wonderful Jewish word that means the nerve and the guts to venture forth in spite of the difficulties. Some of you have physical difficulties that would scare the socks off a lesser person, and yet you continue on with your amazing deeds of goodness. All of us have chutzpah, and know how it has enriched our lives and blessed our years of service.

A deaconess friend, in her Christmas letter, started with this quote: "Faith is the bird that feels the light and sings while the dawn is still dark." And a bit later on she says, "Loss has been an ever-present companion this year. And yet we sing."

Many of our gospel songs are based on the theme of faith and trust. I think of "Trust and Obey," "Faith of Our Fathers," and on and on. You can name a dozen with hardly a thought.

Some of us know the illnesses of children and young people and adults who cannot trust the goodness of others. One of my friends is starting a training program that will qualify her to work with children in the area called "attachment therapy." It is just what it sounds like: work with children who cannot make attachments to others because they lack the trust in others they need to build the supports that all of us need for a healthy life.

Trust and faith are essential to our lives. Thank God for them.

Let us pray.

Gracious God, thank you for our lives and for our trust in your goodness and in each other. How good it is to be alive! Thank you for life and its living here and now and in this place.

—given at Brooks-Howell Home, January 19, 2000

The Prophet Amos

Last Sunday our pastor, as part of the lectionary readings, read a selection from Amos. The brief snippet published in the Jubilee! bulletin read, "Alas for those who lie on beds of ivory, and lounge on their couches . . . but are not grieved" (Amos 6:4–6 NRSV).

The theme of the celebration was greed, and our attention was called to the lack of joy (the woe, if you will) experienced by those who cannot grieve for the sorrows of neighbors and friends, or for the pain and suffering of others. It sent me back to reading Amos again, and then I found this selection from a book written by Sister Joan Chittister, a Benedictine sister who is a friend. One of Joan's books is *Passion for Life, Fragments of the Face of God*, with icons by Robert Lentz. The book has brief sketches of many of the saints of yesteryear as well as today. I should like to share her brief writing about Amos.

> Prophets are a motley sort who bear little resemblance to one another except that all of them have a sense of what's missing in life and are committed to saying so. They come from every walk in life and every social level. For years they seem harmless enough, normal people in normal situations, until suddenly they get an insight into life that will not go away. Then there is no stopping them.
>
> The problem is that they do not always communicate their newly found understandings with finesse and polish. In fact, what is more likely the case, they often make their announcements entirely without nuance or political adroitness. Prophets, in other words, are not always the world's smoothest people nor are they, as a result, its most popular. They talk about things that hurt. They talk about what people are not supposed to talk about at all. And they talk about it unceasingly.
>
> Amos was perhaps the farthest out of line of them all.

Amos, a person of some substance it seems as a shepherd or sheep-owner from the southern kingdom of Israel, felt impelled by God to make a social critique of a society that was more than satisfied with itself. Amos prophesied to a world that was totally complacent. *[If this bears any resemblance to the situation of our country at the present time, so be it!]* In the time of Amos Israel was at its most powerful and prosperous peak since the time of David. Its boundaries had been extended to an unprecedented degree. As far as the merchants and the military and the monarch were concerned, Yahweh was blessing Israel. Amos, in other words, was totally out of step with his times.

Amos had the effrontery to question how power and prosperity had come to Israel. Amos cited war crimes and tax foreclosures and "failures at the gate," where the elders met for the purpose of meting out justice but decided routinely against the poor, while, all the time, worship went on regularly at the shrines. . . . Amos warned the pilgrims and the pious about going so frequently to worship! He said, "Instead, let justice reign at the city gate." But no one listened.

Their theology told them that they were special to God. Their worship told them that they were good since its frequency alone lulled them into thinking that their relationship with God was intact. Their wealth told them that their thick, rich, comfortable lifestyles were actually the sign of God's beneficence to them.

Indeed, the book of Amos reads like [today's] newspaper. Yahweh is baffled, the scripture says, that the very people who had themselves been brought out of slavery in Egypt were now the oppressors of others. [*Sound like Israel today and the Palestinians?*] They were waging war. They were turning farm families into exiles. They were corrupting justice by taxing the wheat of the small farmers, and turning away the needy. They were living off the backs of the poor.

Amos, impelled by the will of Yahweh, saw the situation in a burst of holy awareness and begged the powerful to recommit themselves to the vision of God. More than that, he preached that formalism in religion was worse than useless.

The message of Amos is a very strong one to people who think they are already holy. Amos tells us, in essence, to forget the amount of money we put in collection baskets, to quit presenting as credentials the number of [worship services] we attend; to stop trying to kid ourselves by the size of our building donations. God, Amos says, wants much more than that. God wants our lives. God wants a new point of view from us. God wants us to want the will of God more than we want our own comfort and consolation. God wants us to pay attention to the poor. "Let justice flow like water," the scripture reads. Give more than the minimum. Give everyone their human due. Give everyone God's will for them.

And so then and there, Amos is called to give up his nice private life as an owner of sheep in the pure and open desert, and gets sent into the city to remind us all what religion is really meant to be about.

But the establishment—the high priests of Bethel itself—ran Amos out of town. "We want no more prophesying in Bethel, this is the national temple."

Anyone who has dared to question society with its ill-gotten oil and high-tech military and runaway economic system knows the scenario. The world does not want a prophetic religion; the world wants the type of religion that makes life comfortable. The system wants a religion of private consolation rather than a religion based on the kind of public commitment that brings inequity into question.

And there, for any novice to see, are all the contradictions and all the ironies of what it still means for anyone to be called by God. In the first place, Amos is a strange, unlikely messenger. Shepherding is nice work but hardly the stuff of which public influence is made, then or now. Secondly, the priest is a strange adversary. If no one else can, surely the priest would be able to recognize the voice of God. Then, too, this rich country is pitiably poor for all its wealth. They have money but they do not have values. And, finally, the people to whom Amos is trying to speak don't want to hear bad news when things are going fine for the privileged of them.

The parallels are all too clear. To be a religious person in today's world too is to claim commitment in a society that taxes the poor more than it does the rich. Like Israel we too wage war on the innocent in the deserts of undeveloped nations and profit handsomely from it. We too terrorize whole peoples into exile for the sake of national political advantage. We too turn away the needy at the city gates of the richest country in the world in the name of job security while the industries of the country gain unconscionable profits from the unjust wages of Third World laborers.

Like Amos, we too are the ones being asked now to listen to the voice of God in our own lives, to leave what we were doing and to stand for something other than what this world takes for granted. We are the ones now who are expected to speak for the poor and the forgotten of our world. We are the ones being asked to do justice rather than to fool ourselves with the kind of pious niceties of religion that are just as likely to keep us from God as they are to take us there. . . .

From Amos, then, we must learn first to hear the word of God ourselves so that we can tell the voice of God from all the other voices that are clamoring for attention all around us, the voice of money, . . . the voice of comfort, the voice of independence, the voice of status, the voice of a world gone deaf with lesser messages than the will of God.

Like Amos we have to make a new decision every day about whether or not we are willing to be called from our own good works—as Amos was—from being good professionals and responsible civil servants and devoted workers to do an even better work as witness to the just and loving mind of God. Shepherding flocks, after all, is honorable, steady employment to this day. But it was not enough for Amos. Amos was being called out of his good, private life, with all of its value, to live a life planted in the mind of God for the sake of others. Amos was being called to be an icon of the just and compassionate face of God. [5]

Amen and amen and amen.

—given at Brooks-Howell Home, October 3, 2001

The Bible as Midrash

On Monday night of this week, I felt extremely privileged as I went with a busload of our residents to Lipinsky Hall, at UNCA, to hear Bishop John Shelby Spong, the Episcopalian bishop. Bishop Spong has been raising questions for some time, about our traditional Christian faith. I heard him first at Chautauqua three or four years ago and was immediately stimulated and excited about his reputedly controversial understandings of our Scriptures and their meanings. He has written a number of books throughout recent years, and these have been increasingly well received. I felt very privileged to be sitting again at the feet of such a renowned and extremely competent scholar of the Bible.

I did not encounter the Bible in serious study until I entered National College in Kansas City, Missouri. I had attended Sunday school for several years, and went through confirmation classes and memorized many of the questions and answers for that experience. At National College, however, we studied the New Testament, among other parts of the Bible, in several different translations. I understood, early on, that there were various versions and interpretations of the same events. I found myself not wanting to memorize Scripture, and I have never been able to do that. I had to ask, "What is this story saying?" and, "What version do I memorize?"

Bishop Spong spoke well the other night, about the fact that our Christian faith is really a Jewish-based religion. Jesus was Jewish, and the Bible must be read and understood through a Jewish lens. Yes, of course Jesus was Jewish! We know that is true. Interestingly, our speaker reflected the experience of most of us as we learned, through our Sunday school experience, to "dislike and denigrate" the Jewish people of Jesus' day, and those of our own day. After all, we learned, it was Jewish people who crucified Jesus. Bishop Spong corrected our understanding when he said that the Romans were the only ones who could crucify, but we lost that along the way. He speaks in his books of this Christian dislike of Jewish people, often turning to persecution, to exiling and casting out, and of the fact that these attitudes eventually led us to the Holocaust. He says that one of the big reasons we have so much trouble with some of the passages of both Old and New Testaments is that they are so Jewish and we have so little knowledge of that faith.

Many of the stories of the New Testament that are so difficult for us to understand are in the style of Jewish writing called the midrash. I first encountered this word when I went to Garrett-Evangelical Theological Seminary a few years ago. Bishop Spong explained this well when he said the midrash is the method of clothing events in our right-now world in the stories and understandings of the past that are meaningful and known to be "true" from long ago.

In other words, so many of the "miraculous" events of Jesus' life—so often difficult for us to understand—can be more easily understood if we relate them to stories of Moses from many years earlier, when they were seen as divine—revealing of God's truth.

In other words, there were events in Moses' life and experience that were recognized by the Jewish people as divine, or "impregnated with God's spirit." Moses was the greatest figure they knew; he had revealed God.

They saw the events in Jesus' life, too, as full of God's spirit—and described them in that way. What they recognized in Moses' life was the understanding that God was in him. What they recognized in Jesus, very clearly, was that God was in him. Therefore they wrapped some of the stories of Jesus, the crucial events of his life, in stories reminiscent of the stories of Moses. Some of Jesus' life events were even more revealing of the God they knew through Moses, and so the miracles of Jesus are even greater than those we have of Moses. Here Bishop Spong spoke of the parting of the Red Sea, and its relationship to Jesus' baptism story, where Jesus "splits the heavens," so to speak, saying, in other words, that Jesus is even greater than Moses, who only split the waters. Moses is the greatest one we have heretofore known, who clearly revealed God to us.

I want to insert here a note about the trouble I am having in writing the book of my life. Yes, I remember a lot of my younger life, and I am writing what I do remember. But I have to be careful. There is so much that I do not remember. In talking with my sister awhile back, I related an incident that I remembered happening, and my sister corrected me, saying that was not at all the way it happened. Well, in writing about the stories of Jesus, do you remember how many years it was before anything at all was written of these narratives of the Gospels? And Bishop Spong reminded us the other night that there were no Kodak pictures, or tape recordings, or other ways of jogging our memories. It is not surprising that the Gospel writers differ in the significant experiences they remember, or how they remember them. I can remember raising questions long ago, in college, about how the Gospel writers could remember the stories in such detail.

All of this is to say that telling what they remembered of Jesus was certainly difficult for the Gospel writers. This is why some of the stories differ so, and are sometimes almost contradictory, although they are both telling the same stories.

And so, Bishop Spong is saying that Jesus' story was written with the essence of its meaning as its central core, and not ever intended to be a literal, scientific account of his life. This is the way the Jewish people wrote many stories. And so he despairs of those of us who tend to "take the Bible literally" and are so insistent on telling others that "this is what the Bible says."

When I say it that way, I think immediately of the Jewish rabbi who was speaking in a meeting I attended here in Asheville sometime ago. He was speaking of those who say, "This is what the Bible says." He said he had been taught to, when he heard his students say that, bring a Bible to his class and place it on the desk for all to see, and say, "Well, let us see what the Bible says." He would ask the class to listen. One minute would go by, and another, and another, and no one heard a thing. Finally he would say, "The Bible does not say a thing except through those who interpret it through their own lives and their own lens."

Thus, Bishop Spong asks that we read and see and understand the Bible we know through the Jewish lens through which it was written long ago.

On Easter Sunday our pastor again used a phrase he had used earlier in another context, and which rings as something to remember. That statement is, "There are some things that are true, whether or not they actually happened."

Let us pray.

Gracious God, help us to know that there are many ways, and many different ways for us to find and know you. There are many doorways into your presence. We thank you for the Scripture stories we have of Jesus that have helped us to know who you are, and to know the solid truth of Jesus' life and ministry that have revealed to us your way and will. Amen.

—*given at Brooks-Howell Home, May 7, 2003*

Risk Taking

There is a story in the New Testament that I should like to share with you. This reading is from *The Message,* Eugene Peterson's modern translation. Matthew 25:14–30. This is commonly called the story of the talents, and has been used for many purposes throughout the church years.

"It's also like a man going off on an extended trip. He called his servants together and delegated responsibilities. To one he gave five thousand dollars, to another two thousand, to a third one thousand, depending on their abilities. Then he left. Right off, the first servant went to work and doubled his master's investment. The second did the same. But the man with the single thousand dug a hole and carefully buried his master's money.

"After a long absence, the master of those three servants came back and settled up with them. The one given five thousand dollars showed him how he had doubled his investment. His master commended him: 'Good work! You did your job well. From now on be my partner.'

"The servant with the two thousand showed how he also had doubled his master's investment. His master commended him: 'Good work! You did your job well. From now on be my partner.'

"The servant given one thousand said, 'Master, I know you have high standards and hate careless ways, that you demand the best and make no allowances for error. I was afraid I might disappoint you, so I found a good hiding place and secured your money. Here it is, safe and sound down to the last cent.'

"The master was furious. 'That's a terrible way to live! It's criminal to live cautiously like that! If you knew I was after the best, why did you do less than the least? The least you could have done would have been to invest the sum with the bankers, where at least I would have gotten a little interest.

" 'Take the thousand and give it to the one who risked the most. And get rid of this "play-it-safe" who won't go out on a limb. Throw him out into utter darkness.' "[6]

I should like to speak of risk taking in our lives. All of you who have been missionaries, and all of you who have been deaconesses are indeed risk-takers. No one could have told you before you went out to your assigned places, wherever they were, what you would encounter or what unknown experiences would be yours. Surely you have used your talents well, with so many of you starting needed programs here and there, and often serving what is sometimes called "the least of these"—although they are not at all the least ones, they are rather the blessed ones!

A few years ago, I had the opportunity to study at Garrett-Evangelical Theological Seminary as the Georgia Harkness scholar in residence, and that was a very special experience in my life. Because of the shocking change to my normal pattern of living, I wrote an article about it called "Culture Shock," which was published in our *Michigan Christian Advocate*. I want to repeat some of those words here.

> I'm not sure why I keep putting myself through these new experiences where I am entirely vulnerable to others and their (hopefully) good intentions. Just knowing who to trust is sometimes a major concern!
>
> The first time I went to Nicaragua alone, I happened to be the last in line as a large group of us stood and waited at customs, to enter the country. A young soldier approached me and asked if I was alone. I nodded yes. He asked me to follow him. Before I had a chance to wonder what was happening, he had placed me at the head of the line to go through customs first, an amazing courtesy and a nice surprise. On the other side, I met the person who took me to my new home.
>
> In recent months, I have asked myself over and over questions I asked at that time—"Wouldn't it be simpler just to enjoy life in my own accustomed space and territory? . . . Wouldn't it be better not to have to worry about who to ask for directions, or how to get to the post office, and a million other unknowns?"
>
> And then I answered that, in spite of the anguish of a new

situation, it is indeed worth it all. . . . There is a very special feeling involved in a new adventure: What fun it is to start anew, to project sometimes a different self, and to try out new ways of living. And indeed with new adventures, life has become so much more worth the living. It is a rich and joyful experience. The exposure to different times and places, and different people and ways of doing things have all left me with a joy in people that just does not quit. And then my conclusion, "There is no place where we can go where our God cannot be found. What a great assurance!"[7]

I have thought of this article lately as I prepare to go in February to Nicaragua again. I told someone that it is a scary experience, and he rightfully asked why, since I have now been there several times. Well, you must know that it is not at all the same country that I knew several years ago, because of U.S. intervention. Nor am I the same person. I am no longer up to walking four to six miles a day to get where I need to be. I have developed some eating problems and that, too, will be an adjustment. I expect to lose some weight because the same kind of food does not exist there. God willing, I will be there and possibly in other Central American countries for two months, and will come back in April, after attending a conference on women's solidarity in Cuba.

Risk taking: Yes, we make our choices, and invest our lives where God leads. For some of us that is very difficult, very chancy, certainly very risky. It's a big world out there, and we do not know what we will find, or what adventures will be ours. But, as we say in worship at Jubilee! each Sunday, "Here we come, God, into another week! We do not know what the week will bring, but we know that you are there."

And so I urge you, do not hide your talent or bury it in the ground until our Lord returns. The talent or gift you have is what you alone have, whatever it is, so use it! Put it to use however and wherever God leads. The reward or payoff is a confident and joyful walk with God and that is indeed reward enough. Amen.

Thank you, God, for taking a chance on us, and sending Jesus to show us how to risk life itself as we live and work with You. Amen.

—*given at Brooks-Howell Home, November 20, 1997*

We Can Kill Giants

Some of you know that I belong to a UMW circle at Central United Methodist Church in Asheville, North Carolina. I regularly receive Central's bulletin. I have come to appreciate very much the brief writings of Rev. Dr. Rob Blackburn. The fact that I belong to Jubilee! and attend regularly does not mean that I cannot appreciate another pastor or church, of course.

This morning I should like to share with you the editorial in the most recent bulletin. It is titled "David's Story."

> We have often treated the David and Goliath story as a children's story. Truthfully, the story is not for children as much as it is for anyone who knows what it is to feel small, powerless and overwhelmed. This story is not neutral, not disinterested in contests between giants and the small.
>
> Some of you have read Viktor Frankl's book about his survival of the Nazi death camps. One sentence particularly stood out for me. Frankl says the Nazis could strip their victims of every dignity except the last, and perhaps the most dear, "the last of the human freedoms—to choose one's attitude in any given set of circumstances—to choose one's own way." Did Frankl, the Jew, know the story of young David? Yes. Time and time again, what hope God's people must have found in this narrative of how David—not large, not well armored—used not only his wit but also his faith. To those who live with radical trust, there is a way when it seems there is no way.
>
> When Chief Justice Thurgood Marshall died, Justice Sandra Day O'Connor, who disagreed with Chief Justice Marshall on most things, said, "What I will miss most about Thurgood Marshall is sitting down with him and listening to his stories, stories about the tough days of the Civil Rights Movement when there was only Mr. Marshall and a couple of other

30 *A Faith Expressed*

NAACP lawyers against a great, ingrained, legally established system of racial injustice. I will miss most those stories, *stories that changed the way I look at the world."*

Well-armed, big Goliath on one side. Well-armed, cowardly King Saul on the other. But there is another participant in the struggle. And I am not talking about upstart little David. I'm talking about God, the God who is determined not to leave history up to the carnage that is left after the armies have had their clash, the God who is busy prodding little shepherds into the fray.

As long as there is God, there are surprising twists to our story. There is space enough, even for the small and the vulnerable to do something with history, if you dare let God put you to noble purpose.[8]

Interestingly, I read this to a good friend who calls himself an atheist. After he had heard it and my note of appreciation to Dr. Blackburn for the assurance that God is always prodding little shepherds like you and me into the fray, he commented that people these days know that giantism is a disease of the body and that giants are very vulnerable. So David was lucky enough to hit him in the head—a very vulnerable place—and fell him.

Yes, I know that's so. For me, however, it does not negate this story of a young man who had the chutzpah to tackle a formidable adversary and trust God in his doing so. I'm sure David did not know about giantism!

I think I was amazed at the lack of belief of my friend regarding this story. Then I remembered that he seems to feel that a belief in God is all in your head, and I asked him if this was the case. He confirmed that immediately, with a remark that said that we simply deceive ourselves if we think God is in charge, really helping the poor and the weak. He said, "Just look at our world today. The rich are in charge. Why do you think the poor and the weak are going to get anyplace in this kind of world?"

Well, I admit it is a stretch of the imagination today to think that the poor will inherit our earth today— and yet, that is our faith. I can only say, "Yes, I believe it, and I will stake my life on it. Enough said!

Let us pray.

Gracious God, it is a tough world out there! The odds are all against us, and yet we keep on keeping on, trusting you and the goodness of our world to bless us and keep us, and help us to kill the giants of greed and graspiness. Thank you for this faith, fragile as it seems sometimes. Thank you that we know it is possible to trust you and live a life of faith. Amen.

—*given at Brooks-Howell Home, January 23, 2002*

Eve

My friends Laura and Tillie and I have just returned from a week at Chautauqua. Chautauqua is a nine-week feast of worship, lectures, music, discussions, get-togethers of all kinds of people for all kinds of good purposes, and a learning vacation.

I should like to bring a brief piece of one of the lectures, one by Sister Joan Chittister, a Benedictine sister and president of Benetvision, a resource center for modern spirituality. I have known her since 1983 when the two of us, and a number of others, were involved in forming the Chautauqua Society for Peace and Justice. She was a lecturer for the Chautauqua religion department. The overall theme for the week was God, and Joan lectured on icons of God. Much of her lecture material was taken directly from her book *A Passion for Life: Fragments of the Face of God.* The book has brief writings about many people whom you know and may want to read about.

The Scripture is from Genesis 1:26, 27, and 31a.

> Then God said, "Let us make humankind in our image, according to our likeness; and let them have dominion over the fish of the sea, and over the birds of the air, and over the cattle, and over all the wild animals of the earth, and over every creeping thing that creeps upon the earth." So God created humankind in his image, in the image of God he created them; male and female he created them.
>
> God saw everything that he had made, and indeed, it was very good (NRSV).

In the second chapter of Genesis, another version says, "*We* shall make humanity. Male and female *we* shall make them." Thus God is very clearly both male and female. I shall read briefly from this lecture. You will find that Sister Joan does not mince words, but lays things out straight. She cares not who may object, who may agree or not agree. She backs up her understandings by solid readings and understandings. Recommended readings are listed.

It is hard to imagine anyone who has been scorned more often or rejected more universally than the woman Eve. Men have heaped disdain on her as an enemy of the human race, and women have despised her for the weakness they see in her as having been bred in them as well. . . . [T]he campaign of derision and contempt has been almost universally successful. The cause of human suffering is the woman Eve, the fundamentalist theology of sin insists, and therefore women in general are to be punished, avoided, controlled, pitied, mocked, and feared. It is a rationale that has kept women out of public arenas, out of intellectual centers, out of ecclesiastical holy places, and out of touch with themselves for eons. That simple . . . rationale theologized—has kept them down, kept them quiet, kept them in bondage forever. Eve was not to be trusted and neither were they. Eve was out of control and so were they. Eve was a danger to the proper order of society and so were they.

But the picture of Eve the temptress that has served sexism so well for so long is an unkind one to men as well. If woman is by nature a calculating temptress who requires control, then man, who fell to her simpering wiles without a whimper, is, by nature apparently, an unsubstantial, unthinking, sniveling weakling who doesn't qualify to be in charge of anything. If Eve is the enemy who took him down, with a simple, empty-headed, inviting smile, then a man by nature is far too easily duped to be in charge of important things. He is far too embarrassingly gullible, his will power is far too essentially flabby, he is a weakling at the mercy of the weakest of opponents.

The philosophical problem is clear, though it is seldom, if ever, admitted. Either Adam was rebellious and so was Eve, or Eve was weak and so was Adam.

It is not a pretty picture. It does not sound like creation at its best in either case. It does not sound like what Scripture means to describe when it reads that "on the seventh day, God made humans, and God said, 'That is good.' " . . .

The fact is that Eve, no less than Adam, is the glory of God; and Adam, no less than Eve, is the sign of humanity becoming human. . . .

... Eve may, in fact, be the most powerful icon of them all. If the world begins to see Eve as an icon of the feminine in God, then every system will have to change. ... Every negative and limited and manipulated religious teaching about women will have to blush in the sight of God. Every sexist lie will have to give way to the God of Truth.

Eve makes clear that systems based on male power structures and male god-figures are at best only half the ideas that God had for the management of the human race. If Eve is simply a sign of humanity subject to error but certain to grow, then the idea of woman the temptress is as much a commentary on men as it is on women and can never be used again to justify the exclusion of women from seats of male power or centers of male decision-making.

Eve recalls us to our real selves, to our full selves, to our incomplete selves. It is Eve who makes the feminine as normative as the masculine. She makes equality the measure of humanity. She makes us mourn the limitations that we have put upon ourselves in the name of God.[9]

Let us pray.

Gracious God, thank you for new insights on religious figures and biblical saints we have long known. Thank you for thinkers like Joan Chittister, Catholic sister and friend, who helps us to understand more about religious saints that we admire, too. Amen.

—*given at Brooks-Howell Home, July 8, 1999*

What's in a Cracked Pot?

There recently came across my desk a story that was very helpful to me. When asked how he comes up with some of his ideas, our pastor says that he preaches to himself. I think I do, too! Most of us are "cracked pots"—some of us real *crackpots*! The title of this piece is "What's in a Cracked Pot?" The author is unknown.

A water bearer in India had two large pots, each hung on either end of a pole which he carried across his neck. One of the pots had a crack in it, and while the other pot was perfect and always delivered a full portion of water at the end of the long walk from the stream to the master's house, the cracked pot arrived only half full.

For a full two years this went on daily, with the bearer delivering only one and a half pots full of water to his master's house. The perfect pot was proud of its accomplishments, but the cracked pot was miserable, ashamed that it was able to accomplish only half of what it had been made to do. After two years of what it perceived to be a bitter failure, the cracked pot spoke to the water bearer one day by the stream.

"I am ashamed of myself, and I want to apologize to you."

"Why? What are you ashamed of?" asked the water bearer.

"I have been able, for these past two years, to deliver only half my load because this crack in my side causes water to leak out all the way back to your master's house. Because of my flaws, you have to do all of this work, and you don't get full value from your efforts," the pot said.

The water bearer felt compassion and said, "As we return to the master's house, I want you to notice the beautiful flowers along the path."

Indeed, as they went up the hill, the old cracked pot took notice of the sun warming many beautiful flowers on the side of the path, and this cheered it some. But at the end of the trail, it still felt bad because it had leaked out half its load, and so again it apologized to the bearer for its failure.

The water bearer said to the pot, "Did you notice that there were flowers only on your side of the path, but not on the other pot's side? That is because I have always known about your crack. Accepting what was given to me, I planted flower seeds on your side of the path, and every day while we walk back from the stream, you've watered them. For two years I have been able to pick these beautiful flowers to decorate my master's table. Without your being just the way you are, he would not have this beauty to grace his house."

In the Creator's great economy, nothing goes to waste. So as we seek ways to minister together, we must embrace what may seem like flaws and honor our unique design and purpose.

—Anonymous

Let us pray.

Gracious God, we give you thanks for the unique way in which you have made each one of us. Each of us has shining moments of goodness and creativity, and each of us has irritating habits that send others up the walls. How boring it would be if we were all perfect. Help us, then, to accept ourselves as we are, and to use the talents and skills that you have given us to serve both you and our brothers and sisters. Thank you now for this food, a small symbol of the abundance with which you bless us daily. Amen.

—*given at Brooks-Howell Home, October 12, 1999*

The Return of Tears

One of the areas of my life for which I thank Jubilee! Community is the return of my tears. When I was a young child, growing up, I was sometimes called a crybaby. I had four older brothers, and they often teased me unmercifully—the only one still living still does so occasionally. Then our mother died when I was twelve, and I cried my eyes out when I was twelve and thirteen, and maybe later. I do not know when, but at sometime a year or so later I put away my tears, and went on with life. As someone said, "Crying does not change the baby's diaper!"

When I got to college I never cried. I also, interestingly, never talked about my family, whom I had essentially lost in the following years. I became a social worker, and in that career, if one is to be professional, you surely can't cry with every sob story you hear. I learned to accept and absorb the feelings of others and help them to move on to answers and solutions to the problems presented. That's what social work is all about, and I was a good social worker.

Even with homesickness, as I moved from place to place, I cried little for years. I do remember crying in Harrisburg when I had a letter from Tampa, where I had worked for four years, but I soon got over that!

In retirement, through two specific instances, I came to realize that I had no memories of my mother, who had been my strong support in my early years. One of these instances was when a nursing student came to my home to do an interview about my medical history. I had seen a notice on our church bulletin board about one of our members who was teaching student nurses. As a part of their experience, she advertised for the older people in our church community to share their medical histories. As I did so, I realized that I really did not know much about my own medical history or that of my parents. I knew appallingly little about the medical history of my mother. The circumstances around her death were not even a part of my memory bank, although my sister was able to fill these in for me later on.

Several months later, I took a creative writing course at one of our colleges, and wrote a wonderful story about my father and the fun our family had together when we were children. When I read it to the class, the same question came from several students together. They asked, "Where was your mother?" I almost said defensively, "This story is about my father; it is not about my mother." But I was silent and went home and reread the story. I realized that I had talked about not only my father, but every one of my siblings—and there was not a hint of my mother in that account. I decided I needed to find my memories of her, and I went into therapy for perhaps a year and a half to find those memories. We never found them and I never cried. Yes, once I was brought to tears thinking about the death of one of our wonderful pastors who had been a very good friend, and very helpful to me. As I brushed away the tears and quickly recovered myself, the therapist said, "It's all right to cry." I can remember registering surprise. We went on with the session . . . with no more tears.

Then I came to Brooks-Howell, and after canvassing many churches here, I decided to join Jubilee!. I found I was sometimes brought to tears in the celebrations by the open joys and the caring, the intensity, if you will, of the love shown to others in so many nurturing and helpful ways. As I began to share with others in friendship and in smaller groups, there were others, too, who confessed to crying in the celebrations. Watching more carefully, I became aware often of people wiping their eyes, of eyes filling with tears, of harumphs and a quiet clearing of the throat. Interesting that I had not noted it before!

Finding one's feelings, when they have been put aside for a long, long time, is sometimes not easy. I find that it brings a different and much deeper pattern to life. When the blurb on the back of Jubilee!'s bulletin says that we are a community and we share together our joys and our sorrows, I began to realize what that means. It means wonderful hugs, sometimes crying on the shoulders of another, laughing more freely and more deeply, and consciously feeling again the depths of one's own spirit and life within. How good it is, to be whole again!

Emotions are amazing things. A man named Ivan Petrovich Pavlov once said that dogs do not have emotions, and that if you beat a dog, he does not really feel it. This is in many of the older textbooks about animals. Well, Pavlov was very wrong. He did us all a great and terrible disservice. Cats and dogs and horses and other pets, the entire ape family, seals, elephants, and all kinds of animals have emotions. They belong, with us, to a life of feeling, which includes both hurts and joyful pleasures. I can still remember with a horrible feeling inside, the anger and hurt and understanding of betrayal in the eyes of Peter, our wonderful cat from Michigan, our latest cat, whom we had decided would need to put to sleep because of his own coming suffering and illness. He would have lived a few more months without pain, but because Barbara needed help making that decision, and I would not be there when she needed help, I picked up Peter while he was eating, and quickly caged him. We carried him off to the vet. I cannot to this day recall that without crying myself!

I am glad that I have recovered my tears. That recovery has brought a deeper joy and understanding of others and their pain. It has also brought a depth of feeling on my part that was a real surprise to me, and that I never expected to find. it is a deeper wholeness than I have ever known.

Let us pray.

Thank you, God, that you have put tears within us, and have connected us all with feelings of compassion and caring. Help us to nurture these and to recognize and appreciate them. Help us to use them to project the love and caring that You have put within us, so that love moves from our lives to the lives of others who need your love so much. Amen.

—*given at Brooks-Howell Home, January 19, 2002*

NOTES

1. Peterson, *The Message*.

2. *The Methodist Woman* is the former name for the magazine *Response*, published by United Methodist Women.

3. From October 2001 Asheville Friends newsletter. Used with permission.

4. Peterson, *The Message*.

5. Joan Chittister, *Passion for Life: Fragments of the Face of God,* icons by Robert Lentz (Maryknoll, NY: Orbis Books, 1996). Used with permission.

6. Peterson, *The Message*.

7. Helene Hill, "Culture Shock," *Michigan Christian Advocate,* October 27, 1991.

8. Used with permission.

9. Joan Chittister, Ibid.

Thoughts About God

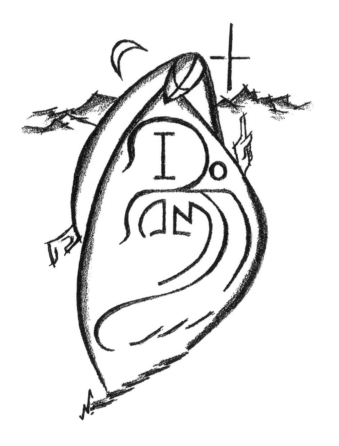

When You Say "God," What Do You Mean?

The question surprised me. In my church, Jubilee! Community, here in Asheville, North Carolina, I am part of a group known as "The Calling of the Elders." We are telling our own stories. When I told mine last week, another person asked, "What do you mean when you say 'God'?"

I came home thinking about a more thoughtful answer than I had given on the spur of the moment. It seemed a good spiritual discipline to formulate a more thought-out answer.

In my senior year at National College (now St. Paul's Seminary), I was one of three students who took a philosophy course with Dr. Ruth Decker. Our final exam was oral, and each of us had twenty minutes to state and defend our own philosophy. I started with the fact of God, and Dr. Decker questioned my postulating the existence of God. I said, "I believe that God exists." I cannot recall that the existence of God was ever a question in my mind, although it is questioned by many, perhaps especially today.

What do I mean when I say "God"? God is a spirit, neither male nor female. I believe that God dwells within each person, and I believe that we are surrounded by God. How can one enjoy the warmth of the sun or see a sunrise or sunset without believing in God? How can one experience the healing of one's body without believing in God? I was interested the other day in a brief clip of a television program in which it was very clear that scientists are now understanding that they ought not be so rigid about science as opposed to religion, and that thoughtful theologians are recognizing that evolution is not inconsistent with God's creation, although evolution has usually been considered to be exclusively in the scientific province. Scientists are questioning how we find such obvious order and consistency and growth in our universe if there is not an overall plan—which posits the God whom many of us know.

I recall also a discussion a number of years ago when I visited the Fellowship of Reconciliation, in Nyack, New York, where a person who had been studying Buddhism and other Eastern religions said these wise words: "When we cut through all the superficial paraphernalia of different religions, we come to a deep agreement about the existence and the goodness of one God, who is both transcendent and immanent enough to satisfy all, no matter what we call ourselves."

For a while I pondered the question *Is God outside us, a separate entity, or a spirit within us?* Now I believe that God is both. Elisabeth Schüssler Fiorenza, a theologian, in the video *Faces of Faith*,[1] cites an instance where her four-year-old daughter asked this question. Dr. Fiorenza answered that God is down inside each of us. Her daughter thought for a moment and said, "Oh, now I understand." Her mother asked wonderingly, "*What* do you understand?" "Now I understand why the boys all call God 'he,' " her daughter replied. "If God is down inside us, then all boys should call God 'he,' and all girls should call God 'she.' " (Amen!)

I recently read a book by Barbara Walker entitled *The Crone*.[2] It is one of the most thoughtful books I have read, but not one I would recommend to many people, because I think one must have a very strong faith before reading it. The author seemed bitter about much of Christianity because, as she said, Christianity is a very patriarchal religion. She contends that it is this faith that disparaged and displaced the feminine in God, and women have been abused ever since. I've read enough feminist theology to understand what she is saying. Her book is truth, although difficult for Christians to appreciate.

What do I mean by God? I mean a creative spirit that surrounds us, and is also within. God is goodness and love, forgiveness and grace, maturity and wisdom, and definitely a part of each created—and creative—human being. I believe that God is also in animals. I have long been a special devotee of elephants, who stand in a respectful circle to mourn the loss when one of their herd has died. I learned some years ago that horses will never knowingly harm a human being. In the Jewish pogroms, horses had to be blindfolded before they would step on human beings, which was one way of disposing of some of the people. Dolphins have been known since ancient times to be rescuers and helpers of humans who are beyond their depth in the oceans. I have also been impressed by the amazing patience and adaptability of Harley, our therapy cat here at Brooks-Howell and God's grace, if you will. He is to me a precious image of God, certainly God's good healing.

At Jubilee! we are assured, over and over and over and over, that God is right here right now, in the midst of the darkness and the pain and the evil. All of us personally know how difficult it is to feel the presence of God in the times when we feel that God has abandoned us to pain and/or evil spirits. As I said to someone the other day, it is not easy to be sweet and gracious and patient and caring in the midst of physical pain. We simply do not easily *feel* God's goodness and grace in such times. That doesn't mean God is not present. As I recovered from my knee surgery sometime ago, in the midst of pain and weakness, I found myself surrounded by the love and caring of many people. For me that *was* God's presence—in the likeness of all of you who came to visit and sent me notes and telephoned and prayed for my recovery. This is why it is so important for us to be present to another's need. We *are* God's presence to others!

My pastor recently wrote a meditation about dandelions. They grow in spite of all our efforts to kill them, the meditation pointed out. And then it paraphrased Jesus' words from Matthew: "Why do you worry? Are you not worth much more to God than the dandelion?"

Of course you are! After reading the meditation, I wrote two haiku, which I should like to share with you.

First,

> Dandelions grow
> No matter what their troubles.
> God made *us* that way.

And second,

> God is here and now—
> Grace and love—always present.
> Thank God for this truth.

We once set up a time for our residents at Brooks-Howell to speak more about what we mean when we say "God." All were welcome. It was a blessing to all of us to share what God means in our individual lives and living.

Think about it: What do *you* mean when you say "God"?

—given at Brooks-Howell Home, June 3, 1999

God Is Love—
No Matter What!

Good morning. I should like to speak briefly this morning about God. I will start with a quotation from Meister Eckhart, from our celebration bulletin this past Sunday:

> Consider the divine spirit in the human soul.
> This spirit is not easily satisfied.
> It storms the firmament and scales the heavens
> trying to reach the Spirit that drives the heavens.
> Because of this energy everything grows green,
> flourishes, and turns into leaf.
> But the spirit is never satisfied.
> It presses on,
> deeper and deeper into the vortex
> further and further into the whirlpool,
> the primary source in which the spirit has its origin.
> The spirit seeks to be broken through by God.
> God leads this spirit into a desert,
> into a wilderness and solitude of the divinity
> where God is pure unity
> and where God gushes up within Himself.[3]

The theme of our celebrations for this next quarter is "going deeper." In an editorial speaking about the quarter's theme, our pastor pointed out that most of us prefer the shallows when we swim. We often do not want to get beyond our depth; we prefer to stay where we can see the land and be sure of our footing. And yet our religious leaders, whether they be the early prophets or the saints of the church or our spiritual leaders today, keep pushing us out beyond the shallows, trying to help us move to the depths, where we may sometimes be fearful of drowning or of getting lost. For that is where we also find depths within ourselves that we never knew existed. St. Augustine said, "Our souls are restless until they rest in God." It is not only our saints who push us beyond ourselves, but our own souls also push us beyond what we know.

Last night, a group of us met with our pastor, to discuss what we had been thinking about since Sunday's talk about going deeper. The following are the questions posed:
1. What does it mean to experience God?
2. If someone told you they want to experience God, what would you tell them to do?
3. If "God" were not the word used for God, what other single word might you use?
4. If humans are made in God's image,
    a. why are we not more loving and forgiving? and
    b. is God fallible like us?

I do not plan to give answers to these questions, nor could I. We had some lively discussion last night. I have quoted them here simply to raise these issues for our thinking.

I shall close with the mantra that we used on Sunday, one which I shall adopt for my own understanding of God and of my relationship to God.

There is nothing you can do (or ever have done) that will make God love you more.

There is nothing you can do (or ever have done) that will make God love you less.

This is the truth I plan to hold. God's very self and nature are love, and God loves, no matter who you are, and no matter what you do. Amen.

—given at Brooks-Howell Home, January 18, 2001

The Holy

Ash Wednesday was a week or so ago, and many in our community went to various churches for Lenten services. Our church held an early morning Ash Wednesday service with Communion.

Various individuals have different customs for Lent. Many people give up something such as chocolate, desserts, the malls, the movies, favorite foods or drinks or activities, in order to sharpen their understandings of the sacrifice Jesus chose to make. Others take on certain disciplines—spiritual exercises, visiting the sick or writing them letters, daily meditation, yoga, or other practices that help to center and focus their lives. There is wide variety in the Lenten observances of Christian people.

Tuesday night, February 27, our church continued its weekly discussion of "going deeper." We found ourselves discussing what is meant by the term *holy*. The question posed was "Is there an (a) inanimate object, (b) a life form, or (c) an idea—that is holy to you? What is it and why?" It was a very interesting discussion, with many everyday activities or items or well-known experiences and shared understandings that were seen as holy by various people. I would commend to you the discussion of holy matters with a few friends or loved ones. It is like a cleansing of the soul, an airing out of long-held untouchables in our minds and hearts.

On the same day I received in the mail our semiweekly newsletter. It had an editorial about an old and well-loved chest of drawers, a highboy, and how it meant the possession of long-forgotten wealth to the owner. One thing that impressed me about our discussion on that evening was that so many everyday experiences and possessions were noted as holy.

Perhaps that is the point of the exercise: for us to recognize, in the process of discussion with others, how very holy our everyday experiences and possessions are, in reality. It is not often that we meet The Holy every day, or very often in our lives. In my life of eighty years, I can recall three specific incidents when I felt I had met God personally. These were very holy experiences for me and remain etched in my memory; they will be unforgettable until the end of my life. I treasure these rare occasions, and I assume you treasure your personal encounters with God too.

To know and understand that the holy is with us every day is a different matter. Our pastor is fond of asking, "How would it change your day if . . . (so and so and so were true)?" Now I will ask us, "How would it change your day if you knew that every experience of your everyday life is holy?" The alarm at 6:30 . . . the warm shower . . . the breakfast coffee . . . the companionship of your neighbor . . . ? Perhaps for you it's combing your hair in the morning, or the drink of water when you are thirsty, or the playful cat who graces your home, or the neighbor next door who brings you a freshly baked roll, or the homeless man walking on the street near you. . . .

A deeper realization of the holiness of all of life will surely change the way we treat our Mother Earth and all of her lifeforms. *All* life is holy, but I find holy the human beings we contact each day especially so. In our discussion at Jubilee! it was enlightening to me, again, to be reminded of how often people—a child, a person dying, a beloved wife or other humans in our lives—come to the fore when we discuss the holy. We are made in the image of God. So often we seem to forget that.

Gracious God, thank you for the holy in our lives, whether it is the picture of a loved one, or the ocean wave, a sunset, a playful dog, or the toothbrush that elicits a sense of your presence in our minds and spirits. Indeed, it is you we are speaking of when we speak of The Holy. Thank you that you have put within us a longing for yourself, expressed in so many wonderful—and often surprising—ways. Amen.

—given at Brooks-Howell Home, March 10, 2001

How Big Is Your God?

Before this past Christmas I went to the New Orleans area to visit my brother, who had been given an iffy timeline for his life. Since I was there over Sunday, I sought out a United Methodist church in the area and worshiped with its congregation. Since my brother's family is Catholic, I went alone. I found myself ashamed to recognize the pastor as a part of my own Christian faith family. In the midst of his sermon, he told the story of the young girl who asked her pastor why the God of the Old Testament was portrayed so differently from the God of the New Testament. "Oh," the pastor told her, "the reason God is so different is that the Old Testament happened before God became a Christian." The pastor went on to assure his congregation that the God in whom we believe is a Christian God.

While I call myself a committed Christian person, I have no trouble accepting as fellow travelers on the way to God's realm the many people who belong to one of the other twelve or fourteen major religious faiths in our world today. I find myself ashamed of the narrowness that we sometimes find among our good church friends.

Again, in another city and sometime ago, I went to buy a book from a well-stocked bookstore. The young clerk who was taking my money asked, "Are you Christian?" Knowing very clearly that she meant, "Are you a member of the Christian Reformed Church?"—the major church of that city—I answered that I am Christian, but not Christian Reformed. And I went on to say quietly that I resented her question and felt angry that she or her specific "brand" of Christianity would try to claim that term exclusively.

The Interfaith Alliance is an organization that has been born in more recent years. It functions both nationally and locally to bring a broader vision to many religious issues. In a recent newsletter of that body, the executive director, C. Welton Gaddy, spoke about the narrow concepts that some have of religion today. He gave the illustration of a woman who indicated that speaking about faith these days scared her because of this narrowness.

It is sad these days that people do not seem to feel free to express their faith. So many have in recent years taken a very rigid, constricted approach to their beliefs, and expect others to believe as they do, and to do the same as they. Thus we are divided, rather than supportive of each other. Gaddy expressed his joy that he could be a part of a movement, the Interfaith Alliance, that worked to facilitate positive interaction between our politics and our faith.

Most of you are aware that I put bumper stickers on my car. I am not enamored of just any old bumper sticker. The ones I have chosen make statements of conviction or draw attention to truths that many people easily forget; for example, NO ONE IS FREE WHEN ANYONE IS OPPRESSED. That is a truth that many of us forget or neglect. One of the most recent additions is one that I like very much, and that is certainly appropriate to this discussion. It says simply, GOD IS TOO BIG TO FIT INTO ONE RELIGION.

God *is* too big to fit into one religion. I believe that. My particular place to stand is Christianity. That is my religion and, within that faith that is very much a minority among the religions of the world, I have generally adopted the United Methodist Church and its beliefs. That does not mean that I cannot worship with other denominations or other faiths, or appreciate them and their good work. In solidarity work in Nicaragua I found myself working with Presbyterians, Catholics, Baptists, Episcopalians, Mennonites, Jewish people, Buddhists, and people whom I call my "unchurched" friends. All of them were committed to justice in the situation of Nicaragua, and we were solidly bound together in our common humanity and in the common pursuit of justice for all in that situation.

I often find myself journaling about issues that bother me and need some thinking through. As I have said about other thoughts that I have shared in worship, this is not the final word on this issue, but it is my thinking at this point.

Let us pray.

Gracious and abundant God, thank you that you are always and ever too big for us to understand or grasp, or know entirely. Thank you that you are so many things to so many people, so that we cannot claim to know all there is to know about you. Thank you that we can keep on growing in our understanding of you for as long as we live. Thank you for the curiosity that you have put within us—the desire to know more—and for the assurance that you are universal and available to any and all who seek you. Amen and Amen.

—given at Brooks-Howell Home, April 19, 2001

God's Surprises

Surprise! Today, at Jubilee!, we talked about God's surprises in our lives and the fact that God likes surprises very much. It is so true! I think of the surprise of the daffodils and forsythia bursting into bloom. And right now, the lilacs' leaf buds are fat and ready to burst. Several weeks ago I heard a robin—what a delightful surprise in the early morning outside my door. And yesterday a mockingbird was singing his heart out!

Three or four years ago, on a Sunday afternoon, I became aware of a lost puppy whining behind the business office near my apartment. Surprise! I gathered him up and took him around the neighborhood, but no one claimed him. So then I had the frustrating problem of what to do with him on a Sunday afternoon. The Humane Society was not open, and I surely could not keep a lively puppy. But I was very sure that I did not want him to get hit in the street. Finally, Jo, here at Brooks-Howell's front desk, took him home with her. She advertised widely, but no one claimed him. Well . . . surprise! Today you can ask her about him. He has grown into a horse, and he's still in her care! He was a great surprise to me, and a surprise to Jo as well—the kind of fun surprise that changed her life!

Surprise! I was in Lucerne, Switzerland, and we were unloading from our big tour bus. As I hit the sidewalk, I heard someone call my name. I looked around quickly and . . . there was my friend, also once a school social worker, just climbing into her big tour bus, having had an earlier meal at the same place! She had worked in another school in another county in Michigan, but we were companions in our occasional meetings together for regional training and understanding. We had both worked in Michigan in the 1980s and now were both at the same restaurant in Lucerne in the 1990s! Surprise!

Surprise! I was living in Nicaragua, and had flown to Tegucigalpa, Honduras, for an international peace conference that was advertised in our Nicaraguan papers. I kept asking my missionary friends in Managua and all the internationals I knew if anyone was going, but no, no one was. They were all tied up with work or schedules that did not permit their being free to go. I debated about it for a while and decided to go by myself. I arrived a day before the conference and went to a hotel that catered to internationals, where I was to spend the night and meet with the peace group the next day. Toward evening, I went down to the open lounge, and . . . there I saw a young woman who was obviously from the United States. We introduced ourselves, and told each other about our respective business in Tegucigalpa. June had come from a small evangelical church and was to be the bookkeeper at an isolated medical clinic. She was in Tegucigalpa to get her language training. We went on talking about our connections and where we were from—the normal small talk in such circumstances. Surprise! Not only was June from my own city in Michigan, but she lived not a half mile from my home. Surprise!

Surprise! I went from Wilmington, Delaware, where I was working, to New York City to visit Ruth Decker, a deaconess friend who had been my college philosophy professor. I had taken the bus, and Ruth was to meet me at the bus station and take me to her apartment in Brooklyn. As we approached New York, I heard someone say there were *two* bus stations in New York. Not knowing the city, I was thrown into confusion. So I went forward and asked the driver which station was the main station. He was a grumpy man and he replied angrily, "They're both main stations." I was more confused than ever and decided to get off at the first station. Of course, Ruth was not there. Since it was near lunchtime and I had not eaten much breakfast, I decided to get a bite of lunch, get directions to her place in Brooklyn, and find my way out there. Thus, about an hour later, I found myself on the platform waiting for a subway train to Brooklyn. My train finally came and, as the car pulled up and stopped . . . surprise! There was Ruth, sitting right near the open door!

Surprise! I was in Nicaragua and, due to an amazing confusion of circumstances, I found myself in Bluefields, on the east coast of Nicaragua, all alone, not knowing a soul. Gringos seem to spot each other and often give help to people alone in a strange land. A young woman told me there would be a rally at such and such a place early that evening, and I would probably be interested. I decided to go. There I quickly met a mature couple, and we started talking. His wife met a friend of hers and they walked off together while the man and I continued to converse. He told me that he taught at Williams College, in Massachusetts. "Williams College," I said. "I don't know anything about it, but a young friend of mine goes there. Bill is the son of a family I've known for some time, and he is at Williams." The man asked excitedly, "Bill who?" "Bill Freeman," I said. The man jumped three feet off the ground! "Bill Freeman? You didn't say Bill Freeman?!" "Yes, I said Bill Freeman. His family lives about a mile from us, and we are good friends with his parents. His brother is my computer teacher." The man said excitedly, "Bill is my star football player!" . . . Surprise!

It seems that God's surprises often come when we are feeling down or discouraged or all alone, and perhaps in need of comfort or a boost of some kind. This afternoon I phoned a friend in another city, to remind her that I have been thinking of her and her son. He has needed much of her extra attention with a syndrome related to autism that leaves him less than fully healthy. I am grateful that he is better these days, although it is uncertain for how long. My call was a pleasant surprise! to her.

So often God's surprises keep us reminded of God's amazing presence in this world. God cannot be taken for granted and is not a dull and predictable friend. I find myself glad that God surprises us in so many ways each day!

—*Journal, March 17, 2002*

God Is a Spendthrift

Our theme at Jubilee! this quarter talks about the amazing fullness of God. On Sunday, the altar was piled high with succulent peaches and wonderful red, full tomatoes. What a spendthrift our gracious God is!

At my former home in Grand Rapids, Michigan, I never ceased to be impressed with the abundance and creativity of God. We had several mature maple trees—and each fall, we raked leaves and raked leaves and raked leaves. There were thousands and thousands of them. Are you aware that there are no two maple leaves alike? Each one can be identified as a maple leaf, just as each leaf of an oak tree can be identified as an oak leaf—and yet each one is different from every other. Check it out for yourself on the trees around here! We know an awesome God.

The thing that always got to me with our trees, however, was the spring, when the winged maple seeds fell—thousands and thousands and thousands of them. Talk about abundance! Clearing them up was never an easy task. Once I had a landscaper at my home, and I asked about this apparent overabundance of seeds. Yes, he said, we had not had enough rain or snow, and the trees were in danger of death—thus the overabundance of seed pods. We were always away in the summer, and the trees needed much more water than we were able to give them, and sure enough, they had to come down a few years later—they did not live. This seeming overabundance of seeds was God's way of ensuring that the life of these wonderful trees would continue. I remember thinking what a wonderful God we know, with a built-in plan to ensure that a tree's life would continue.

And then the snow—in one year, 1967, we had snow each and every day for weeks and weeks on end. Each morning we would get up and see more snow. I finally said to God, "Dear

God, how can you do this to us? Please, not one more day of snow!" Oh yes, it kept coming anyway! Have you thought of how many billions and billions of snowflakes that meant? I am sure you know as I do that there are no two snowflakes alike! Can you imagine the creativity of a God who can send billions and billions of snowflakes, each one with a hexagonal shape, and yet no two alike? That is simply awesome.

Then there are human beings. Have you ever seen or known two alike? Are you not amazed and delighted at how different each one is from every other one? Even when there are twins, every child is different. Every person is different! What a delightful world it is with so much to discover and so many wonderful people to know. What an amazing and creative God!

At this time, I am reading *The Shelters of Stone*,[4] the latest Jean Auel novel about Ayla, a young woman who lived in the very early years of human existence. The author has done her homework with an amazing understanding of anthropology. This is the fifth book in the Earth's Children® series. What has struck me from the very first book is the wonder and awe and respect and tender love with which the "Great Mother" is approached and worshiped by her creation. Each group of people singles out the healing people among them to help them to approach this creator with rituals. In this book there is a long recital of the beginnings of life, one of the sacred stories of the group. It is told in song and rhythm as a part of one of their sacred ceremonies.

The Psalms we know pick up this wonder and awe in many passages. I shall close with reading a few of these. They are from Eugene Peterson's translation of the Bible, *The Message*.[5]

From Psalm 19:
   God's glory is on tour in the skies,
      God—craft on exhibit across the horizon.
   Madame Day holds classes every morning,
      Professor Night lectures each evening.
   Their words aren't heard
      their voices aren't recorded.
   But their silence fills the earth:
      unspoken truth is spoken everywhere.

God makes a huge dome
    for the sun—a superdome!
The morning sun's a new husband
    leaping from his honeymoon bed.
The daybreaking sun an athlete
    racing to the tape. (Ps. 19:1–5)

The revelation of God is whole
    and pulls our lives together.
The signposts of God are clear
    and point out the right road.
The life-maps of God are right,
    showing the way to joy.
The directions of God are plain
    and easy on the eyes.
God's reputation is twenty-four-carat gold,
    with a lifetime guarantee.
The decisions of God are accurate
    down to the nth degree. (Ps. 19:7–9)

From Psalm 23 we read,

God, my shepherd!
    I don't need a thing.
You have bedded me down in lush meadows,
    you find me quiet pools to drink from.
True to your word,
    you let me catch my breath
    and send me in the right direction. (Ps. 23:1–3)

Your beauty and love chase after me
    every day of my life.
I'm back home in the house of God
    for the rest of my life. (Ps. 23:6)

And from Psalm 36:

God's love is meteoric
    his loyalty astronomic,
His purpose titanic,
    his verdicts oceanic.

Yet in his largeness,
   nothing gets lost;
Not a man, not a mouse,
   slips through the cracks. (Ps. 36:5–6)

In closing, let me read a quote from Julian of Norwich, from *The Life of the Soul*.

... There is no created being who can know how much and how sweetly and how tenderly the creator loves us, and therefore we can with his grace and his help persevere in spiritual contemplation, with endless wonder at this high, surpassing, immeasurable love which our Lord in his goodness has for us; and therefore we may with reverence ask from our lover all that we will, for our natural will is to have God, and God's good will is to have us, and we can never stop willing or loving until we possess [God] in the fullness of joy.[6]

—given at Brooks-Howell Home, June 26, 2002

An Amazingly Creative and Changing God

A lot of interesting life has been coming my way lately, and I should like to share a bit about it.

I have been reading two very different books, and they are a contrast. The first is titled *Faithful Guardians*.[7] It is a collection of brief accounts of dogs, cats, and other pets who have been wise teachers, nurses and helpers to their human friends. The other is the book *Jailed for Justice,* written by Clare Hanrahan about her prison experience.[8] She served six months in a federal prison for her protest at the School of the Americas, or the School of Assassins, as it is called in Latin America. The SOA Watch held its most recent protest this past weekend.

One of the verities of life is that nothing stays the same—there are always changes in our lives and living, in our relationships, in our friendships, in our understandings, in our activities, and in our "normal" lifestyle. Life is certainly not boring—I find it different each day!

Our own lives and living are not unlike the leaves on the trees—one can always tell that it's an oak leaf, or a maple leaf, or a sweet gum leaf, but even so, each leaf of every tree is a new creation, and different. For us, each with our own, unique lifestyle and pattern of the days, each day is different. I can only marvel at such a creative God—millions of snowflakes photographed, and never two alike—although all are on a hexagonal pattern. So it is with our days; each is very different.

For many people, the concept of God is that God is a never-changing entity—always the same. Yes, surely our God is the same in the amazing intensity and outward thrust of love and patience and understanding and righteousness and wisdom! But certainly, changing is how we conceive of God. I was interested in the reaction I recently received when I mentioned Karen Armstrong's book *A History of God*.[9] The person asked, "How can there be a history when God is the same yesterday, today and tomorrow?" Well, *is* God always the same for you? Does God not *ever* change? How about the times in our Scriptures when God changed God's mind? There are several very clear instances of that. Is not your concept of God different now than when you were thirteen? Do you not think of God very differently at your age now than you did when you were twenty? I hope so! If not, where have you been? Why did you put God in a box and store God away? I certainly no longer see God as an old man with a white beard as I did when I was young. Sometimes I see God as Harley or Butterscotch or Oliver (pets here at Brooks-Howell), or a good friend, or that last wonderful brightly-golden marigold that hangs on fresh and vibrant, although all of its companions have become dried brown heads.

Oh yes, our relationship with whatever God we know enlarges and deepens and changes and surprises and sometimes shocks us. God is made known to us in so many ways. God's presence is always dependable, and is always loving and caring, yet always different, as it grows and deepens. Do not tell me that the love that Beth knows for Hunter is the same love they started with fifty-seven years ago! Oh no! Do not tell me that my love for Barbara has not had its ups and downs, and ins and outs, and has not changed and grown and changed again! It is no wonder that couples often want divorce these days. Things just don't stay the same, and some of us are lost when our love changes. All of us change and grow, and see things very differently as the days pass on.

Faithful Guardians and *Jailed for Justice*—these two books give us very different views of God, as God is seen through the actions of animals and through the lives of prisoners. Both books have helped me to enlarge and deepen my concepts of God.

One illustration of God's changing might be the newly-bred plants and flowers. I was amazed the first time I noted that the day lilies along our drive from the street are double lilies. How did that happen? Is a doubled flower or some of the modifications of our vegetables and foods these days an indication of a changing God? God's creations may not be the same these days. Does that point to the reality that God also changes? I do not know, but I do know that God is indeed amazingly creative, yesterday, today, and forever.

Let us pray.

Amazing and creative God, we know that you are changeless in your love for your world and for the life you have put on this planet. Thank you for all we learn of you through flowers and plants and animals and people. Thank you for the creativity you have put within each of us. Help us always to hold you in reverence and love. Amen.

—given at Brooks-Howell Home, November 20, 2002

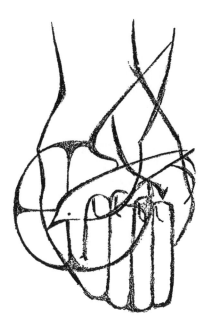

God Will Never Wear Out

We read in Hebrews (Peterson's translation):

You, Master, started it all, laid earth's foundations,
    then crafted the stars in the sky.
Earth and sky will wear out, but not you;
    they become threadbare like an old coat;
You'll fold them up like a worn-out cloak,
    and lay them away on the shelf.
But you'll stay the same year after year;
    you'll never fade, you'll never wear out. (Heb. 1:10b–12)[10]

Christmas is not always a whoop-de-doo holiday! For many, that is putting it mildly. Sometimes we do not want to admit that, for ourselves, it is just not the wonderful, happiness-filled holiday that the crooners sing about and many others seem to be celebrating.

Social services in this town recognize this truth. They know there are many suicides and attempted suicides at this blessed time of year. Hospitals and therapists know there are many who have a double dose of depression at the holiday season. There are some among us here at Brooks-Howell who find holidays difficult—one of us is spending her first Christmas with us, away from her own home and longing for that comfort still. There are others among us who have lost loved ones or who, for other reasons, find little to celebrate at this festive time.

When I received the bulletin from my church in Grand Rapids the other day, I was interested to note that our parish nurse recognizes this phenomenon. She set a time and place for people in our church family—those who do not feel good about trying to celebrate this season while weeping inside—to gather together and share with others of like mind. She calls it a Blue Christmas. It is a time and space for people to gather together and acknowledge their sadness and concern. There is great comfort in sharing with others, and knowing that you are not alone. A church gathering provides a safe place to share our sadness together.

That does not mean that this holiday is not worth celebrating. Far from it! It is rather a simple and honest recognition that some of our brothers and sisters, and maybe you yourself, have been facing a different kind of life experience at this time of year.

Jubilee! celebrates four seasons throughout the year. This is based on Matthew Fox's understanding of what he calls original blessing—an outlook different from the theory of so-called original sin, bequeathed to us by our understanding of Augustine and adopted long ago into our church doctrine. At Jubilee! the fall season is called the *Via Negativa*—the negative time of our lives. In our natural world Via Negativa comes in the fall, as trees lose their leaves, the days grow cold, the rains come, the nights grow longer and days shorter. There is less sunshine in late fall. Sometimes, in our church life, we tend to forget that the bitter comes with the sweet, that the negative is also a normal part of life, and that life is not all grace and glory. Sometimes our lives are full of "bitter herbs."

In my own life, as we began this fall season with its higher potential for depressed feelings, I was on top of the world and simply could not, at first, get into the recognition that this more quiet and often more dull time of the year is also a part of *my* life as well as of the lives of others. I was especially glad for the reminder this year at Jubilee! that this time is temporary. That is what the Jewish Succoth feast is all about. Our worship center at Jubilee! was decorated for this feast day with long sheaves of corn stalks and fall fruits, reminiscent of the simple structure of the Succoth, a temporary hut that reminds us that life itself is temporary.

Soon after the feast I had to go into the hospital. At first I thought, "Why this interruption of my panicky efforts to get my cards sent out, to get the last gifts bought and mailed, and to ensure my attendance at some of the wonderful concerts and music events and, of course, parties, that bless this season?" And then I recognized that this was my own Via Negativa experience.

Yes, it is depressing to realize that we are all vulnerable, especially as we begin to age—sometimes, we know not where or how, we are struck with maladies that can seem unending. So it is good to remember that *all* things—even our lives—are temporary! As someone reminded me today, we are all headed for the inevitable passage.

So what is this meditation about? Simply to recognize the negative in our lives—things we really don't want to think about? Oh no!

A recent meditation that I read in *Upper Room Disciplines* indicated something that we often forget. It said essentially that nothing that we know in this entire universe is permanent. It said that everything will be worn out like a piece of discarded clothing. But the book of Hebrews reminds us that it does not really matter how impermanent everything seems, because the essential in our lives, the love of God, is permanent, and God's faithfulness will always be the same.[11]

For meditation, let us think for a moment about how that faithfulness of God has brought us, each one, through many changes to new life.

(After a moment of silence) Let us pray.

Gracious God, Thank you that your love for us is forever. It is not transitory or temporary. Thank you for the difficult experiences in our own lives that have brought us to new life. And we thank you that we too can, in this new year, learn to love your world and your people, even as you love us, and bring them to new life. Amen.

—*given at Brooks-Howell Home, December 19, 2002*
(used on January 8, 2003)

Is God Monarch or Lover?

Some of you may be familiar with Marcus Borg as an author of books on understandings of Jesus, and on theology. He is a keen thinker, and did a series of lectures at Chautauqua in a recent year. In one lecture he contrasted two different models of God and made clear some of the consequences in our world of each of the models.

He referred to the one model as that of God as monarch and the other of God as lover. He then fleshed out these two ideas with some of their consequences. He noted his reliance on Sallie McFague's book, *Models of God*. [12]

The monarchical model is the one of a patriarchal God with which we are quite familiar. It is the pattern we hear every day in references to God when we hear people refer to God as judge and when we speak of God as Lord, Almighty Ruler, and many other familiar images. It is a model that essentially says, "You'd better shape up or you will not go to heaven"—in other words, your behavior now will bring a reward, or a severe punishment, later. Most of us grew up with this model, and we still tend to carry it around with us. It is like the concept of superego, the conscience, and it carries with it a keen awareness that we cannot measure up to the perfection required of us. That is why many of us carry around a heavy load of guilt and feel that we can never "do it right." I have a psychologist friend who used to speak of "the tyranny of the *should*s."

The other model, that of God as lover, emphasizes our relationship to the God who loves us, even when we are not perfect and have not kept the jot and tittle of the law. It speaks of our eagerness to embrace others as our brothers and sisters because of that relationship with a God who loves all people even as God loves us.

The model of God as monarch has led to much of the destruction of our planet, with its emphasis on the idea that man is ruler over all of creation. Thus we have exploited and destroyed much of our world rather than nurturing and protecting it. It has also led to the kinds of prejudices we know in racism and militarism, and most of all in sexism, wherein man is seen as a god because we have seen God as patriarch, or male. Men see themselves as rulers over others, rather than appreciating others as brothers and sisters, also beloved of God.

As Marcus Borg's lecture continued, he explained that the model of God as lover means that God loves each one of us. He noted that he was in a restaurant while preparing for the lecture, and after he had written that line, he looked up and noted the people in the restaurant. He asked himself what a difference it would make in their lives—and his—if he saw them as God's beloved, even as he saw himself as such.

I have been reading a book for the Women's Division reading program, on the parables, and was brought up short the other night with the parable of the sheep and the goats, when the author pointed out that the story of the Last Judgment is not only about our personal ways of life, although of course it embraces that. If we read that parable carefully, we realize that whole nations are brought to account. We tend to think of this parable as pertaining to our individual behavior only. It is a very different matter when we look at groups of people, entire nations, coming to judgment on the basis of feeding the hungry and clothing the naked and visiting those who are ill. That puts a very different spin on the story, as they say these days. It is food for thought for all of us: How are we doing as community, as nation, in our relationship to the God of our Universe?

Because this worship each morning is very brief, I will not go further at this time. Perhaps I have said enough to open your thinking to the possibilities of seeing God differently than just the one way that we have come to image God.

On Sunday at Jubilee!, we had an interesting and brief exercise, in which we were asked to think quietly for a minute about one wish that we would want for our world for this next year. We were asked to share this wish with a neighbor. We were also challenged then, to make that wish come true this year—to do all we, each one, can do to make that dream or wish a reality. Is it peace for our world that you want? Then what will you do to bring that about? Is it surcease from pain for loved ones? What specifically will you do to make that happen?

I have thought all week about how to implement my wish for our world.

And now, let us pray.

Thank you, God, for the realization that you are always beyond our understanding, and much more loving and mysterious than our small minds can conceive. Thank you that you are always calling us beyond ourselves to understand more of you, and to love you more deeply. Thank you for your delightful and abundant gifts to us, manifest every day in the realities of food and friends and daily news and next door neighbors. Amen.

—*given at Brooks-Howell Home, January 9, 1999*

God Is a Verb

In Anne Wilson Schaef's small book, *Meditations for Women Who Do Too Much,* the meditation for today's date is quite thought-provoking. She starts with a quote from Mary Daly: "Why indeed, must God be a noun? Why not a verb . . . the most active and dynamic of all?"[13] Anne Schaef continues her brief meditation with these words.

> Some of us have difficulty with the concept of God because we have seen God evolve into something or someone who is static, a mega-controller, and frankly someone who is not that nice to be around. Traditionally, we have tried to make God static so we would feel safe. [And I will add, editorially, so that we can control God by our own lives.] That is our problem, not God's.
>
> What if we see God as a process—the process of the universe? What if we begin to understand that we are part of the process of the universe? What if we realize that it is only when we live who we are that we have the option of being one with that process? Trying to be someone else, who we think we should be or who others think we should be, ruptures our oneness with that process.[14]

The author concludes with this brief sentence: "If God is a process and I am a process, we have something in common with which to begin."

On Tuesday evening, a number of us listened to the cassette tape of Marcus Borg, hearing his lecture given at Chautauqua sometime ago. This particular one is titled "Imaging God: Why It Matters." It set me to thinking about different images of God. Many, of course, show up in the Scriptures. Since the early centuries, though, some of these images have been glossed over or covered over or forgotten or simply neglected by the Church. As the Church "grew up," it adopted the patriarchal, monarchical image—to the neglect of many others.

When I studied at Garrett-Evangelical Theological Seminary a few years ago, I did some readings from Marjorie Suchocki's book *God, Christ, Church*,[15] and found myself fascinated by the concept that God is not a static person or thing, but moves and changes even as our own existence moves and changes. If we think about it, we know that *we* have changed. God help me if I have remained the child I was when I started college! I feel as though I'm miles apart from that young woman, in dress style and thinking power, in social relationships, and in concern for our planet. Thinking of this progression, it makes sense to me that, if we are made in God's image—and I believe we are—then God also changes and evolves. When we think of God as Spirit, perhaps that is not so hard to think about. It is only when we conceive of God as a static entity that we come to trouble.

I have said several times in various ways—in prayers and worship essays—that, to me, God is always beyond us, mysterious and beckoning forward, and difficult to comprehend in God's entirety. It seems that, no matter how much we know of God's love or how deeply we love God, there is always more —more of God's strength and depth within us, more of God's love for us, and more of our love for God, and more to understand and appreciate of God.

I am excited about the fact that I have moved, also, from a childhood concept of God, to seeing God as Spirit or, as Anne Schaef's thinking suggests, as a process—an ongoing verb that moves beyond us even as we have moved from childhood to adulthood. And so, why not think of God as a verb, rather than as a static noun, as Schaef suggests? I can only speak for me, but for me that makes life exciting and fresh and sometimes ridiculously fun—full of laughter and surprise, singing and dancing, replete with endless energy and joy. As we say at Jubilee!, Oh yeah!

Let us pray.

Gracious God, it is impossible for us to know you completely because you do not stand still, but are ever moving, even as the air or wind . . . or Spirit. Thank you that you thus call us to move, to continue our own growing and changing, even as we seek to love you and nourish your world, even as you do.

Thank you for your gifts to us that tell us of your love: our daily food; our precious friends and mentors, and our companions, all images of yourself, on the journey of life. Amen.

—*given at Brooks-Howell Home, January 14, 1999*

Nonsexist Names, Titles, Phrases, Applied to God

This list was compiled by Develyn Vignaud for the section on worship, Board of Discipleship of the United Methodist Church.[16]

All-powerful God
Almighty giver of love
Answer to all mysteries
Awesome God
Awesome one
Binder of Wounds
Brightness of faithful souls
Comfort of sufferers
Companion of the lonely
Creative source of all being
Creator and preserver of all
Creator of all
Creator of goodness and beauty
Creator of the light
Desire of all nations
Eternal Father-Mother-God
Eternal God our answer
Eternal Keeper
Eternal One
Eternal Ruler
Eternal source of knowledge
Eternal source of peace
Eternal spirit of the universe
Ever living God
Ever loving God
Faithful God
Fountain of all holiness
Fountain of everlasting light
Fountain of life
Fountain of light and truth
Fountain of wisdom
Friend of the poor
Generous provider of all good gifts
Giver of all good things
Giver of every good and perfect gift
Giver of love
Giver of peace
God arrayed in justice
God of ages past and future
God of all being
God of all compassion
God of all creatures
God of all flesh
God of all generations
God of all goodness
God of all power
God of all righteousness
God of all the world
God of all times and places

God of comfort
God of comfort
God of compassion
God of earth and air, height, and depth
God of earthquake, wind, and fire
God of eternal might
God of forgiveness and understanding
God of freedom and right
God of grace and glory
God of health and salvation
God of heavenly powers
God of holiness
God of holy love
God of hope and joy
God of Israel's past
God of life and death
God of life and health
God of light and sun
God of many deliverances
God of peace
God of power and splendor
God of prophets (and apostles)
God of steadfastness and encouragement
God of the beginning, God of the end
God of the loving heart
God of the morning, noon, and, evening of life
God of the spirits of all flesh
God of this day
God of truth
God of unchangeable power
God of wonders
God our companion
God our helper
God surrounded by glory
God who art perfect love
Gracious giver of knowledge
Gracious God
Great God (of power)
Great God our hope
Great healer of body and soul
Great ruler of the world
Guide and inspiration of humanity
Guide of humanity
Guide of the meek
Healer of the sick
Healer of the weak
Heart that inspires in us a vision of justice and love
Heart's delight
Helper of all persons
Hidden God
High and Holy One
Hope of all the ends of the earth
Incognito God
Inexhaustible God
Infinite God
Inspiration to goodness
Judge eternal
Judge of all humankind
Keeper of (the) Covenant(s)
Keeper of our souls
Life of all who live
Life of mortals
Life of the universe
Life of the world
Light of all seeing
Light of the faithful
Light of the minds that know Thee
Lover of concord
Lover of peace
Lover of souls

Maker of all things
Maker of heaven and earth
Maker of light
Maker of men and women in your own likeness
Mighty forever God
Mighty God
Mighty redeemer
Mind of the universe
Mind that unifies all creation
One and eternal God of time and space
Only one
Our creator and our teacher
Our refuge and our strength
Our source and our end
Power that saves
Power that shields
Proclaimer of justice
Protector of all who trust
Pure and upright one
Radiance of faithful souls
Radiant and glorious God
Redeemer and deliverer
Redeemer of Israel
Redeemer of the oppressed
Redeeming God
Refuge of those who put their trust in you
Repose of the dead
Righteous God
Righteous one of all generations
Rock of all creation
Rock of Jacob
Rock of our life
Ruler of all creation
Ruler of all people on earth
Ruler of the universe
Searcher of hearts
Shelter from the storm
Shield of Abraham
Shield of our fathers and mothers
Shining glory
Source of all existence
Source of all health
Source of all power
Source of all that we have and are
Source of all true joy
Source of blessing
Source of creation
Source of deliverance and Help
Source of eternal light
Source of freedom
Source of good
Source of health and strength
Source of life
Source of mercy
Source of peace
Source of salvation
Source of strength
Source of truth and law
Sovereign God
Sovereign of peace
Staff and support of the righteous
Steadfast and loving one
Strength of our life
Strength of the weak
Strength of those who labor
Strong God of truth
Support of the innocent
Sustainer of all the worlds that are
Teacher of peace
The first and the last

The power that brings healing to the sick
True and only light
True sun of the world
Upholder of the falling
Watchful and caring God
(The) Will that gives us power
Wondrous fashioner and sustainer of Life
World's light

These ways to address God were found in Jubilee! bulletins:

Amazing Grace
Ancient Wholeness
Balmy, Sea-soaked Southerly Gale
Brutal Nor'easter
Consummate Lover
Creator
Creator of All of Us
Creator of All Things
Creator of Now
Dear Heavenly One
Divine Choreographer
Dreamer
Eternal One
Everlasting Life of Life
Excessive, Generous, Lavish God
Father and Mother of us All
Gentle Peace
God Beyond all our Gods
God of Wind and Air
Good God
Holy and Beautiful God
Holy Artist
Holy Assurance
Holy Blessedness
Holy Constancy
Holy Giver
Holy Goodness
Holy Imagination
Holy Kindness
Holy Life
Holy Love
Holy Mother—Holy Father God
Holy Mystery
Holy One
Holy One of the Universe
Holy Peace
Holy power
Holy Presence
Holy River
Holy Serenity
Holy Sustainer
Holy Tenderness
Holy Vivacity
Holy Wholeness
Holy Wind
Holy Wonder
Holy, Loving Artist
Imaginative Lover
Light Divine
Loving Kindness
Loving Mystery
Maker of the Rainbow
Morning Star
Most Holy Fire
My God
Mysterious Guide
Mystery Maker
O Light
Old Friend

78   *A Faith Expressed*

Parent of All People
Quiet, Gentle Breeze
River of Life
Source of Life and Love and Caring

Star-gazing, Life-Giving God
Sweet Forgiveness
Wild Adventurer
Wild and Restless Wind
Wonder-Maker

NOTES

1. This is one of a series of videos produced by the United Methodist Church in the 1980s. About a half hour long each, these videos featured interviews with religious leaders regarding their faith. A copy of the series was sent to each Conference library for use in the Conference. They are now available only through the Conference Headquarters Archives.

2. Barbara G. Walker, *The Crone* (San Francisco: HarperCollins, 1988).

3. Meister Eckhart, quoted in Jubilee! Community bulletin, January 2001. Used with permission of Jubilee!

4. Jean M. Auel, *The Shelters of Stone*, Earth's Children book 5 (New York: Bantam Books, 2003).

5. Eugene H. Peterson, translator, *The Message: The Bible in Contemporary Language* (Colorado Springs: NavPress Publishing Group, 2002). Scripture so cited is taken from *The Message*. Copyright © 1993, 1994, 1995, 1996, 2000, 2001, 2002. Used by permission of Navapress Publishing Group.

6. Julian, *The Life of the Soul: The Wisdom of Julian of Norwich*, translated by Edmund Colledge, OSA, and James Walsh, SJ (Boston: Paulist Press, 1996).

7. Phyllis Hobe, editor, *Faithful Guardians: Listening to Animals*. Trans. by Edmund Colledge and James Walsh (Boston: Paulist Press, 2001).

8. Clare Hanrahan, *Jailed for Justice* (Asheville, NC: Brave Ulysses Books, 2002).

9. Karen Armstrong, *A History of God: The 400 Year Quest for Judaism, Christianity and Islam* (New York: Random House, 1994).

10. Peterson, *The Message*.

11. *The Upper Room Disciplines 2003: A Book of Daily Devotions* (Nashville, TN: Upper Room Books, 2002).

12. Sallie McFague, *Models of God: Theology for an Ecological, Nuclear Age* (Minneapolis: Augsburg Fortress, 1987).

13. Mary Daly is a feminist theologian, well known for her book *Beyond God the Father: Toward a Philosophy of Women's Liberation* (Boston: Beacon Press, 1973). See also, her book *Gyn/Ecology: The Metaethics of Radical Feminism* (Boston: Beacon Press, 1978).

14. Anne Wilson Schaef, *Meditations for Women Who Do Too Much* (San Francisco: HarperCollins, 1990).

15. Marjorie Hewitt Suchocki, *God, Christ, Church: A Practical Guide to Process Theology*, rev. ed. (New York: Crossroad Pub. Co., 1982, 1989).

16. This list, circulated in the late 1980s by the Board of Discipleship of the United Methodist Church, is in the public domain, according to the church Board.

God's Reflection In Our Natural World

Heaven Is Under Our Feet

Ina Warren, in her book *Care and Feeding of the Natural Rituals of Our Lives*, has a section titled "Heaven is Under Our Feet," in which she includes four pages of awesome delights. I have pulled out the ones that can be possible for many of us here, in a retirement home. (I left out, for example, backpacking in the Grand Canyon!) I should like to share these with you.

> making soap bubbles out of doors
> sitting in front of the oven as fresh bread is baking
> saying grace and giving thanks at every meal
> a homegrown tomato patch
> a bookstore with a coffee shop attached
> anywhere there is mistletoe
> Easter sunrise services
> giving a child a box of 64 colors with a sharpener
> eating an orange—anywhere, anytime, anyhow
> a break anywhere honeysuckle grows
> midnight candlelight Christmas Eve services
> memory lane
> stringing cranberries and popcorn for a wildlife holiday tree
> sitting at a window at a hummingbird feeder
> a long, hot, luxurious bath for no occasion
> surprising someone with fresh flowers
> listening to the ocean in an empty conch shell
> watching a sunset from anywhere
> back roads for scenic drives
> feeding birds in your feeder
> watching stars twinkle with a cup of hot chocolate
> a safe, dry haven in a pounding rain
> listening to Vivaldi's *Four Seasons* suite
> popping corn—anywhere, anytime, any way, anyhow!

blowing bubbles
anywhere you happen to be drinking clean water
a sunny brunch in an atrium filled with plants
a native American medicine wheel
laughing till your belly hurts
looking for birds nests in all four seasons
realizing that every day is an epiphany.[1]

—given at Brooks-Howell Home, November 28, 2001

Epiphany

Reading from the Beatitudes, from *The Message*.

"You're blessed when you're at the end of your rope. With less of you there is more of God and his rule.

"You're blessed when you feel you've lost what is most dear to you. Only then can you be embraced by the One most dear to you.

"You're blessed when you're content with just who you are—no more, no less. That's the moment you find yourselves proud owners of everything that can't be bought.

"You're blessed when you've worked up a good appetite for God. He's food and drink in the best meal you'll ever eat.

"You're blessed when you care. At the moment of being "carefull," you find yourselves cared for.

"You're blessed when you get your inside world—your mind and heart—put right. Then you can see God in the outside world.

"You're blessed when you can show people how to cooperate instead of compete or fight. That's when you discover who you really are, and your place in God's family.

"You're blessed when your commitment to God provokes persecution. The persecution drives you even deeper into God's kingdom.

"Not only that—count yourselves blessed every time people put you down or throw you out or speak lies about you to discredit me. What it means is that the truth is too close for comfort and they are uncomfortable.

"You can be glad when that happens—give a cheer, even!— for though they don't like it, I do! And all heaven applauds. And know that you are in good company. My prophets and witnesses have always gotten into this kind of trouble." (Matthew 5:3–12)[2]

O Holy One
The thought of a flower is nothing compared to its smell—
Hearing a story of a full moon doesn't even come close to
    basking in its glow—
Reading about a kiss is ridiculous when balanced against
    the real thing—
And who can even describe the taste of a banana?

Why, then, Holy One, are we content to merely think of you—
Or hear stories about you—or read about you—
    and think that's enough?
Where did we develop such an anemic sense of the divine
that we could content ourselves with
hymns, Bible stories, and preacher babble?

May we pay close attention to the yearning of our souls,
the longing of our hearts to—not just think holy thoughts—
but to be immersed in your love—
to be filled to gushing-overflowing with an abounding
    sense of your presence.

Open us, therefore, to your touch in the wind
your taste in a lime,
your smell in a garden just after rain.
Open us to your here-and-now closeness
to our bodies, souls and memories.
May you become for us not just an idea,
but an experience.

—Howard Hanger[3]

Lord, the earth smells good today,
    straight from the mysteries within the inner courts of God,
A grace like new clothes thrown
    across the garden, free medicine for everybody.
The trees in their prayer, the birds in praise,
    the first blue violets kneeling.
Whatever came from being is caught up in being, drunkenly
    forgetting the way back.

— Rumi (13th century Sufi mystic)[4]

—given at Brooks-Howell Home, June 6, 2002

Recent Trip to the North

On my recent trip up north there were two things that impressed me greatly, and I'd like to speak of them this morning. These were the beauty of God's world in its luscious green, and the delight of renewing friendships and the beautiful reunions with friends.

It is not surprising that I would want to speak of the beauty of our world after my recent trip north through North Carolina and Tennessee, West Virginia and various parts of Ohio, western New York, across Canada, and on into Michigan. Then, from Grand Rapids, we went up to Traverse Bay and as far as Suttons Bay, and the Little Finger area of Michigan. On Labor Day we went south and west to Saugatuck, on the Kalamazoo River. Of course we took time to visit Barb's family cottage on Lake Michigan, north of Holland. I never cease to be awed by the vast expanse of lake, with its ever-changing beauty. We did not take time on this trip to go down the ninety-seven steps to walk again on the wonderfully warm sandy beach.

Driving down again through Ohio on I-75, I felt the power of the flat farmland, and then moved into the gently rolling hills of Southern Ohio, and the more deeply cut areas in Kentucky, and on into the mountains of Tennessee and Western North Carolina. Years ago I had expressed a desire to live in the mountains. I worked for seven years in Harrisburg, Pennsylvania, with the gently wooded and beautiful Pennsylvania mountains all around. Did you know there are seven tunnels through mountains on the Pennsylvania Turnpike? I used to travel that route frequently, and I could name them all then. I just loved it. Now I consider myself very fortunate to be able to live in this beautifully sculpted mountain area here. I love it!

As I drove through, this year, I often found myself driving

with my mouth open, gaping at the wonders of God's good, green world. The beauty outside seemed to be complemented by the joys within, as I connected in friendship and love with so many along the way—kinfolk, of course, and friends, both old and new. One of my special surprises was the privilege of standing in the living room of the old, old home in Amish country near Canton, Ohio, where my maternal great-grandfather, great-great-grandfather, and great-great-great-grandfather had all lived in succession. This high, square brick house, built in the mid-1800s, has foot-thick walls. It now houses, still without electricity or water in most of the house, an Amish family with two young children. There is an addition to the house that has both water and electricity, but the big wood stove for heat still stands in the center of the living room. My cousin Bob is a newly found relative, discovered by my great-niece's work in genealogy recently. He is the grandson of my maternal grandmother's sister. To me, there is nothing more soul-satisfying than seeing old friends or precious relatives, or meeting new ones, and renewing or finding our love for one another.

Someone asked if it was a good trip. The resounding answer is, "Yes!" Not only am I grateful for safe journeys and no car trouble; I continue to be so very grateful for connecting with so many good people. Our love is enhanced by my understanding that I may not see some of these good people again!

At first, when I arrived back here in Asheville, I said to several that I did not want to come back! So true! I still occasionally find myself schizophrenic about where my home is. Of course it's here in North Carolina, but when I go back to Michigan, to the house I lived in for twenty-five years, which my "daughter" Barb now owns, when I sleep in my former bed in my former bedroom, when our big white cat keeps me company there, it is hard to believe I no longer live there. Even Wednesday morning, yesterday, at the computer at ABCCM (Asheville-Buncombe Community Christian Ministry), I found myself asking someone if Mulberry Street is a street in Grand Rapids! I quickly corrected myself, but you see where my mind still is!

In reality, now that I've been back for several days, I find myself rejoicing with all of you, and with other good new friends. I would be devastated if I should need to move again, for any reason!

Let us pray.

O, our gracious and abundant and joyful God, you have put within us such wonderful memories, and such appreciation for your beautiful world. Thank you for that. The memories and connections mean so much more to us as we grow older. So it is with the people you have created. We come to value them as friends, and see in them your likeness, in both health and pain. Keep us aware of you, our creative God, and help us to pay attention to you as we move along, knowing that you are not only in the mountains and hills and waters and wide expanses, but also in each one of us. Help us, then, to learn to love as you love, and care as you care, about each one of your children. Amen.

—*given at Brooks-Howell Home, September 11, 1997*

Honoring Trees

I should like to share a few selected verses from Scripture—first from the Psalms, and then from Matthew.

From Psalm 1 comes this gem:

> Happy are those
> > who do not follow the advice of the wicked,
> or take the path that sinners tread,
> > or sit in the seat of scoffers;
> but their delight is in the law of the Lord,
> > and on his law they meditate day and night.
> They are like trees
> > planted by streams of water,
> which yield their fruit in its season,
> > and their leaves do not wither.
> In all that they do, they prosper.
>
> The wicked are not so,
> > but are like chaff that the wind drives away.
> Therefore the wicked will not stand in the judgment,
> > nor sinners in the congregation of the righteous;
> for the Lord watches over the way of the righteous,
> > but the way of the wicked will perish. (NRSV)

And from Matthew, we find:

> Either make the tree good, and its fruit good; or make the tree bad, and its fruit bad; for the tree is known by its fruit. (Matthew 12:33, NRSV)

And,

> He put before them another parable: "The kingdom of heaven is like a mustard seed that someone took and sowed in his

field; it is the smallest of all the seeds, but when it is grown it is the greatest of shrubs and becomes a tree, so that the birds of the air come and make nests in its branches." (Matthew 13:31, 32, NRSV)

Some of you are aware that we at Brooks-Howell have just lost two Bradford pear trees, which were part of a threesome lining our drive in the parking lot. Oh yes, they looked good—all three matched in shape and size—and have beautifully bloomed the last few weeks.

In talking with David Williams, our wonderful gardener, I learned that they were genetically engineered trees, and were therefore not so sturdy and strong as our older trees are. They could not withstand the last heavy snow we had two weeks ago. I am one of a growing group of people who has a real thing against genetically engineered trees, and genetically engineered foods, including many of our cereals. We are now often eating these as unknowns because the food corporations in our country managed to get a foothold without the public's awareness, and labeling was not demanded here, as in England and European countries. There is now a strong group of people fighting this, and we hope that we can be successful in demanding labeling. We need to know *what* we are eating. Many of these foods have very little nutritional value.

From Polly Whitacre's recent informative sketch on our residents' bulletin board, I learned that the first Arbor Day was held April 25, 1872. In these days, Earth Day is celebrated on April 22, and there were events then and this week acknowledging and celebrating that. I remember well the commemoration of Arbor Day in our school when I was in grade school. Our class groups gathered outside in April of each year to witness the planting of one more tree.

Quality Forward is an organization in Asheville responsible for the metal sculptures around town—the big iron that stands at the corner of Wall Street and Battery Park, commemorating the Flatiron Building; the three cats chasing a mouse on Wall Street; the delightful dancers with a fiddle in front of the Asheville Civic Center; the three women shoppers in front of Malaprop's bookstore; and other markers around town. From their newsletter I found this wisdom regarding trees.

They ask, "What's the big deal about trees?" And their answer:
1. Trees clean our water. . . .
2. Trees clean the air. . . .
3. Trees cool the air, land, and water. . . .
4. Trees provide vital habitat for wildlife. . . .
5. Trees save money. . . . [They reduce] the cost of storm water runoff, reducing home and office energy use, and improving property values.
6. Trees count! Every tree . . . counts toward . . . a greener future.
7. Trees celebrate life. Planting trees shares the joy of a birth or birthday, remembers a loved one, or says thank-you to a friend.
8. Trees make good neighbors. . . .
9. Trees fight climate change. . . .

I should like to share again a poem I wrote sometime ago.

     My Friend the Tree
An elderly tree shelters my home.
What a blessing she is!
Her well-built trunk
still stands straight and sure,
offering to me her solid strength.
She reminds me of my own body,
scarred and wounded from the years
and yet still reaching for the light.

When I hug her gnarly form,
I can hear the gentle flow of sap.
The life within has a steady beat
that lends assurance to my fickleness.

Her sturdy branches hold on tight
as she sways sveltly with the winds.
Her twigs and branches sometimes crackle off,
and fall with gentle thuds
to the friendly earth,
as she shrugs off what she no longer needs.

Her leaves in spring and summer
dance joyfully in their colorful costumes
as breezes play through her hair.
In autumn, she showers me with self-same flags
of green and buff and red and gold.

This tree is a blessing to me
and a shelter to my home.
She gives shade in summer
and protected warmth in winter,
and always a quiet energy
with her gentle life.
I thank my Creator
for such a gracious blessing.
—Helene R. Hill, October 30, 2001

I am grateful for trees. I would confirm again the amazing creativity of our God. Are you aware that every leaf on every tree—no matter what species, is a new act of creation? The God who is ours is an amazing and creative God. Along Wall Street yesterday morning, the newly created leaves of the ginkgo trees were just plain delicious!

Let us pray.

Thank you, God, for your creation of trees. Amen.

—*given at Brooks-Howell Home, April 23, 2003*

Lawns

Imagine the conversation the Creator might have with St. Francis about this:

"Frank, you know all about gardens and nature. What in the world is going on down there in the USA? What happened to the dandelions, violets, thistle, and stuff I started eons ago? I had a perfect, no-maintenance garden plan. Those plants grow in any type of soil, withstand drought and multiply with abandon. The nectar from the long-lasting blossoms attracted butterflies, honeybees, and flocks of songbirds. I expected to see a vast garden of colors by now. But all I see are these green rectangles."

"It's the tribes that settled there, Lord. The Suburbanites. They started calling your flowers 'weeds' and went to great extent to kill them and replace them with grass."

"Grass? But it's so boring. It's not colorful. It doesn't attract butterflies, birds, and bees, only grubs and sod worms. It's temperamental with temperatures. Do these Suburbanites really want all that grass growing there?"

"Apparently so, Lord. They go to great pains to grow it and keep it green. They begin each spring by fertilizing grass and poisoning any other plant that crops up in the lawn."

"The spring rains and cool weather probably make grass grow really fast. That must make the Suburbanites happy."

"Apparently not, Lord. As soon as it grows a little, they cut it—sometimes twice a week."

"They cut it? Do they then bale it like hay?"

"Not exactly, Lord. Most of them rake it up and put it in bags"

"They bag it? Why? Is it a cash crop? Do they sell it?"

"No, sir. Just the opposite. They pay to throw it away."

"Now let me get this straight. They fertilize grass so it will grow. And when it does grow, they cut it off and pay to throw it away?"

"Yes, sir."

"These Suburbanites must be relieved in the summer when we cut back on the rain and turn up the heat. That surely slows the growth and saves them a lot of work."

"You aren't gonna believe this, Lord. When the grass stops growing so fast, they drag out hoses and pay more money to water it so they can continue to mow it and pay to get rid of it."

"What nonsense. At least they kept some of the trees. That was a sheer stroke of genius, if I do say so myself. The trees grow leaves in the spring to provide beauty and shade in the summer. In the autumn they fall to the ground and form a natural blanket to keep moisture in the soil and protect the trees and bushes. Plus, as they rot, the leaves form compost to enhance the soil. It's a natural circle of life."

"You better sit down, Lord. The Suburbanites have drawn a new circle. As soon as the leaves fall, they rake them into great piles and have them hauled away."

"No! What do they do to protect the shrub and tree roots in the winter and keep the soil moist and loose?"

"After throwing away your leaves, they go out and buy something they call mulch. They haul it home and spread it around in place of the leaves."

"And where do they get this mulch?"

"They cut down trees and grind them up."

"Enough. I don't want to think about this anymore. Saint Catherine, you're in charge of the arts. What movie have you scheduled for us tonight?"

"*Dumb and Dumber*, Lord. It's a real stupid movie about—"

"Never mind, I think I just heard the whole story."

—Source unknown, supplied by Richard Fireman.[5]

Let us pray.

Gracious God, we thank you for the life you have given us, and for the resurrection of our earth at this time of year. We thank you for green grass, for the wonders of opening flowers, and the amazing circling ways in which your world works together to renew and replenish and resurrect itself. Forgive us for tampering with that cycling of life and death and life and death and life again. Easter has come to mean for us the renewal of life itself for people through Jesus the Christ, even as our earth is renewed. And now we thank you for our food: for the growing grains that have provided our breads and cereals, for the bushes and trees that have provided our fruits and coffees and teas, for the animals that have provided our meats and eggs, for the minerals and clays that have provided our dishes and silverware, and for your love over all, providing our very breath and life itself. Thank you for this time of year when we celebrate the renewal of life for all. Amen.

—*given at Brooks-Howell Home, March 27, 2002*

Wonderful Sand

The earth is the Lord's and all that is in it,
> the world and those who live in it:
for he has founded it on the seas,
> and established it on the rivers. (Psalm 24:1–2, NRSV)

I have here, this morning, a jar of sand. It is not much sand—we only had a big cup from Perkins Restaurant to put sand in. There were no other containers in the car when Barb and I drove up north, to Michigan, and decided to bring a little of that wonderful sand home as a souvenir. This sand is very special to me because it comes from the shores of Lake Michigan. It comes from Sleeping Bear Dune, one of the most well-known of the dunes, and now a national park area. In other years, Barb and I both have climbed up the long high dune to the top, to catch from there a majestic view of that wonderful lake. It is not easy to climb a sand dune.

This summer there was no climbing for us, but it was fun to watch whole families struggling up through the sand in bare feet, slipping and sliding, laughing and playing as they plodded step by step to the top. What fun it was to throw footballs or other balls to family members still struggling along. I hope my photos come out well.

I grew up in Toledo, and we often went to swim in Lake Erie. From childhood, I remember the pleasantness of sand in my toes, and sometimes irritating sand in my shoes, often without socks, of course. Our mama was sure to have us dump the sand out of our shoes before she would let us in the house. Even so, there was often gritty sand in our clothes. It always lodged in our swimsuits and shook itself out all over the floor when the suits were dry—What a mess! Somewhere along the way I learned about sandpaper, and then emery boards, also made with sand. I've often wondered why sand was so abrasive. Well, now I know.

Helen Mandlebaum knew that I was headed "home" to Michigan, and thoughtfully sent to me in Grand Rapids a wonderful small book written by her friend about the Great Lakes sand dunes. I decided to share a bit of it with all of you.

Sand dunes have graced Great Lakes shorelines for thousands of years, but the source of their sand is much older. The sand originated as extremely hard bedrock, which has existed for millions of years in the depths of the northernmost regions of North America. Some of the rock layers may even be billions of years old—already ancient by the time dinosaurs roamed the earth 120 million years ago. Pressure on the earth's crust pushed bedrock to the surface in some places, and erosion eventually broke it down.

A million years of ice ages greatly accelerated that erosion of bedrock and transported it to the Great Lakes region via vast sheets of ice. When these glaciers began to melt 13,000 years ago, they washed enormous amounts of debris through glacial lakes and down rivers. This conveyor belt sorted out larger sediments while washing the smaller sediments into the basins that became the Great Lakes. The glaciers left tremendous amounts of meltwater and the raw material that ultimately eroded further into the small, loose, gritty grains that we commonly call sand.

This very old sand served as the main ingredient in our Great Lakes sand dunes. Quartz, an abundant mineral that is chemically stable and very hard, became the dominant sand mineral as less resistant minerals dissolved or broke down further.

This abundance of sand, combined with the other ingredients—wind, vegetation and geography—was amazingly arranged into the largest collection of freshwater coastal dunes in the world. These dunes have been a part of the Great Lakes scenery for 3,000 to 4,000 years.[6]

Wow! And I thought sand was just a bother! Gritty, grainy, irritating, impossible to shake out sometimes, and certainly the bitter that goes along with the sweet of swimming in fresh water lakes! We had to shake it out, sweep it out, clean it out, every time we went swimming! Reading about its origin billions of years ago and understanding how it came to be blows my mind.

Sand is just one tiny part of the creation in which we find ourselves living. It is one of the miracles of life—just as tomatoes, roses, watermelons, a green tree, drinking water, our pets Butterscotch and Harley, and you and I are miracles.

The earth is the Lord's and all that is in it,
 the world and those who live in it:
for he has founded it on the seas,
 and established it on the rivers. (Psalm 24:1–2, NRSV)
Amen.

—*given at Brooks-Howell Home, September 10, 1998*

Christmas Mail

Various selections received at Christmastime, some from people you know:

From a Christmas card from Virgilia Wade, a longtime friend from Grand Rapids, and a child psychologist:
> This is the *star* that inspires the *wish*
> that's the beginning of the *dream* that turns your *life*
> into the greatest *adventure*;
> that lights a fire in others who go on to do even more amazing things
> that help to make our planet a happier *place to be*.
>
> That's how *magic* happens. That's why you're here.
> That's what *Christmas* is all about. Hope yours is wonderful.

From Hospitality House newsletter:
> What may bring many of us a sense of comfort during this holiday season is our deepened need for experiences that connect us. These days take on a special significance as we embrace our families, celebrate our friendships or simply reach out to another to better understand ourselves.

Received from several sources:
> Three wise women would have asked directions, arrived on time, helped deliver the baby, cleaned the stable, made a casserole, brought practical gifts, and there would be Peace on Earth.

From a Christmas card from Aliyah Schick, a friend from Jubilee! (I think she designed it!):
> Jo**y**, Peac**e**, Love, F**a**ith, **H**ope, Grace (emphasized are the letters YEAH!). Inside, in a delightful frame, the card says, Joy, Peace, Love, Faith, Hope, Grace. Outside the frame, "Life's true gifts . . . the great giveaway! Help yourself and pass them along!"

From a card sent by Cynthia Justice, another friend from Jubilee!:
I was always looking outside myself for strength and confidence, but it comes from within. It is there all the time. —Anna Freud

Excerpt from *By the Still Waters* by Vance Hayner:
God uses broken things. It takes broken soil to produce a crop, broken clouds to give rain, broken grain to give bread, broken bread to give strength. It is the broken alabaster box that gives forth perfume. . . . It is Peter, weeping bitterly, who returns to greater power than ever.[7]

From Affordable Housing Coalition, a quotation from Alice Walker's book *Anything We Love Can Be Saved*:
It has become a common feeling, I believe, as we have watched our heroes falling over the years, that our own small stone of activism, which might not seem to measure up to the rugged boulders of heroism we have so admired, is a paltry offering toward an edifice of hope. Many who believe this choose to withhold their offerings out of shame. This is the tragedy of our world, for we can do nothing substantial toward changing our course on the planet—a destructive one—without rousing ourselves, individual by individual, and bringing our small, imperfect stones to the pile.[8]

From another section of the same brochure, an Ethiopian proverb:
When spider webs unite, they can tie up a lion.

From a Chautauqua friend:
To see the sacred, we must slow down. . . . At this gentle season, may you find time to enjoy life's simple blessings and the beauty of each quiet moment.

From Friends Committee on National Legislation:
We seek a world free of war and the threat of war.
>We seek a society with equity and justice for all.
>We seek a community where every person's potential may be fulfilled.
We seek an earth restored.
Amen.

—given at Brooks-Howell Home, December 26, 2001

NOTES

1. Ina W. Warren, "the Jubilant Botanist," comp., *Care and Feeding of the Natural Rituals of Our Lives: An Earthy Almanac Guide for Greening Worship Services.* Unpublished. Permission sought.

2. Peterson, *The Message.*

3. Used with permission of Rev. Howard Hanger, pastor, Jubilee! Community, Asheville, NC.

4. Accessed August 1, 2005, from http://www.spiritoftrees.org/poetry/rumi/lord_rumi_sufi.html.

5. Supplied by Richard Fireman, leader of the Jubilee! Earth Team.

6. Elizabeth Brockwell Tillman, and Earl Wolf, *Discovering Great Lakes Dunes* (Michigan State University Extension Bulletin E-2653), 4.

7. Vance H. Hayner, *By the Still Waters* (Fleming H. Revell Co., 1934).

8. Alice Walker, *Anything We Love Can Be Saved* (New York: Random House, 1997).

Reflecting God to Others

I Am Who I Am

I returned on Tuesday morning from my first Elderhostel, which I attended with Nancy Parrish, a friend from Grand Rapids. It was held in Arizona.

We found that we were compatible friends and we enjoyed being together. In our nine days together, we never seemed to run out of things to talk about. In addition to the four and a half days at the Elderhostel, we had three and a half days to do some sightseeing and traveling on our own. We had a wonderful time. Nancy had been to Sedona two years before, but had not seen the Grand Canyon. Seeing the canyon is an experience beyond compare. As some have said, it is indeed a big hole in the ground, but it is a hole in the ground with amazing layers and rocks and ridges and colors beyond description. Hopefully, before long, I will get my pictures and materials about it into a photo album. Then you can enjoy it, too.

Before going on our all-day trip to the canyon, we had lectures on the geology and the ancient conditions of the area. The piece of information that blew my mind, so to speak, was the evidence of five oceans—yes, *five* oceans—that existed in this area at various times in the early life of our planet and left behind their debris. There is evidence that one of the oceans invaded and receded, invaded and receded, at least sixteen times. Now the area is all desert and gets very little rainfall.

Sometime ago, as a hobby, I gathered a good rock collection that includes several sea shells and a fossil or two. The fossil and shells were found in a coal mine in the heart of Germany —again, evidence of unbelievable changes in the topography of our planet in the millions of years that it has existed. Evidence like this gives one an assurance of God's care for life. While we sometimes think life is here today and gone tomorrow, because our own lives are all too short, we can see evidence all around us that the planet itself has existed for millions and millions of years and, we hope, will last long beyond our own lifetimes.

For me the highlight of our trip was meeting and hearing Ramson Lomatewama from the Hopi tribe. He gave two lectures about the Hopi. During the first lecture, when he introduced himself, he said something that confused our group. He kept saying that he was not a Hopi.

He acknowledged that he is of the Hopi tribe. He is a very integral part of his own tribe and participates regularly in its customs and rituals. But he said very clearly, "A Hopi is what *you* call me; it is not how I call myself." He went on to explain that being a Hopi is an ideal to which he strives—but he is not yet there. He then told us of some of the Hopi precepts and customs and ideas, making it clear that he saw being a Hopi as an achievement far beyond him. His humility came through most clearly when he said, "I am just who I am, nothing more and nothing less."

This good man teaches at North Central College in Naperville, Illinois, which is several miles from where we were and where he lives on a reservation. He commutes from his home to the college for his teaching. He noted that his class was just ended, and he would be able to receive the class's term papers by e-mail. So, since he was between classes, he was available to give lectures to our Elderhostel. This was obviously not his first time as one of the lecturers, nor his first time to talk with a group like ours. He is an accomplished speaker.

He is in his late forties or early fifties and has three girls and a boy between the ages of seven and twenty-two. His wife, Jennifer, helps him with his creative artwork and the business associated with that. His oldest daughter has finished school and works as a nurse in the local hospital. She also does wonderful, creative artwork and has won prizes for it through her exhibits and shows.

Mr. Lomatewama is a well-known artist, and if you see a wonderful Native American piece of art in bright colors with the name Ramson Lomatewama printed across the bottom, you will know that it is one of a thousand prints he has had made up for sale. He also works on commission, doing wonderful stained glass windows and large pieces. He noted that he had to fight for the right to do stained glass and call it Hopi art because the authorities said, "That is not a 'traditional craft of the Hopis.' " He won his point, and has continued to work in glass.

Both he and his daughter take many of their designs from craft books and from sources of early history that depict early Native American designs and themes. He moved from piecing stained glass to blowing glass, and he brought with him two very expensive vases he had done. They were blown glass tubes wrapped around the outside of clear amber glass in most amazing and wonderful designs.

He lectured first in the morning. We had the afternoon free, and he suggested that if any of us wanted to visit his studio that afternoon, he would be happy to host us. Nancy and I took advantage of this and found our way onto the Hopi reservation. Traveling on dirt roads, we found the two-story house his family lives in, and his studio next door. It was indeed a workplace, with the work tables and materials necessary for work. It also had a display of both his work and his daughter's. I bought some turtle earrings and a necklace, examples of the craft work he continues to do, in addition to his glasswork.

For the purpose of our worship this morning, I do not need to share his lecture about the Hopi people. The important thing to me was to find and meet with and talk with—and rejoice with—a person who knows who he is, a person who is genuine and honest and humble and who puts on no airs. A person who is open to life and to other people and is thus a magnificent example of a child of God. He is very magnetic; he attracts people because there is nothing false about him. The two things that struck me most were his humility and his creativity.

I marveled, at first, thinking that this man was a genius. But perhaps not. It seems to me that the creative powers of all of us would be freed up if we released ourselves from the need to strive to be something we, or others, falsely expect of us. This man does not need to protect his reputation. He does not fear losing his job or money. He does not keep up appearances for anyone. He is just what he said, "I am (just) who I am."

Let us pray.

Thank you, God, for your life within us, which can free us to be ourselves, and for our ability to learn that we are okay just as you created us—each one different and each one with creative powers within. Help us to learn who we are, and to be just ourselves . . . in your goodness. Amen.

—*given at morning worship, Brooks-Howell Home, October 9, 1997*

You Are Loved

The writings of the Rev. Dr. Rob Blackburn, senior pastor of Central United Methodist Church in Asheville, are great. Sometime ago, he wrote a brief meditation about love that I had put aside. I'd like to share that with you now. It seems particularly appropriate on what used to be called Lincoln's Birthday, in a month that is still celebrated as African American History month.

The Scripture used is Romans 12:9, which is commonly translated "Let love be genuine." (ESV) The Peterson translation renders these words as "Love from the center of who you are—don't fake it."

Rev. Dr. Blackburn says,

> Love from the center of who you are. Who we are is this wonderful paradox; we are all imperfect; we are all capable of causing another pain. Yet, we are all children of God; we are all God's beloved. Both statements are true.
>
> Once we embrace that, then we can relax, because we can be merely human—not angelic and not demonic—just from the earth. Community is only possible when we relax. Community is only possible when we put away our masks and our preoccupations.
>
> When we meet someone it's not, "How can I keep you in a box so I can maintain my self image?" But, "How can I see the Christ in you and allow you to see the Christ in me?"
>
> Remember in *To Kill a Mockingbird* when the white men come in the night and surround the jail where Tom, an African-American wrongly accused of a crime is held?
>
> The men are a mob. They do not see Tom. They only see an enemy. They do not know themselves. They are blinded by rage and fear. Scout, a little girl whose father is Tom's lawyer, watches them. Her father tells her to run, to go home. But little

Scout doesn't run, and she doesn't fight. Instead she finds a way to love.

She looks at one of the men in the mob and says, "Hey, Mister Cunningham—don't you remember me? I go to school with Walter. He's your boy, ain't he? We brought him home for dinner one time. Tell him 'hey' for me, won't you?"

There is a long pause. Then the big man separated himself from the mob, squatted down, and took Scout by both her shoulders. "I'll tell him you said 'hey,' little lady."

Then the mob dispersed.

That is the power of genuine love. It is what happens when we remind one another of how we are connected and when we call one another by our true name. Only when we speak and love from the Center of who we are will our divisions be healed.[1]

Let us pray.

Gracious and living God, we need you among us to remind us that we are all imperfect, and capable of hurting others, and that we are all beloved, and capable of recognizing and cementing our connections and relationships to each other and to you. Help us to learn to love from the Center of who we are, with genuine, spontaneous love, your gift to each of us. Amen.

—given at Brooks-Howell Home, February 12, 2003

Jubilee! Community Church

I became aware on Sunday, when I took a visitor to Jubilee!, that there are some misconceptions about this independent church. Perhaps this would be a good time to clarify information about Jubilee! for people at Brooks-Howell.

I do not see myself as a part of another faith because I belong to Jubilee! I retain my United Methodist identity, and take an active part in a UMW circle at Central, and participate as much as possible in district and conference activities. Until recently I have taught in our mission schools, and continue on the list for teachers. I continue to speak to UMW groups and others as I am asked to do.

This August the Jubilee! church congregation will be fifteen years old. For all fifteen years it has continued in its present location. Before that, it was, for five years, part of Central United Methodist Church, where Howard Hanger was assigned as associate pastor, with the particular task of developing an alternative worship. He did so, and an alternative worship group met in the church's fellowship hall for five summers.

Howard was raised in Florida, and is the son of the Reverend John Howard Hanger, a pastor now deceased, in the Florida Conference of our United Methodist Church. He was trained as a musician, and in younger years, he had planned to be a jazz musician. Today, as a pastor, a graduate of Candler Theological Seminary at Emory University, he uses his musical training in many ways. For one thing, it is a rich source of theology, and he often pulls out popular songs that say just what needs to be said in regard to our love relationship with God. They so often clinch the point of the depth and tenderness of God's love for us, and point to the kind of love that each of us wants in his or her love life with God.

Howard was ordained by Bishop James Armstrong when Armstrong was bishop of the Dakotas Conference, and he maintains his relationship with the church. He values and cherishes that relationship and the connections it brings for friendships and service. He is often used as worship leader at annual conference meetings, and in various churches for special occasions of all kinds. He marries and buries parishioners and others, and continues as a pastor in good standing. He is on what is called extension ministry.

He follows the lectionary readings. While themes and sermons follow the quarterly themes of Matthew Fox's creation spirituality, these are biblically solidly based. One of the criticisms I have heard here is that he never uses the name of Jesus. That is simply not true. Jubilee! is a Christian church, and Jesus is seen as the image and likeness of God. Howard reads from the Gospels every Sunday, and offers Communion. Parishioners are urged to follow in the way of Jesus.

I have trouble, sometimes, with closed minds. I always regret it when people are either unable or unwilling to accept new ideas or new people. I think that one characteristic of congregants at Jubilee! is their open-mindedness and support of people who are different. As Jubilants, we sometimes tease about that, and say very clearly that we are all misfits, different, and that's why we are Jubilants! It is a church that has been a great solace to many people who have trouble with the small-mindedness and narrowness of some of our congregations. I find it a very appreciative and supportive audience for whoever speaks to the group.

All of me—why not take all of me?
Can't you see? I'm no good without you.
Take my lips. I'll never use them.
Take my arms. I'll want to lose them. . . .[2]

This just fits this morning's theme of commitment to God—really going whole-hog for God and taking a big bite of the joy and abundance of life that God has made possible here. And of course that's what got Jesus crucified—his amazing understanding of the power of God's love.

Let us pray.

Gracious God, thank you for the path of Jesus that you have shown us. We thank you for Jesus who has shown us the way to You. We can only live in awesome praise. Amen.

—*given at Brooks-Howell Home, June 26, 2002*

We're All in This Boat Together!

On Tuesday afternoon, I drove to Boone, North Carolina, to talk with a UMW (United Methodist Women) group there. It was a small group of rural women who strongly support our church, but who have had some difficulty understanding that their service and sense of mission goes beyond their immediate area and their own limited vision in helping others. The person who asked me to come asked that I emphasize the sense of world mission and the connections of world mission to our own local church and setting. That is what I tried to do, illustrating the worldwide sense of mission and concern for others with my own experience and work through the years. This was an interesting thing for me to do because normally we think of the deaconess as working in the United States and its "possessions," and we think of our missionaries, in contrast, as having a world outreach.

Well, it may surprise you to know that this is not always the case. Sometimes overseas missionaries *do* have a sense of world outreach and an understanding that all of us are brothers and sisters, children of God together. Sometimes they do *not*. Sometimes deaconesses *do* have a sense of world outreach, and the understanding that we are all brothers and sisters and children of God together. Sometimes they do *not*. The fact that you have a world vision is not dependent on whether you have served in Japan or India or Timbuktu, or in Kalamazoo or Kentucky or the mountains of Tennessee.

As someone has said more clearly than I, we are all in this boat together, and the sooner we realize how dependent we are on each other, how interrelated, and come to appreciate each other as each having strengths as well as faults, the better off we'll all be!

Here let me comment on my experience of living in Grand Rapids, Michigan, and one thing my living there taught me! I lived there for almost thirty years. Grand Rapids is one of the centers of Dutch communities of our country, and many have brought with them their Calvinistic understandings of theology—especially the bias that some of us (of course they are white and fairly well off!) are ordained for heaven and some are not. Thus, at its extreme, one would think Christians could "do *for*" the black population of the city but not "do *with* them." One would not ever think that those for whom you "do good" will go to the same heaven for which you are destined. The concept of "doing *with*" black people or other minorities—as partners with you, as your coworkers—is not something that extremist Calvinists understand easily. Giving to others—charity—is a duty for Christians, they say; so, "I give to another because that person is poor, and it is my duty as a Christian to give to the poor," but there is no understanding that the poor also have something to give to the giver, to fulfill the giver's needs. If you are a giver and destined for heaven, you don't have any needs—only the poor do! After all, say they, we *know* we will go to heaven. And as for the poor, if they do not want the charity we want to give, then indeed they are ungrateful wretches.

This concept is put in its proper light by Dom Helder Camara's[3] very incisive comment, "When I feed the poor, they call me a saint, but when I ask why the poor are poor, they call me a Communist." Indeed!

This puts a different light on our missions, and our giving to mission, doesn't it? When we see the people we are sent to serve as part of the family of God, and realize that we are interdependent, and interlocked, and both needy pilgrims seeking God, then some of our mission ideas go out the window. In truth, we are as dependent upon the poor, the minorities, and other people with social needs, as they are on us.

I have encountered societies that understand this interconnection in their family setups. At my recent Elderhostel, Ramson Lomatewama, a Hopi, and also the lecturer from the Navajo and Hopi cultures helped us to understand that a tribe of at least these two native groups (perhaps others as well!) is bound together by family as well as neighbors. The father of one family is uncle to others, and has the responsibility of being the mentor for the young boys in his sisters' and brothers' families. The aunts mentor the young girls. Thus each family is tied together by many more interlocking responsibilities than is our concept in a nuclear family. Also, my niece is appreciating very much her Filipino in-laws, and their understandings that families look after each other. She grew up in a standard U.S. nuclear family, with all of the burden for raising the children on her two parents. Now, with parents-in-law who understand extended families, she rejoices with sharing the responsibilities for child care and the interlocking give-and-take of a large family. As Hillary Clinton says, and it is surely true, "It takes a village to raise a child."

I think that one of the reasons it has been more difficult for our church to understand and appreciate the deaconesses in our midst, in contrast to our missionaries, is that deaconesses work among us here. Most of us understand that the people with whom we work are just like us—all of us are needy children of God, seeking to help each other to find our way to God and God's abundance in this life. We have needs just like those whom we have come to serve. We try to help our brothers and sisters to meet their needs in a more satisfactory way, and they help us to understand who we are and why we serve among them. We do not serve out of Christian "duty" but out of our common needs.

Let us pray:

Gracious and abundant God, you who give us all of our understandings and our love for each other, open our eyes and our hearts to our brothers and sisters, no matter who or where they are. Help us to understand that each of us has gifts to share, and each of us has needs that can only be met by others. Thank you now, for this food, and this our meal together. Amen.

—*given at Brooks-Howell Home, November 16, 1997*

Different, Yet One!

Yesterday I had the opportunity to speak at a UNCA class on human rights in Nicaragua. For me, it was like coming home. As I prepared to talk about my experience in this small country and its implications, I found myself with tears in my eyes when I reviewed a video about Nicaragua and the effects the World Bank and the International Monetary Fund have had on it.

I did not go to Nicaragua until my retirement years, but I have now made six trips to this beleaguered country, starting in 1987. The most recent trip was last year, when I went for two months. In those several visits, I fell in love with the people of the country, and especially with the families with whom I lived.

Last year I was especially touched by a photograph I took. In our Witness for Peace trip, we stayed five nights in one of the smallest and poorest and most primitive communities that I have experienced. Our leaders wanted us to take a picture of the families with whom we stayed. My partner and I arranged to do that. I had just given the young host a picture of myself for his family's memento. When I took the picture of his family, I was surprised to see that I had also taken a picture of myself, for he held up in his hand the picture that I had given him, as though to say very clearly, "You are a part of our family."

The opportunity to talk about Nicaragua again gave me great pleasure, but it also spurred my thinking about what I learned in this small country that changed and enriched my life. At least as much as the political understandings, when I made the connections between what was happening worldwide and what was happening there, I also learned that we, personally, are not different. People are the same the world over. Two-year-olds there are sometimes called *diablo* here, as in the first family with whom I lived. Students study little but expect decent grades. They sometimes cheat. They are very happy when there is a diversion from their studies in the classroom. Most adults are sincere, but some are, as in the words of one of my friends, "nothing but a bag of wind."

We in the United States tend to think of ourselves as different from the people of other countries. The professor of the class I addressed yesterday asked some very sharp questions. The students had just read a book about the El Mazote massacre in El Salvador.[4] One question he asked was if they thought the soldiers who killed so many people were evil. In the ensuing comments, the students likened that massacre to the U.S. massacre at My Lai in the Vietnam war. There was discussion back and forth, and one student commented that he tended to think that the soldiers in El Salvador *were* perhaps evil, but he had a very hard time thinking of our own soldiers as evil. In other words, he understood that we find it much easier to impute evil to those who are different from us, or people we do not know, than to those who are like us.

How about you? Are you a victim of xenophobia (a fear or hatred of strangers or foreigners)? Do you give them the cold shoulder? Are you fearful, or for some other reason, do not like people who are different? How is it in your church? Is your church one that makes it clear that people of other cultures or faiths are not welcome there? How about the young people who sometimes have different ideas about life and/or worship—are they still in your church? Perhaps they worship through creation and its realities of life, rather than solely Jesus Christ. Perhaps they have not found a faith at all. Do we shun those who do not worship as we worship?

A week or so ago I attended the first meeting of people in a new group called United Religions Initiative. The group's purpose is to bring together people of various faiths for a better understanding and appreciation of each other. As the individuals introduced themselves, it seemed as though we were trying to recreate the Council of Churches; Protestant denominations were well represented, and there were several Catholics, but only one of a faith other than Christian was present.

I think if there was one thing I learned in Nicaragua, it was that we are one: one family, under God, rejoicing in life and full of life, even though we are different in the amount of money we have, in the clothing we wear, and sometimes in the foods we eat. Sometimes we are different in the language we speak or how we celebrate weddings or even in the color of skin. Are some of us, then, *not* God's creation?

God forbid! I rejoice in the diversity of life on this small planet and I hope you do, too. All of us are capable of evil at times, but also all of us are capable of being life-givers and nourishers of life. Let us then know that we are one.

Let us pray.

Gracious God, help us to understand that this is one world, created and sustained by yourself, no matter how we perceive you or each other. Thank you for the diversity and joy of life, no matter where we find it. Amen.

—*given at Brooks-Howell Home, February 17, 2000*

There Is Only One You

I have been greatly impressed by the weekly editorials of Rev. Dr. Rob Blackburn, on the front of the *Jot and Tittle,* Central Church's weekly news sheet. He writes concisely and to the point, and always has something worth saying. And he says it well! The current issue is a good example. I quote.

> We are living in a time in which hero worship has grown to near cultlike proportions. Many persons, in not being able to accept the gift of their own sample of life, spend great energy trying to ride on the coattails of someone's life which seems much more exotic. Eugene Peterson in one of his writings noted, however, that "our faith refuses to feed our lust for hero worship. It will not pander to our adolescent desire to join a fan club. *Fan clubs encourage secondhand living.* Through pictures and memorabilia, autographs and tourist visits, we associate with someone whose life (we think) more exciting and glamorous than our own."
>
> Something very different than hero worship takes place in the life of faith. Each person is invited to take part in an original adventure and is called into a unique association with the living Christ. God's creative genius is endless. There is no evidence that God grows fatigued, resorting to mass-produced copies. Each life is a fresh canvas on which He [God] uses lines and colors, shades and lights that he [God] has never used before.[5]

As an aside, I want to comment that my former pastor in Grand Rapids, Michigan, once preached on the abundance of God, and he noted the billions of snowflakes in winter, the amazing number of leaves from the trees, and the marvelous abundance of male sperm, in order to make sure that at least one egg is fertilized and life continues. Of all of the snowflakes that have ever been photographed, no two have ever been found to be alike, although all are formed in the same hexagonal pattern. Every leaf on each tree is different, even though it is always possible to identify the kind of tree by the shape and integrity of each leaf.

And every human being is different, even though there are billions of us. I thought about my own family. I had a brother six feet tall. My oldest brother had my mother's brown eyes, and the next had my father's blue eyes, while several of us got a mixture, and came with hazel eyes. I have often marveled at this mixture.

Blackburn continues:

> God says to each of us: "You are unique, the one and only you. From all eternity into all eternity, there will only be one you. You have been given a role to play in the world. You have a unique message to deliver, a unique song to sing, a unique act of love to bestow. This message, this song and this act of love has been entrusted exclusively to the one and only you.[6]

Let us pray.

Wonderful, creative Friend, we marvel at the continuous and unending joy and fun you show in your creation, especially as you create such amazing and delightful human beings, each one different. Help us to value the unique gift of life that you have given us, each one, and to recognize that you have given us your gift of creativity as well. We can only say thank you, thank you, thank you. Amen.

—*given at Brooks-Howell Home, August 3, 2000*

Put the Big Rocks in First!

Recently, I had the opportunity to catch up on some reading, and among other newsletters I read the one from the Michigan Association of Retired School Personnel, of which I am a part. The president's message is surely worth sharing. I quote:

> Awhile back I was reading about an expert on the subject of time management. One day this expert was speaking to a group of business students and to drive home a point, he used [the following] illustration.
>
> As this man stood in front of the group of high-powered overachievers he said, "Okay, time for a quiz." He pulled out a one-gallon, wide-mouthed Mason jar and set it on the table in front of him. Then he produced about a dozen fist-size rocks and carefully placed them, one at a time, into the jar. When the jar was filled to the top and no more rocks would fit inside, he asked, "Is this jar full?" Everyone in the class said, "Yes." Then he said, "Really?"
>
> He reached under the table and pulled out a bucket of gravel. Then he dumped some of the gravel in and shook the jar, causing pieces of gravel to work themselves down into the spaces between the big rocks. He smiled and asked the group once more, "Is the jar full?" . . . "Probably not," one of them answered. "Good!" he replied.
>
> Once again he reached under the table and brought out a bucket of sand. He started dumping the sand in and it went into all the spaces left between the rocks and the gravel. Once more he asked the question, "Is this jar full?" "No!" the class shouted. Again he said, "Good!"
>
> Then he grabbed a pitcher of water and began to pour it in until the jar was filled to the brim. He looked up at the class and asked, "What is the point of this illustration?" One eager beaver raised his hand and said, "The point is, no matter how

full your schedule is, if you try really hard, you can always fit some more things into it!" "No," the speaker replied, "that's not the point. The truth this illustration teaches us is: If you don't put the big rocks in first, you'll never get them in at all."[7]

And so we are led to ask, "What are the big rocks in my life?" For each individual, the answer may be different. I will not even suggest answers to you. You have your own.

Two weeks ago, in our celebration service at Jubilee!, each one asked his or her neighbor, "What do you want?" It's a good question, and surely one to ponder at Christmas. What do you really want?

I used to think that on one of these beautiful days full of sunshine, I would go walking in the woodsy area down at Asheville's Beaver Lake just to enjoy. Yes, I did that several times when I first came! But I did not do it often enough! Now I am at the place where the thing I enjoy most is *not* a long walk in the woods because it is simply not possible.

And so, put the big rocks in first, or you don't get them in!

Let us pray.

Gracious God, thank you for your amazing world of checks and balances, and clear understandings. Thank you that, no matter who or where we are, you give us help in keeping first things first in our lives and in our living. And now we give you thanks for the blessings of morning sun and for this meal we share together. Amen.

—given at Brooks-Howell Home, December 3, 1998

Connections

Loise George and I are two of those eighteen or twenty who went from Brooks-Howell recently to Philadelphia for the sixteenth assembly of United Methodist Women. Those of us who took the bus from here arrived home as planned on Monday night, between nine-thirty and ten P.M., and are again getting settled into our community.

There is so much to share that it would certainly not be possible to share it here and now. There will be bits and pieces coming to you from many participants in myriad ways in the near future. I do not want to steal anyone else's thunder. Actually, that is not likely because there is such a richness that it matters not that we went to some of the same sessions. We all participate differently and see different people and hear different things, according to our own needs and interests.

What I will share with you was that, for me, the highlight of such a meeting is connections with others, and the deep joys of the sustenance one feels with a time to be again with longtime friends and coworkers. I was privileged to stay with two good friends from Michigan. Luci Baer and Elaine Youngs belong to my church in Grand Rapids, and some years ago I went to another assembly with Elaine; the two of us roomed together. I heard Elaine say to Luci, "Well, when you go to one of these assemblies with Helene, you meet the world." It was great.

Elaine and Luci kept me in stitches. Each one has a great sense of humor, and the three of us enjoyed belly laughs and giggles, joys and fun and puns together. We skipped one session to do the city of Philadelphia on the trolleys which take people to historic sites. For the crowded meals, which always involved long lines, we quickly worked out our own system. Elaine was the most sure-footed of our threesome, so we sent her to get in line. Whatever she bought for all of us to eat was just fine. We settled the cost with her later. I went to find a table, not easy, and held it for the three of us, and Luci brought the food for all on her wheelchair. On the first night, I had to bargain for a table ahead. As I waited, the two strangers and I introduced ourselves, and we talked so fast and furiously and so long, that when I went to find my friends with food, they were not to be found anywhere. I checked out both sides, and never saw Luci's wheelchair. I decided they had eaten and left me. It was getting late and I had not eaten, so after looking all over again for the two of them, I found some other friends in line, and saved a nearby table for them. Then Elaine found me, and never let me forget that I had abandoned them! We did eat together, after all, and got to our next meeting on time.

Again, a longtime friend from the North found me, and brought a mutual friend along, and the three of us sat and talked until the meeting started. Ginni Eddy is moving to Minnesota to be with her family. With Phyllis Jackson, when I am in Grand Rapids, we meet at our favorite spot for breakfast. That always takes at least two hours as we share the joys and sorrows in our current lives and learnings.

I had a brief visit with Flora Clipper, a deaconess whom many of you know. We were commissioned together, along with Lucy Gist, and had the privilege of working together for one year, in a long-ago time and place. What a joy it was just to sit and chat again briefly. She does not plan to come to Brooks-Howell, even though Lucy and I are here; Flora is settled in her hometown.

The deaconess dinner connected me with Barbara Brooks, a deaconess who once lived with Barbara Boultinghouse in South Carolina. I think many of you knew both of them. Barbara now works in Cali, Colombia, teaching English to six hundred children, more or less. It was very good to spend time with her. At that dinner, too, I talked with a number of deaconesses known through Fenton Home at Chautauqua. And it was so good to see Debra Sue Chenault, one of our younger deaconesses from this area.

At my first forum luncheon, I had come early, and had a wonderful time talking to the woman sitting next to me, who was a stranger when we sat down. Another woman quietly slipped in on the other side, and partway through the meal we turned to each other and introduced ourselves. Guess who that was? Many of you know Elizabeth or Libbey Johannaber. She sends greetings to all of you, but especially to those of you she knew through her work and life ventures. She is in good health.

The connections at UMW Assemblies are to me a wonderful highlight, no matter the wonderful music, which we had in abundance—and such a variety!—and the great speakers! Marion Wright Edelman was one among several speakers—and the participation of children and young people in so many creative ways! I value and cherish friends from other times and places, and I find myself very grateful for the opportunity to again participate with them in such a meeting as the Assembly.

Let us pray.

Gracious God, thank you for the wonderful images of yourself that you have sent to our hearts in years past, and the opportunity to again connect with you through them. Such an experience reminds us that people with whom we live now are also images of you, and we give thanks for that assurance and understanding. Thank you that you have put yourself into the hearts and minds and spirits of each of us. Send us forth from here to recognize that image in others and continue to celebrate life in your presence. Amen.

—*given at Brooks-Howell Home, May 1, 2002*

Let Us Honor Our Bodies

Last Sunday at Jubilee! we considered the story of the two disciples walking to Emmaus, and noted that they did not recognize Jesus until he broke the bread for them at supper. The breaking of bread for the feeding of the body is a very earthy thing to do. It is a physical thing. The theme for this particular Sunday concerned the understanding that our bodies and spirits belong together.

Let me read a few of the meditation readings.

> You have to go through the dark in order to see the light. You have to go to the source of all our wounds, the big wound, the divorce of spirit from flesh, and heal this wound if you ever want to fulfill the longing for a real self, a soulful self, a big, huge self.
> —Gabrielle Roth

> Plato, Paul the Apostle, Saint Augustine, all troubled by the flesh, taught that we cannot trust our bodies, that our bodies will lead us to violate our spirits—but where else is the spirit to reside? Where does the truth lie, if not in our good flesh?
> —Marilyn Sewell

> The body is a sacred garment.
> —Martha Graham (the creative modern dancer)

> All that is good in creatures—all their honeysweetness—comes from God.
> —Meister Eckhart

"The reason I don't go to church," said a young vibrant dancer, "is that I never felt as if my body was welcome. Dancing—moving my body—is life for me. But in church, I am seated in a pew and told to sit still." Our pastor went on to remind us that early worship (and worship today in many parts of our world) was primarily drums and dancing—dancing for the hunt and harvest, for births and deaths, for rain, for the moon, the sun, the trees, the animals, the crops.

Many of us have tended to neglect our bodies, and we take them for granted as though the bodily functions and the ways we are put together are not miracles. And miracles they are. I have often been impressed with the way the body heals itself. Most of you know that I came home from my recent journeys really "wiped out," so tired that I even looked bad! I needed sleep and rest, and for a week I have taken it easy, with naps in the afternoons as well as a lighter schedule and a long sleep every night. And now I find that my body has begun to stabilize, and I feel like myself again. To me, that is a miracle, and a reason to give God thanks for bodies that serve us well when we use them as they are intended to be used.

I was recently sent a simple news sheet that has been started for retirees, and the authors asked for some advice for people about to retire.

Well, one piece of advice I included was the words on a poster I once saw. It showed a young man riding a bike fast enough that the wind behind him was obvious. The poster said, EAT SENSIBLY. EXERCISE EVERY DAY. GET PLENTY OF SLEEP. AND GO LIKE HELL!

Those are all very physical, bodily things to do!

In closing, I should like to use the community prayer that we used on Sunday, celebrating our senses.

Let us pray.

Gracious God,
For the smell of cinnamon and lilacs,
For the sight of dogwoods and children at recess,
For the sound of night winds and waterfalls,
For the hugs of old friends and the touch of new lovers,
For the taste of freshly squeezed orange juice, buttered toast,
*   strawberries and chocolate—*
We praise and thank you.

For ears to hear and toes to tap,
For legs to dance and mouths to sing along,
For laughter that brings tears, and tears that bring release,
For pain that alerts and heartache that opens,

For shoulder massages and back scratches,
For blinking and sniffing, and smiling and licking,
We praise and thank you.

Open our conscious minds to what our bodies already know:
That you are present in every molecule and cell,
    in every muscle, bone and tendon,
    every organ, artery and corpuscle . . .

Holy fire of life,
Our flesh and blood is filled with your goodness.[8]
Amen.

                          —*given at Brooks-Howell Home, April 30, 1998*

Keep the Main Thing The Main Thing

Jubilee! has a bumper sticker that reads, KEEP THE MAIN THING THE MAIN THING. I have had it on my car for some time, and I have had questions from some asking, "What is the main thing?" Usually I ask the questioner, "What is the main thing for you?"

Recently, the community of Jubilee! sat down to discuss the possibilities of purchasing the present building and the future of Jubilee!. Our pastor spoke briefly about what we mean by the main thing. He used items on our worship table, in the center of the room. (We worship in the round.) These items have been a part of Jubilee's worship from the beginning of the church, and are basically a part of all of the churches to which you belong, too. The items include a lighted candle, the bread and the cup, and a basket in which we place our money for feeding the hungry.

These are all very simple items, but with profound meanings. Who can fathom the significance of a lighted candle? While it means many things to many people, it always signifies the amazing personal love of an unknowable God, with insights and understandings, with guidance and spiritual awareness, with the mystery of a flickering light blown about by wind and gentle breezes, even as the Holy Spirit is often depicted.

The bread and the cup center us in Jesus the Christ, with understandings of our own sinfulness and inadequacy, along with our redemption and support from life beyond our own brief span. The ritual embodies our communion with one another as well as with God. Of course it is not always wine and bread that are used. I have been a part of communions (not at Jubilee!) where we used elements as widely varying as water or Coca Cola, and sweet potatoes or cookies. The ritual's meaning is the same, that of communicating with (understanding and appreciating) our brothers and sisters in both our humanity and divinity, and in God.

And the hunger basket signifies a congregation's outreach to others, in whatever form that may take. It is both giving to local groups to feed the hunger of the poor who surround us, or giving to far-away people who are also our brothers and sisters in need. The basic hungers for food and the necessities of life are no less important than the basic needs for spiritual communion with others of God's human family. We all need to live together in justice and peace. We do not worship God's light and partake of communion only with people just like us, but through our hunger basket we are constantly reminded of people who are not like us, for we are not ever hungry—and we reach out to embrace them in the circle of love which sustains our own spirits and our daily living.

And so, let us keep the main thing the main thing—whatever those words may mean to you.

Let us pray.

Gracious God, you who are the Main Thing in our finite lives, keep us always centered on you, no matter what tasks or responsibilities, or lack of same, may come our way. Through pain and sorrow, through healthy, joyful days, through the Mondays and the Thursdays, as well as the Sundays of our lives, keep us aware of you and the constancy of your love among us and within us. We thank you now for the abundance of your gifts, for food to eat and clothes to wear, for delightful friends and joyful activities, and for the freedom with which we move and love each day. Amen.

—*given at Brooks-Howell Home, August 26, 1999*

Life Is Give and Take

Just the other day, I heard someone remark that all of us here at Brooks-Howell have had our times of "being boss." The person went on to say that it is amazing that we get along as well as we do together, considering that all of us have been "chiefs" and not "Indians." All of us have been caregivers and "ministers" in our various careers, and now the situation is very different for us. For others give us care, now, and minister to us.

Most of us find it difficult to accept help from others. It is almost beyond the pale for us to *ask* for help or even to acknowledge our need for it. Thus, we never want to move in from the apartments until there is an emergency in our lives or we have had a fall that makes it necessary or for some other compelling physical reason. You notice that I do not like to use my cane. It is difficult to find ourselves needing the care of others, or finding ourselves dependent.

Thus, I had a lot to learn when I went to Nicaragua recently as part of a Witness for Peace group. I knew before I went that I would need some help, but I could not have foreseen how much help I would need. I should like to share with you two specific experiences during my time there.

I knew not a soul in the group, but had applied to the group's leader, and had been accepted, before I left the States. And so on the morning after my seventy-eighth birthday I appeared on the doorstep of the Witness for Peace house in Managua, as instructed. Michael, from the long-term team, put my bag and sleeping bag on the porch and suggested that I make myself at home while he and Ellen, his partner, got themselves ready. They then called a taxi, and we went to the *hospedaje* (small hotel) to meet the group. These potential witnesses for peace were really excited about their opportunity to learn about Nicaragua. For most of them, it was the first time in this country. Some spoke Spanish well; others, not a word. The first instance of my needing major help came when I learned that we would be traveling in a van large enough to hold all sixteen of us. It did not take me long to learn that I could not get in or out of the van on my own. So I asked for someone to "please give me a boost" whenever we had to get into the van, and I asked for an arm to lean on whenever it was time to get out. At first, as I did this, I found myself much ashamed to have to ask for help. There were often tears in my eyes. I soon learned that hands reached out to offer help, unasked. Sometimes I did not know who it was, but someone simply gave me a boost to enter, or an arm to lean on, as I got down—no questions asked.

The second instance was, at first, a bigger worry to me. I learned that, when we went to the country, we would not be staying just one night, as is often the case in such a trip, but *five* nights. I thought, and said aloud, "That's a long time." I expressed my fear more than once because I was quite sure I simply could not handle that much time without what I considered the basics. I feared not only the famous outdoor toilets but also the uncomfortable beds, the unfamiliar foods, the difficult walks, and of all things, on this trip, a work project—unusual for Witness for Peace. Our group was planning to build, with some of the community's men, a cement ramp for the road so that the community could be accessible when the rains came. It was not that the road was not needed. It certainly was. This community of seventy families was completely cut off from any kind of help in the winter because the road was impassable. But at my age, I don't do much digging or cement work or heavy lifting! I really had a lot of anxiety about the experience coming up.

Well, on the first morning of our being there I surprisingly had a very good night's sleep. The bed was a woven plastic camp cot. It had been a night with no electricity and, of course, no running water. We were up at dawn, had a shower with a bowl of water thrown over our heads, and we washed our clothes in the *pila* (basin) with water poured from a small bowl. The clothes had been hung to dry on the barbed-wire fence. Ruth, a medical doctor and my housemate for those five nights, and I were sitting on the front porch of the small two-room house, eating our breakfast of dry bread and black coffee brought to us by our host. I found myself laughing a deep free laugh that bubbled up from inside. Jorge, our young host, looked at me questioningly and I said to him, "It's a beautiful day." And it was. He was satisfied. But to myself I said, "Helene, what were you so worried about? Did you think that, after caring for you for seventy-eight years, God would abandon you, and give you something you could not handle with God's help?" And I chuckled again, to think what a lack of faith we sometimes show, in our worries and frets about life and the need to ask for help from others.

After all, I realized, how are we ministered to by God if not through the hands of others? From then on, even when I needed to ask for help, as in crossing a barbed-wire fence almost daily, there was a freedom to accept the help that was needed and always freely offered. I found it a very good experience to be an Indian for a change and not the chief!

Let us pray.

Gracious God, thank you that life is a give and take experience, and that's what our living together in community is all about. What a burden it would be if we were always in charge. That would simply be too much responsibility for one person! And so we thank you for the times that we need help. Grant us the grace to ask for help, knowing that others, too, have the right to give to us. And now we thank you for the abundance of life as expressed in this breakfast meal that we share together. Amen.

—*given at Brooks-Howell Home, May 14, 1998*

Dancing Sarah's Circle

The following worship is adapted from a letter I received in June, from Ellen Dozier, a Presbyterian mission specialist in Guatemala. She titled her letter "Life in a Circle is Life in the Kingdom."

Ellen noted that she attended the high school graduation celebration for the son of missionary parent coworkers, held in a hotel in Quezaltenango. There was plenty of food and very loud music and plenty of dancing. The music was so loud that it was not possible to carry on a conversation, and so she settled for watching the dancing. She comments, "I wondered how they could tell who their partner was, since there was little physical contact. It appeared to be a moving, swaying sea of humanity on the dance floor." And then she saw, at one end of the room, a circle of dancers, some older. She thought, "I can join that circle." And so she did. She says, "People came and went from our circle. There was always room for one more, and there was always a hand reaching out to welcome newcomers, and to twirl them into the circle."

She notes that she thought about how life in God's kingdom is meant to be life in a circle. She says, "Anyone can participate. Your age, where you come from, the color of your skin, or the language you speak—all of these are simply not important. All are welcome in the circle. It is not even important if you can dance. Few of us could. What is important is your desire to be part of the group, to share yourself, to accept others into the circle, and to enjoy yourself."

She goes on to say, "In Guatemala—and in our world—we need more circles. A circle implies community, equality, sharing, being connected, and being bound to one another. A circle implies living in such a way that we can look into the faces of one another, and see the joy as well as the tears.

"In Guatemala, many people live in or on a kind of pyramid, rather than in a circle. Living on a ladder or pyramid means that a few folks are on top while many others are on the bottom. Usually the ones on the bottom are the poor, the unemployed, children, and women. Some of those on the bottom struggle to climb up the ladder or pyramid. Others struggle to survive day by day at the bottom with little or no hope of climbing up the rungs of the ladder.

"Much of life in Guatemala [and, I would add, in our United States] is not conducive to living in a circle, or living in community. Many people are accustomed to seeing the authority figures up front, whether that person be the teacher in front of the class, the preacher in the pulpit, the army officer directing his troops, the owner of the *finca* (large farm), your boss or the president of the country. Below that authority are the nameless masses who are often treated, not as human beings, but as animals or property."

Ellen continues by saying that there are glimpses of life in a circle, and noted recent meetings of groups from her church who sat under trees, and how they were able to communicate so much better than when sitting in formal rows. She noted, too, the community that is often created on buses so crowded in seats and aisles that one cannot move. She says, "Not always, but at times, we find ourselves helping one another and laughing at the impossible situations we find ourselves in."

She noted that in the Gospels, "We read that in God's kingdom 'the first shall be last and the last, first.' " She says, "I like to think that means there will be no one on top while others are at the bottom, but we will all join hands and live in God's circle."

I recall how, as a younger person, we often sang "We Are Climbing Jacob's Ladder." A few years ago, with better understandings of circles and ladders, I stopped singing that song. I am no longer interested in climbing above others, or in having others' heels on my head as I seek to climb. Today I prefer to sing "We Are Dancing Sarah's Circle," with all of us on the same ground, and holding hands to support each other.

At Jubilee! I am always heartened by the Sending Forth part of each Sunday's celebration. With hands grasped in several circles, we find ourselves supported and upheld, and reaching out to uphold others as we move forth into a new week, which is sometimes messy and difficult and sometimes full of blessings to be shared. I thank God for circles, and the blessings of people sharing and living in circles, rather than in the hierarchical patterns that we know in so much of our lives.

—*given at Brooks-Howell Home, July 14, 2001*

A Moment of Grace

When I was a child, I loved the fireworks of the Fourth of July. In my hometown, the city of Toledo, they exploded the fireworks from an island in the Maumee River and people lined the gentle hills of Walbridge Park at night, just after dark, to watch the display. Many families took picnic suppers, or simply lined up at the end of their long day of play and fun at the park, to watch this wonderful panorama of color and sound, with bursting stars and big booms.

As I have grown older, I have been appalled at the cost of displays of fireworks, at their easy availability wherever one wants to buy them (they are now at our local supermarket, Ingles!), and at the damage they do to the purity of the air around us. I have learned that one of the most pressing problems of Asheville, our own community, is polluted air. And so I no longer rejoice at hearing the big booms of the firecrackers exploding high in the air. Last night I did not bother to go out to see them, although some are visible from my front yard.

In these good days, as my own days are getting shorter, I find more pleasure in reading good books, using our therapy pool as often as possible to keep my body moving, and sending encouraging letters to friends. In that vein, I ran across an excellent editorial from Rev. Dr. Rob Blackburn, pastor of Central UMC, in which I rejoiced! It is the most recent one. I'd like to share it with you now. It is titled "A Moment of Grace."

> A story is told about Fiorello LaGuardia, who, when he was mayor of New York City during the worst days of the Great Depression and all of World War II, was called "The Little Flower" because he was only five foot four and always wore a carnation in his lapel. He was a colorful character who used to ride the New York City fire trucks, take entire orphanages to baseball games, and whenever the New York newspapers

were on strike, he would go on the radio and read the Sunday funnies to the kids.

One bitterly cold night in January 1935, the mayor turned up at a night court that served the poorest ward of the city. LaGuardia dismissed the judge for the evening and took over the bench himself. Within a few minutes, a tattered old woman was brought before him, charged with stealing a loaf of bread. She told LaGuardia that her daughter's husband had deserted her, her daughter was sick, and her two grandchildren were starving. But the shopkeeper, from whom the bread was stolen, refused to drop the charges. "It's a bad neighborhood, Your Honor," the man told the mayor. "She's got to be punished to teach other people around here a lesson."

LaGuardia sighed. He turned to the woman and said, "I've got to punish you. The law makes no exceptions—ten dollars or ten days in jail." But even as he pronounced the sentence, the mayor was already reaching into his pocket. He extracted a bill and tossed it into his famous sombrero, saying: "Here is the ten dollar fine which I now remit; and furthermore I am going to fine everyone in this courtroom fifty cents for living in a town where a person has to steal bread so that her grandchildren can eat. Mr. Bailiff, collect the fines and give them to the defendant."

So the following day the New York City newspapers reported that $47.50 was turned over to a bewildered old lady who had stolen a loaf of bread to feed her starving grandchildren, fifty cents of that amount being contributed by the red-faced grocery store owner, while some seventy petty criminals, people with traffic violations, and New York City policemen, each of whom had just paid fifty cents for the privilege of doing so, gave the mayor a standing ovation.

What an extraordinary moment of grace for anyone present in that courtroom. The grace of God operates at a profound level in the life of a loving person. Persons like Mayor LaGuardia help to transform the world because they live a life that spends itself without counting the cost. They are the ones that know the deep joy of sharing the life we have been given rather than bottling it up for our own consumption.[9]

Let us pray.

Gracious God, teach us also to share the life we have been given, in whatever way is possible. We thank you that, as we grow older, our priorities become more compatible with your life within and we become more aware of the needs of others. Oh, how we pray for more mayors like LaGuardia, who had a sense of justice and compassion for those in need. And now we thank you for our food, for the constancy of your presence, and for the joy you grant us in these good days. Amen.

—*given at Brooks-Howell Home, July 5, 2001*

Being Present to the Moment

Sometime ago, from a meditation I read, I began to understand the idea that "being present to the moment," without carrying the baggage of the past or the worries of the future, is very important. Perhaps that is one of the reasons people seem to see me, usually, as a happy person.

Being present to the moment is not always easy to do. So often, guilt or disappointment regarding something we have just done colors our thinking about the present. In the corners of our minds the worries about tomorrow, or the next hour, or the future, or about what life is bringing to some person who is on our minds—these worries often lurk in the corners. They trip us up and make us distracted, so we do not pay attention to the present moment. The bottom line is that we fail to recognize that God is right here right now, and all is well with our world.

I was impressed with one of my pastor's statements sometime ago. It has been good to remember it. It says in essence that always there is sufficient love, and always it is present right here, right now, where we need it, and we can trust that fact. I do believe it.

As someone said sometime ago, when you find that you and God seem to be far apart, guess who moved?

The last few weeks have not been the best ones in my life. They have been much more crowded and busy than I had expected July to be. July is the month when most of us can relax. They are sometimes called the lazy, hazy days of summer. Many groups do not meet and less is going on. It is a time for relaxation. With so many things going on in my life, however, I have not felt the leisure that I had expected to find in July.

It was first the dentist, then an infection, and then other doctors' appointments, some unexpected meetings, company in the form of five or six unexpected beloved people—at different times, of course, and then the computer breakdown. Altogether, July has been a difficult month. Oh, poor me! Don't you love to hear me whine?

God willing, the new computer is now ready to go. Until help came today, it would not give directions to my printer, and so it was quite limited. The other day, with help, I was able to have the *Gentle Reminder*, our in-house newsletter and calendar, printed on another printer, although it did not come out as it was on my computer. When I asked my consultant about that, he said it was because she did not have the same kinds of fonts that I had used for the document. Ah well, it did get out, but I was quite disappointed in myself—not only were the fonts different, but I found I had left out some important messages from residents.

With the tension and lack of rest that some of these changes have occasioned, I have found myself uptight and overly tired. Last night I fell asleep in my easy chair a little after eight o'clock.

Then today, Wednesday, was quite a day. Sometimes our "ministries" are not what we expect them to be, nor what we may have intended. I went to the spa early, before going to ABCCM for the morning, as I usually do. There I found myself talking with a number of women in the dressing room, some before I swam, and some afterward, one even in the hot tub. When I thought about it, I had talked with five women there; two of them were known to me, and three were not. When I left, I felt as though I had ministered to these women by being present to them and listening to their stories.

Then, at ABCCM, I had worked a good hour and a half with hardly saying a word to anyone else—nor being much aware of who else was in the room, really—until I broke away from the computer and took a document to my boss to ask her about it. She told me what I needed to know, and then she said to me, "I've not heard your laugh yet this morning." She seems to feel that my laugh is contagious and makes her feel good.

Through that meditation I read, I began to understand that "being present to the moment," without carrying the baggage of the past or the worries of the future is very important in living a Christian life of awareness and ministry. It is not easy.

We so often forget that God is right here right now, and all is well with our world.

It has struck me that Jesus was not distracted by worries and concerns of the past or future. Even while he knew that his untimely death was coming, he threw a party, if you will, with all of his buddies. They ate and drank as he told them realistically that he would not be with them for long. When he healed people, he did not worry about how that person got that way, or whether he or she would always do good in the future if healed. He did not ask what had caused the ailment. Instead, his concern was that the here-and-now situation was one of disability or illness that could be corrected. The immediate problem was making the blind see and the lame walk; he did not discuss the causes or possible cures—he simply judged the situation in the here and now, and did the thing that would help, whatever that was.

I find that, when I get nervous and angry with people, I am often worried about what others will think or I am tired from too much running around. Or I have simply not paid attention to my diet, or something else. In other words, I have simply not been present to God here and now. While it is a struggle to keep my mind and my heart on God in all of the hours of the day, I plan to continue to pursue this way of living, because it brings much joy and assurance.

Let us pray.

Gracious God, keep us aware of you as we go about our daily tasks. Help us to pay attention to the images of God, the individuals, who cross our paths daily. Help us to be aware of how we can minister to them, even as we minister to you. We ask you to bless us to your awareness and service. Amen.

—*given at Brooks-Howell Home, July 24, 1997*

Giving

Good morning. I wish for all of you a new year blessed with a giving spirit, and a clear sense of God's presence in your lives. I want to talk briefly this morning about giving. This is not the final word, you know, but a few random thoughts on the subject.

Some people are givers! One can often tell very quickly, on meeting a new person, whether or not that person is a giver! Sometime ago, when I was in the hospital, I received some visitors that I had not met before. They have been giving nourishment to my life in myriad ways since that time. They are residents here, and I continue to cherish their friendship. That friendship started with their giving to me.

My pastor is a giver. He is an amazing combination of ridiculous clowning and the most profound wisdom and sound theology—all in one brief celebration on a Sunday morning. He gives freely and abundantly of himself and his talents.

This year I seemed to go hog-wild on Christmas giving! It will take me a while to pay off the Visa bill—but what fun it was! A couple of weeks ago I went to see my good brother, who has been given an iffy timeline on his own life. I found it a great blessing to visit with him. And in between the visits, it was great fun to be a part of his family and to give gifts to children and grandchildren, and great-grands. Normally I have not given gifts at Christmas to any of these because they have not been, until recently, a significant part of my life. What fun it was to choose gifts for a 4-year-old, a 2½-year-old, and two babies! I felt like Barb and I did a few years ago, when we had great fun buying gifts for a young man from Zimbabwe who was then living with us while he went to college. What fun for two unmarrieds to shop for clothing for a man! I still recall that we did it gleefully!

Christmas is sometimes called the season of giving. It is a time when people seem to open their hearts and think of others and give as they do not give during the rest of the year! People seem to be more open to seeing the needs of others and to giving to meet those needs. It is a time when many money appeals are made because of this; so if you think you have received a lot of requests for money this year, I'm sure you are right. Many organizations take advantage of the willingness and desire to give at this time of year.

Some of us give because of the Christ Child. We know that God gave his son. Jesus came as a baby at this time of year. Wise men came from far away to offer their rare gifts to this child. Angels gave their heavenly music, and music has been an integral part of Christmas ever since. Shepherds came in from the open fields to give their adoration and encouragement. The scriptural stories of all of these events are indeed a beautiful gift to all of us each year.

What started my thinking about giving was my recollection of a dear friend who died here. She came into Cummings, our twenty-four-hour care unit, following a stroke. In her active, former life she had had much to give, and she had given generously as she worked first as a home missionary and then as a chaplain in a large hospital. While she lived with us here, she had little to give. Bodily needs and concerns had sapped her strength and vitality; she spoke little and almost never initiated conversation. It was time in her life for others, even us, to give to her. She was not different from other Cummings residents. All these are people who have given much, and now are in need of our care and thoughtful giving to them.

Giving is a very self-affirming activity, and it has its own rewards for the giver. I remember from long ago, a young girl in one of my Scout troops. She had done a kindness to another girl, and her face glowed as she turned to me and said, "Wasn't that good of me?" Oh yes, yes! And I wanted to say also that it is so good *for* you! Giving makes us feel good all over about ourselves!

This is the whole point, I think, of the popular phrase that says "Practice random kindness and acts of beauty." I have seen people just glowing when they have played Santa Claus to another in some unexpected and greatly appreciated way. Giving raises our own self-esteem, and is indeed good for us.

I recall the joy that seemed to grace the faces of the wonderful people of Nicaragua, especially as they welcomed strangers and showed such great and amazing kindnesses. I shall never forget the young woman who talked briefly at one of our demonstrations in front of the U.S. embassy. She was part of a Witness for Peace trip,[10] and the group had spent a few days in the *campo* (rural area), with very poor families. As they were ready to leave, the woman of the home where she had stayed presented her with a parting gift of a dozen eggs. The young woman asked that the family keep them, for she knew that the children needed food, but the woman insisted that she take them. As she told about this gift received, the girl cried, knowing that she could not refuse such a gift given. The poor give so much in love. That is what the story of the Good Samaritan is all about: giving of oneself.

Giving means a relationship of love to others. One does not give to oneself Christmas gifts, but gifts are given to others. Gifts are given to loved ones, and carry with them that love for another person. There is a saying that there is no small or insignificant gift. It is true. Once long ago, when I was a stamp collector, I put together small packets of stamps for a visiting group of women from other countries. I felt that it was such an insignificant gift, and was amazed at the apparent and joyful gratitude from the women. Gifts cement loving relationships, one to another.

Giving is a connection to others in a loving way, a reaching out to another in contrast to a selfish isolation. It has often occurred to me that much of our mental illness and much of the evil of our world are based on isolation and the lack of giving to others—and therefore the lack of connections. One need only think of the two young men in Littleton, Colorado,[11] who felt alone and isolated, lacking the connections that giving to them would have brought.

These are simply some random thoughts on giving, which seemed appropriate at this time when most of us are writing our thank-you notes to those who have given to us so generously at this Christmas season.

Let us pray.

Abundantly giving God, we give you thanks for your daily gifts to us: another day of life, sunshine and rain and snow and fog, warm food to eat and sufficient shelter. Thank you for people in our community here, residents and employees and others who are givers. Thank you for yourself, always abundantly giving to meet our every need. Thank you for a world of people for us to love, and to whom we may give ourselves. Amen.

—*given at Brooks-Howell Home, December 28, 2000; January 4, 2001*

Diversity

I should like to start with a quote from a recent letter from a group to which I belong, the Methodist Federation for Social Action (MFSA). The author says,

> While in Atlanta for [a recent conference] . . . the MFSA board of directors met. One of our actions was to pass a resolution to inform state legislators that we would not meet in Georgia again should they decide to reinstate a state flag including the confederate symbol. Late that same night, the state legislature passed a bill calling for the confederate symbol to be eliminated from the flag. *The measure passed by one vote.*
>
> One vote. It was a powerful symbol that *one person can make a huge difference.* . . . [You] make a huge difference. . . . Each and every one of you, through your witness . . . contribute to that difference. *The world needs a church that embodies the just love of God. Each of you makes that happen.* It's time to stand up and be counted! [italics added][12]

A week ago last Sunday was one of my most favorite days in our church year. It was Pentecost Sunday, the birthday of our Christian church. Sometimes we forget how our church was born. It was born with fire and difference as individuals spoke in various languages. I know you remember the story. Let me quote from Acts 2:1–8, Peterson's translation, as follows.

> When the feast of Pentecost came, they were all together in one place. Without warning, there was a sound like a strong wind, gale force—no one could tell where it came from. It filled the whole building. Then, like a wildfire, the Holy Spirit spread through their ranks, and they started speaking in a number of different languages as the Spirit prompted them.
>
> There were many Jews staying in Jerusalem just then, devout pilgrims from all over the world. When they heard the

sound, they came on the run. Then when they heard, one after another, their own mother tongues being spoken, they were thunderstruck. They couldn't for the life of them figure out what was going on, and kept saying, "Aren't these all Galileans? How come we're hearing them talk in our various mother tongues?" [13]

What an amazing and wonderful experience! They heard, one after another, their own mother tongues being spoken.

Today most of us need no one to tell us that people are different. Many people just do not like that. We certainly have our troubles with other people because they are not like us. Perhaps they are too fat or too thin, or their skin is the wrong color, and they just don't pronounce their r's right! Maybe they're old and slow, or maybe they never learned anything about music—or talk too much! They're just not like us, and they irritate us. I recall a family reunion, long ago, when my nephew, now deceased, was two years old. Also at the family reunion was a small girl, his age, cute as a button, and getting a lot of attention. Bill walked up to her, and I remember thinking, "It would be a delight if he kissed her." Instead of that, he took hold of her arm, gave her a hard swat on her bottom, and walked away. Enough for getting along with a pretty girl!

Our own country has been built on diversity, with the talents and gifts of many different people from many different lands. Those people who came first to our shores came because they couldn't get along with those of their own country.

But in Acts, when our church was born, people rejoiced that there was difference—that people spoke in their own native languages although they were many different languages. I was amazed at how many different groups were represented in our early beginnings. Acts 2:8–11 says, "Parthians, Medes, and Elamites, visitors from Mesopotamia, Judea, and Cappadocia, Pontus and Asia, Phrygia and Pamphylia, Egypt and the parts of Libya belonging to Cyrene, immigrants from Rome, both Jews and proselytes. Even Cretans and Arabs!" That's a lot of very different groups!

As we move on in Acts, we discover that the church—different as the individuals were—generally worked together. No matter how different they were, they supported each other and worked together to make this new faith group come alive and stand strong. They were known by their love for one another!

In these days when differences in people seem to scare our leaders and our government into taking strange actions like the recent so-called Patriot Act, we need, each one, to stand up and be counted and to make a difference in our world—to stand strong and to appreciate our differences and our diversity. This is how our church was born.

Let us pray.

Gracious God, we thank you that you never heard of "cloning." Thank you that every snowflake is different, and that each oak leaf is a new creation, and that each person has his or her very own special and different gifts to share. Thank you for our differences here, and the understanding that you bless each one with her or his unique and special gifts that make the total a blessing to all. Grant us the chutzpah to use our unique gifts for the good of the whole. Amen.

—given at Brooks-Howell Home, June 18, 2004

Racism

I want to talk briefly about racism. It is very much on my mind today for a number of reasons. First, I recently heard Dr. James Forbes,[14] the first black pastor of Riverside Church in New York City, speak about Dr. Martin Luther King Jr. Secondly, I am reading Cornel West's book, *Restoring Hope*,[15] consisting of interviews by Cornel West with various public figures in our African-American community. Today I ran across a snippet from one of Dr. King's writings, in my reading. This past Sunday I spoke at a church out of town, and in speaking of the work of one of our community centers, I recalled the experience of the center in the midst of the riots some years ago. Thus, racism is much on my mind.

Our Scripture is from Galatians: "There is neither slave nor free . . ." (Galatians 3:28, NRSV)

There is no doubt that racism is alive and well in these United States, and in Asheville. We are aware of the prison industrial complex, which one African-American called the return of slavery. There is forced labor in the prisons; a high incidence of black prisoners held on death row; the drug war, which often targets inner-city black men and women; and we are becoming more and more aware of what is called "profiling," one aspect of which is that black drivers are targeted for traffic violations, or for stopping and searching because they might "fit the profile" of a drug runner. Recently, New Jersey has made a study of this practice, and found that 75 percent of drivers stopped are black or Hispanic. In his recent talk Dr. Forbes noted that many black people carefully wear ties and suit coats because thus they are less likely to "fit the profile." During his talk Dr. Forbes dramatically pulled off his own tie, loosened his shirt, and pulled out his shirttail, to make that point.

One of the things that Dr. Forbes called to our attention was his understanding that racism, harsh and intransigent as it is, is not the real problem, but is just a warm-up for the much bigger issue, that of class, rich versus poor. Those of you who are aware of politics in our own country, and around the world, have clearly seen the separation of the rich and the poor in recent years, and the virtual elimination of our own middle class. The revolutions and protests, whether in Chiapas, Mexico, or in cities here, are just the beginning of the battle of the rich and the poor, which is well on its way.

One of the interviewees for the book *Restoring Hope* is Wynton Marsalis, a jazz player, and that dialogue is most interesting. One of the points is that jazz players are very special people, with understanding beyond that of a "made" musician, because jazz is free and creative, born of the listening and the blending with others. He spoke particularly of Louis Armstrong and Duke Ellington as kings of jazz, and noted how their music is seen as indicating that the two men are recognized as great musicians because they were great human beings.

In the last instance, I should like to recommend that you read Martin Luther King's book *Strength to Love*.[16]

Back in the later 1960s, the time of the summer riots in Chicago and Detroit, I found myself directing one of our United Methodist community centers in Grand Rapids, Michigan, halfway between those two cities. We had riots too, but the news media did not highlight our riots—they were small potatoes compared with Detroit and Chicago. Nevertheless, our inner city was under curfew for several days. Our center was in the midst of day camp, and at work with Job Corps young people (almost entirely black), combined with white young people from our conference churches who had come to help. These young people, black and white, worked together with the younger children in our day camp. Each day we bused them out to a county park because, as the fires and looting and rioting came closer to us, they were safer outside Grand Rapids' inner city. Our day-care parents, however, began to question our wisdom of staying open. Finally, when the fires came within two blocks of us on two sides, we surely did close our doors and cease our activities until things quieted down. I recall asking one of our energetic Job Corps workers what he saw himself doing after "the revolution," which he was very sure was coming. He said simply, "I've not thought about that because I'll not be here." He was convinced he would lose his life fighting for the rights of his people.

Many of us hold a deep conviction that Dr. Cecilia Sheppard, my first Bible teacher and a former resident of Brooks-Howell, made clear long years ago in our Bible classes. That is, that God is the parent of all of us, or God is the parent of none of us. When it is put that simply, we begin to understand that we are all children of God.

—given at Brooks-Howell Home, April 22, 1999

NOTES

1. Used with permission of Rev. Dr. Rob Blackburn.

2. Gerald Marks and Seymour B. Simons, "All of Me." ASCAP 310026950.

3. Dom Helder Camara is a liberation theologian. According to his book, he was ordained in 1931 and served as auxiliary bishop of Rio de Janeiro from 1952 to 1964. He then became archbishop of Olinda and Recife in northeast Brazil, the poorest and least developed region of the country. In the larger sense, he is the bishop of all who share the conviction that inhuman structures can be changed by the violence of truth and justice. See Dom Helder Camara, *Hoping Against All Hope*, trans. by Matthew J. O'Connell (Maryknoll, NY: Orbis Books, 1987).

4. El Mazote, El Salvador, is known far and wide as a small village where men, women, and children were massacred and buried by the militia of the country as a part of the repression of the peasant population.

5. Rob Blackburn, "Life—An Original Adventure," in *Jot & Tittle*, 24:30, (July 23–29, 2000) (Central UM Church, Asheville, North Carolina). Used with permission of Rev. Dr. Rob Blackburn.

6. Ibid.

7. Date of newsletter unknown. Used with permission of the Michigan Association of Retired School Personnel.

8. This prayer is used with the permission of Rev. Howard Hanger.

9. Rev. Rob. Blackburn, Central UM Church, Asheville, NC. Used with permission.

10. Witness for Peace is an NGO (non-governmental organiza-

tion) born in 1983, which first took groups of volunteers to Nicaragua, and now takes them to Mexico, Cuba, Guatemala, and Colombia to "witness" to the need for peace in these conflicted areas. This witness helped keep people from shooting others. When Americans were present, the Contras were less likely to harm the indigenous people.

11. A few years ago two young men "went berserk," in Littleton and shot a number of high school classmates, as well as teachers and school personnel.

12. Date of newsletter unknown. Used with permission of the Methodist Federation for Social Action.

13. Peterson, *The Message.*

14. James Forbes is also the author of *The Holy Spirit and Preaching* (Nashville, TN: Abingdon Press, 1989).

15. Cornel West and Kelvin Shawn Sealey, *Restoring Hope: Conversations on the Future of Black America* (Boston: Beacon Press, 1997).

16. Martin Luther King Jr., *Strength to Love* (Minneapolis: Augsburg Fortress, 1989).

Outreach in Our World

God So Loved the World—Then and Now

John 3:16–18, Peterson translation:

> This is how much God loved the world: He gave his Son, his one and only Son. And this is why: so that no one need be destroyed; by believing in him, anyone can have a whole and lasting life. God didn't go to all the trouble of sending his Son merely to point an accusing finger, telling the world how bad it was. Jesus came to help, to put the world right again. Anyone who trusts him is acquitted; anyone who refuses to trust him has long since been under the death sentence without knowing it. And why? Because of that person's failure to believe in the one-of-a-kind Son of God when introduced to him.[1]

Yes, this is how much God loved the world. God gave his only son. God did this long ago, to help us to understand God's ways. As I was reading a sermon with this title preached by a friend a short time ago, it struck me that we usually put this word of the Lord in the past tense, when it needs to be put in the present tense. Yes, God loved the world so much that he sent Jesus to our world.

And today God loves the world so much that God sends you and me, and many others who teach us about God's ways. God loves the world today, right now. It is not just an event of the past, done once and forever, long ago, but it is an event in the here and now. God loves our world here and now and today.

God loved the world, long ago, so much that God sent our earth spinning through space, with mountains of glorious misty beauty and pristine oceans and lakes and streams, with mighty rivers and beautiful flowers and plants, with amazing and delightfully creative animals, and finally, long years after, human beings, people like you and me, to live and enjoy these blessings, and to know about God's love.

And God loves the world right now, in this time and place, so much that God sends saints to our own day and time—people like those neighbors of ours who have recently died—May Titus, Annie Herbert, Mattie Lou Summey, Clara Ruth Anderson, Elizabeth Nowlin, Joe Lance, and so many everyday saints among us, people whom you and I know, who also help us to understand God's way.

With our Sunday celebrations, our morning services are never complete without an understanding of what our "gig" —or job—is for the week. For what are we responsible in this world? What is our job? The purpose of our worship together is not to just come and sit and listen, and go away refreshed, but, oh yes, if we are made in God's image—and we are—then we have work and responsibility, too.

A few weeks ago, another resident, Ruth Clark, used a hymn that many of us once knew and then forgot, because it was left out of our more recent United Methodist hymnals. It is the one that says, "Be strong, we are not here to play, to dream, to drift; we have hard work to do, and loads to lift." God does not leave us without our own work to do in this world—God loves the world here and now so much that God sends you and me, brother, and you and me, sister, to be the God-spirit in this world, here and now, for others. Yes, long ago, God sent Jesus into the world to show us God's ways. Today God sends you and me, and people we live with every day.

Long years ago, when I was young, I took a workshop to help with my counseling young people. The first thing the presenter offered as a basic tenet of being a counselor was, "Be there." I took note of this, but for several years I found myself wondering, what did he mean? I thought, "If you are a counselor, why would you *not* be there? Of course you are there!" But then I began to discover that many counselors simply were *not* there—one way or another, they were not available when needed. Counselors worked specific hours, and often could not be found for help outside of that specific, brief time. And as I began to know people better, I began to understand that many counselors who were there physically, were really not there in ways that were needed. Their own worries or concerns from other areas of their lives interfered, and they just were not present for the person who needed help.

I know you've known that too, at times. I can hear you saying on some occasion, "She just wasn't listening," or, "Didn't she hear me say that I had no money? What did she think I meant?" or, "I thought she understood that my parents are both dead—didn't she read my bio?" or, "But I told him that three times." Oh yeah—the counselor was just not there! And I began to understand what that wise teacher/counselor was saying about the importance of "being there."

And I recall, too, how deep friendships are formed. In time of need, a person may recall, "She was there for me when I needed her," or, "I'll never forget how helpful he was when I really needed someone to lean on," or, "I could always go to my grandmother and tell her about my problems."

Oh yes, we have known people who in our own lives were there when they were needed and were present to us, hearing our call for help, and listening and responding. "Being there" meant something real to them.

Many of our most beloved hymns are based on that common experience. And so we have "Blessed Assurance" and many others that tell us that our Comforter, our gracious God, is always present for us when needed.

Yes, God loved the world so much that God sent God's son—and today, in the present, God loves the world so much that God sends you and me and other saints —not to be the unique Savior of our world—there was only one Jesus—but to help others to know the love of God. And yes, God sends you and me to be there when we are needed. And yes, there is only one you.

Let us pray.

Gracious God, help us to recognize that we are images of you. We are images of you who are goodness and help and comfort and love to so many in this world. Help us, too, to recognize our unique place in this beautiful planet, a place of belonging and fitting in, and also a place of unique contribution to the well-being of the whole. Thank you for the privilege of knowing you, and finding comfort and joy in that relationship. Thank you that you sent Jesus, long ago, to help us understand your ways of life for all. Thank you for each new day, for each gathering with others of your children, and for your love that surrounds us each new and fresh day. Amen.

—*given at Brooks-Howell Home, June 4, 2003*

Bumper Stickers

Some of you are aware that my car is almost covered in the back with bumper stickers. One day a man asked why I would want to ruin a good paint job. I did not answer. It is more important to me to be salt and light.

Traveling on the highway, I have often had truckers pull up and sit on my rear bumper for a few minutes in order to read them. For those of you who have not read them lately, let me fill you in.

Only two are about places I've been: One of these is from the Bayside Hotel on Corn Island, an island on the Caribbean coast of Nicaragua. The hotel was new, and my friend and I were two of the four guests present. When we ate breakfast, the proprietors asked what we wanted for our main meal, and they prepared the meal to our likes. The other place sticker is from Chautauqua. That is a favorite place, and Jeannie Wintringham and Jewel Brown will soon be off to host Fenton Deaconess Home for the summer. I have attended since 1980.

Other bumper stickers:

CHILDREN FIRST

HUMAN BEINGS ARE NOT THE ONLY SPECIES ON EARTH—WE JUST ACT LIKE IT

THE EARTH DOES NOT BELONG TO US. WE BELONG TO THE EARTH.

SCHOOLS NOT BOMBS

SUPPORT RED WOLF RECOVERY

NATIVE EARTHLING

PROTECT NATIVE FORESTS

APPLAUD THE FRENCH BROAD (This is concerned with the Western North Carolina river's preservation, and it says that in smaller print. Last summer, Barb and I were in the upper area of Michigan and we had stopped for lunch. We came out to find two women reading the bumper stickers. The one had a puzzled look on her face. She looked up at me

as I approached, and said as she pointed to the sticker, "Do you mean the Paris prostitute?")
TV: THE PLUG-IN DRUG. TURN IT OFF. GET A LIFE.
FUSS BUSTER (from the Mediation Center)
DEMOCRATIC WOMEN MAKE GREAT LEADERS. YOU'RE FOLLOWING ONE NOW.
CLOSE THE SOA (the School of the Americas, which trains Latin American military in torture and police tactics)
PRO UN AND PROUD OF IT
TRUST IN GOD. S/HE WILL PROVIDE.
MINDS ARE LIKE PARACHUTES. THEY ONLY FUNCTION WHEN OPEN.
ABOLISH LANDMINES
RESPECT KNOWS NO COLOR
LISTEN TO WOMEN FOR A CHANGE
WAGE PEACE!
BUTTERFLIES ARE FREE
HANDICAPPED: AGITATE FOR EQUAL ACCESS
BIG BUSINESS OUT OF CONGRESS!
THE DEATH PENALTY IS DEAD WRONG
DON'T LET TOXIC WASTE MAKE US ALL ENDANGERED SPECIES
UPPITY WOMEN UNITE!
DON'T POSTPONE JOY
IT'S NEVER TOO LATE TO HAVE A HAPPY CHILDHOOD
One is in Spanish: LOS DERECHOS DE LAS MUJERES SON DERECHOS HUMANOS (Women's Rights Are Human Rights)
My license plate is MUJERES, the word for "women," in Spanish.
And from Jubilee!: KEEP THE MAIN THING THE MAIN THING

These new ones will go on soon:
CHILDREN SHOULD BE SEEN AND HEARD AND BELIEVED (This refers to child abuse stories.)
WHY ENCOURAGE VIOLENCE? DON'T BUY WAR TOYS.
IMAGINATION IS MORE IMPORTANT THAN KNOWLEDGE (from Einstein)
FEMINISM IS THE RADICAL NOTION THAT WOMEN ARE PEOPLE
HOMOPHOBIA IS A SOCIAL DISEASE
IF YOU WANT PEACE, WORK FOR JUSTICE
Now, why in the world would I think that this list is suitable

for our morning worship? Bumper stickers often capture a thought succinctly.

The ones on my car express some of my beliefs. As we get older, many of us do not have so many opportunities as we should like to share with others our beliefs and the guiding principles of our lives.

Recently I was both surprised and pleased when we were visiting with a young black woman whom I have known since third grade. She is now married and has a delightful little girl, and as we were talking, she came out with several understandings that guide her life. More than once in our visiting she said, "You taught me that, Helene."

There are some words in our Bibles which fit this meditation. I am reading from Eugene Peterson's New Testament, from Matthew 5:13–16.

> Let me tell you why you are here. You are here to be salt-seasoning that brings out the God-flavors of this earth. If you lose your saltiness, how will people taste godliness? You've lost your usefulness, and will end up in the garbage.
>
> Here's another way to put it: You're here to be light, bringing out the God-colors in the world. God is not a secret to be kept. We're going public with this, as public as a city on a hill. If I make you light-bearers, you don't think I'm going to hide you under a bucket, do you? I'm putting you on a light stand. Now that I've put you there on a hilltop, on a light stand—shine! Keep open house; be generous with your lives. By opening up to others, you'll prompt people to open up with God, this generous Father in heaven.[2]

Let us pray.

Thank you, God, for the opportunities we have to witness to our faith each day of our lives. And now we offer thanks for the generous gifts from your hand—gifts of food and shelter and our here and now community together. Amen.

—*given at Brooks-Howell Home, March 15, 2000*

Soup – Soup – Soup – Soup

We slept on the floor for two short nights.
Someone lent a double-bed mattress
and put it down for these two old ladies
who had come to work together
as volunteers for the weekend.

And what was this place?
A very big and very old house
in the middle of the city.
It was called "The Open Door."
It is a place where homeless men
can find a welcome and a shower,
clean clothes, and quiet rest and—
—always—big bowls of nourishing soup
and sandwiches they can take along.
No questions asked.

Soup – soup – soup – soup!
I watched as volunteer cooks worked.
I helped to cut fresh veggies.
I poured in can after can of good food
and stirred the big metal pots
with great long spoons that reached the bottom.
This was not a watery soup!

Leftover meats from roasts,
fresh hamburger,
chicken legs, with bones removed,
turkey pieces,
frozen veggies—canned veggies—
fresh veggies—healthy herbs and spices,
and a lot of love
mixed with burns and frustrations,
and anger that soup was needed!

All was combined in the biggest pots that
I had ever seen for making soup.
The pots were full—
the spoons had great long handles.
I stood on a chair to stir.
It took two strong men to lift each pot.

And then the men came.
They moved in quickly and sat down noisily.
They filled the tables.
Every chair was taken.
They became silent
as they waited through a few good words of thanks to God.
The room was quiet
even though they were very hungry.
Some had been here before.

Bowl after bowl after bowl after bowl
of nourishing hot soup filled the tables.
Sandwiches sat in the middle,
wrapped and ready to go.
We heard slurps and swallows
and belches and grunts—
not much talking.
A few gracious thank-you's,
a few smiles.
It was not a chattery bunch.
The men had come to eat
—not to talk.

We filled and refilled the bowls.
The men did not come
to help themselves.
Instead, we carried soup to them.
We picked up each bowl,
and filled it again and again.
Five bowls to one man.
He was very hungry.

Later, resting, I asked, "Why, God?"
"Why does hunger like this exist
when our earth is so bountiful?
These men are strong,
and very much alive.
They could make a good living
just growing the vegetables needed
for a soup kitchen like this!"

I found a truth the other day.
The words said,
"Wealth creates poverty."
"Wealth creates poverty?" I asked.
Oh yeah!
I knew it was true.

Isn't that the ying/yang of life?
Of course—There is always an opposite.

When I was young, most people were poor—
poor as the proverbial church-mice.
Our family was very poor.
But we had what we needed.
There were a few homeless men—
"Bums"—we called them.
And a few very rich.
The earth itself was abundant
and full of life and goodness.
Everyone had a garden,
and we did too!

Today our earth is wasted.
People like you and I have grabbed giddily
for the selfish stupidity of having too much.
Most of us are overweight.
We have more than our fair share,
so there is little left for others.
Some now are very wealthy,
but most are very poor.
Some are squeezing life itself
from the poorest of the poor.

How can one rejoice in life
with no place to sleep,
no food to eat,
no fresh water available,
and no place for body wastes?

How can one rejoice in life
when pants no longer fit the fattened waist,
when surplus stuffs our closets,
when fences no longer protect our treasures,
when brothers and sisters have no soup,
when precious children cry for bread?

"Wealth creates poverty!"
Yes, that is truth.

And, Gracious God, there's one more thing!
The balance of ying/yang does not fit.
Wealth/poverty is not a ying/yang.
Wealth is not forever.
Poverty is not unchanging.
The balance is not there.
Both can be changed.

Wealth creates poverty.
That is truth.
Wealth is not unchanging.
Nor is poverty!

But for the here and now
soup creates blessing!
Hot, nourishing, wonderful soup!
Soup – Soup – Soup – Soup!

—*Helene R. Hill, July 28, 2003*

Salt Shakers?

On Saturday morning, a number of us went to the prayer breakfast sponsored by the Asheville district's United Methodist Women, held at Central UMC. The breakfast was generous and the program excellent. There were 289 breakfasts served. Since the theme for the day was "Lightmakers and Salt Shakers" I should like to read the Scripture verses from which this theme was taken.

> You are the salt of the earth; but if the salt has lost its taste, how can its saltiness be restored? It is no longer good for anything, but to be thrown out and trampled underfoot.
>
> You are the light of the world. A city built on a hill cannot be hid. No one after lighting a lamp puts it under the bushel basket, but on the lampstand, and it gives light to all in the house. In the same way, let your light shine before others, so that they may see your good works and give glory to your Father in heaven. (Matthew 5:13–16, NRSV)

What does it mean to be a lightmaker or a salt shaker? I do not have much problem with being a lightmaker. I think many of us have little trouble seeing ourselves as the light of the world. Some of us have become burned-out bulbs but, be that as it may, I'd like to speak now about the salt shakers.

Salt is a very interesting mineral in our world. You will recall that India, some years ago, had a controversy over the mining of salt. It was one of the major factors that led to India's winning its independence from Britain.

Salt gives flavor and taste to foods and makes the baked potato a treat. Without salt it is a dull and tasteless hunk of starch. The lack of salt in food is always noticeable, even though other spices and herbs can be a great substitute.

Salt is often used as a metaphor that tells us that life without spice and taste is a dull drudgery, day by day. In a group I attended the other day, we spoke of how boring our world would be if all of us were alike, and how thankful we are for the variety and diversity of the people we live with or that we find in the groups we belong to, including our churches. When one thinks about it, we really do know that it does not make sense to try to have us all alike—and yet I see this apparent desire in many groups. Instead of being open to people who look different, or dress differently, or believe differently, or eat regularly in fast-food restaurants, or belong to other churches, many of our groups are closed. They are exclusive, and want only others who are like them to be embraced by their group.

Our own United Methodist Church seems to be fighting that problem right now. People who are born with a preferential attraction to their own sex are simply not welcomed in our churches. In this case, we have made it clear that, even though they believe as we do, we do not want them with us. Are they the salt we need to give life and taste to our total group?

And what about the phrase "rubbing salt in the wound"? We know that salt can be an irritation, a harmful substance, a raw hurt in the midst of difficult, open sores. Our pastor often speaks of that "irritating bozo at work," and how difficult it is for us to try to deal with him—or her—as the case may be. Is he or she salt in our wounds, or the spice we need to enlarge our own lives and living?

And there are those difficult people who are always raising questions that no one wants to answer. They sometimes bring a halt to a group's progress. They make us take notice of things we'd rather let alone or let lie quietly. They are surely salty additions.

Enough for now! Let us pray.

Dear salty and often sweaty God, thank you that life with you is full of different flavors and tastes. How boring would be the sameness of genetically engineered bodies and souls, and how deadening to the creativity that you have put within each of us. Thank you that you have put spice in each of our souls. help us to recognize and honor that difference, and to use it creatively for you. Amen.

—*given at Brooks-Howell Home, April 17, 2002*

Compassion

A deaconess friend, Debra Sue Chenault, recently worked on a project called "Making the Connections." When I heard about it, I wondered what "the connections" were, and got to thinking about the needs of all individuals to make connections in our lives. That is what trust and faith and compassion, the solid basics of our Christian faith, are all about!

Often, I am brought up short by the frustrations of my e-mail. I hear people say it is so much easier and so much less expensive than a phone call, and less burdensome than letter writing or notes. Oh yes, of course it is—but it is also one more step away from a personal connection with other people. For that reason, I use mine much less than I thought I would. I much prefer a phone call that gives me a human voice and immediate interactions with another human being. E-mail means you really do not need to "interact with" others and receive their feedback in dialogue, whether angry or approving or understanding of their joy or suffering—or with the intimacy of human beings that has been ours in the past.

I have a bumper sticker that says QUESTION TECHNOLOGY. That distancing of human beings from each other, from our connectedness, is exactly why that bumper sticker is on there. Technology often means there are fewer connections these days between people, and they are often less intimate than they once were. When we leave messages on phones, some of us speak of "phone tag" in jest, but the messages simply mean that the human beings from which they came just "pass in the night." We get the content but do not need to deal with the person and his or her feelings.

A sentence in the recent newsletter of Holy Ground (a non-profit retreat ministry here in Asheville) caught my attention. It spoke of compassion and the mantras that guide many of us today *away* from compassion. One is "be brave." In other words, do not let the tears of fearfulness fall! Often we do not cry when we should be sobbing. Nor do we let others shed their tears, but tell them to "keep a stiff upper lip" or we put our arms around them and quietly lead them out of sight of others. "Be productive" is another mantra mentioned. We seem to think it is more important to *do* something, than it is to *be* something. Some of us are led to believe that being successful is the only important thing in life, no matter what it takes to do that.

The sentence in the article that stopped me, though, was, "The farther we move from our hearts, the more closed and constricted we become."[3]

I should like to repeat that sentence: "The farther we move from our hearts, the more closed and constricted we become."

At the last deaconess convocation, I was surprised by the number of people who opted not to participate in the small-group interactions at the very close of the conference. Some just said, "No, I don't participate in such groups." Such groups provide us the opportunity to hear others' stories of sorrow and fear, and to share our own. For many that is very threatening. Again we have chosen to opt out of deep sharing with others in compassion that can be given and received. Many are afraid to share their own stories and to hear the stories of others.

Deaconesses and missionaries know it is important for us to "feel with" other human beings. That is what sharing the compassion of Jesus really means. Our pastor reminded us on a recent Sunday that the word *compassion* comes from the Latin, *cum passio*, which literally means "with suffering." Yes, compassion is suffering *with* others.

We do not suffer with others unless we have made connections with them that make that sharing possible and meaningful. We have all heard stories of missionaries like the one in James Michener's book *Hawaii*, who would not let his wife benefit from the understandings of native midwives. So she gave birth in a very difficult and needlessly painful way. Or more recently, the missionary described in Barbara Kingsolver's *The Poisonwood Bible*, who kept his family isolated from the native people and thus brought about his family's separation, and the wide scattering of his entire family.

Have you noticed recent reports on the Iraq war? There is nothing, I mean *nothing,* about the sufferings of the Iraqi people, with their lack of food and water and the basic medications needed to sustain life. Nothing is said of the loss of mothers and fathers, or of the suffering of children dying for lack of medical care because our "sanctions" do not permit many basic medications. I read recently that five thousand children die each week in Iraq.[4] Have you heard that on TV? There is no reporting of this. Again, this is a lack of compassion—of not making the connection that these too are human beings like you and me.

Today, as I listened to "This American Life" on WCQS-FM, I was struck by the so-called conversations. I wondered if these pieces are now so meaningful to people because we are so rapidly losing the close relationships of family and extended families that have sustained our lives in past eras.

I find myself grateful for the "lack of civilization" of much of our world, where the compassion of basic life experience is still in evidence. Thus, in Haiti and in Nicaragua, the two poorest countries in this hemisphere, the joyous sounds of singing and dancing and drumming are still combined in everyday life with the tears of friends and family suffering with the horrors of desperate poverty. Perhaps this is why so many who visit Haiti or Nicaragua, and see life with its open compassion, come back so changed. Here we have moved away from compassion and our basic emotions and feeling, and we find ourselves often living an ersatz life—it is simply not real or true to life, and we recognize that when we are given the chance to see it in action!

Perhaps one reason we find ourselves so devoted to our pets is that they pull us back from "false identities" to the real and compassionate people we were meant to be—because they are real and compassionate with us. This may be the primary reason we love children—they are real, and we know that. We love them especially when they have not yet moved away from honest compassion and reality into the false sophistication of teen or adult life that questions and "laughs at" everything and anything! We even have a name for those who do not do this. We call them, derisively, *naive.* As we grow older, we tend to move away from the life of awe and wonder, into a life of wariness and suspicion and violence! Is this really what we want for our lives?

Let us pray.

Gracious God, keep us full of the awe and wonder with which you have blessed us, and with which Jesus lived his entire life. Return our lives to compassion and reality. And now we ask your blessings on this meal, on those who have prepared it and those who eat it. We ask your blessing on the many in our world who will not eat today because there is no food. Grant us your compassion and your connection with all of your children. Amen.

—*Given at Brooks-Howell Home, April 30, 2003*

Is This the Home for Unwed Mothers?

This bit of worship is dedicated to all of the unwed mothers among us here. There are a good many of us.

The other morning a friend phoned and, to be smart, asked, "Is this the home for unwed mothers?" Not recognizing his voice, I said, "I'm sorry, but you have the wrong number." Then he told me who he was. We both laughed, and went on with our business.

I got to thinking about it, though, and decided I should have said, "Yes, indeed it is the home for unwed mothers. How can I help you?"

Oh yes! Don't you remember when you cuddled that little boy on the playground who had just been hit by a bully, and helped him to understand that it wasn't the end of the world?

Don't you remember when you changed the dirty pants of a crying little schoolboy who had had an accident and was sent to your office for you to deal with?

How about the time Michelle, in junior high, came in to Sunday school crying her heart out? When you finally got her story, you understood that her mom had made her give away her books, which she loved dearly. "But, Michelle," you said. "Why would she do that?" Michelle said, "My mom says when you have eight children in our small house, you don't have room for books!"

And the young college girl who was such an eager student who found herself pregnant, and needed help thinking that through and deciding what she should do. You were the one who sat down with her and counseled her.

And how you dealt with the young boy in your group who could not stand it when someone else got his kite flying before he did on that wonderful outing in springtime. That young boy, frustrated that his own kite would not stay up, ran at full speed to catch his classmate who proudly had his kite in the air. He pulled the kite down to the ground and stomped on it so that it would not fly again. It was your task to mother this boy, and also the one who had been wronged. Of course you mothered the entire group of boys, as together you reviewed and talked through what had happened, and came to an understanding of the worth of each boy—never mind the kites!

That's mothering! And you have been a mother so often!

Is this a home for unwed mothers? You bet your boots it is! The fact that one has never tied the knot with another species of life does not mean we have not acted as mothers throughout all our working lives. Remember those verses in Proverbs 31 that describe a good woman?

>Never spiteful, she treats [others] generously all her life long,
>
>She shops around for the best yarns and cottons, and enjoys knitting and sewing. . . .
>
>She looks over a field and buys it, then, with money she's put aside, she plants a garden.
>
>First thing in the morning. she dresses for work, rolls up her sleeves, eager to get started.
>
>She senses the worth of her work, is in no hurry to call it quits for the day.
>
>She's skilled in the crafts of home and hearth, diligent in homemaking.
>
>She's quick to assist anyone in need,   reaches out to help the poor. . . .
>
>She makes her own clothing, and dresses in linens and silks. . . .
>
>Charm can mislead and beauty soon fades. The woman to be admired and praised is the woman who lives in the Fear-of-GOD.
>
>Give her everything she deserves! Festoon her life with praises!
>
>   (Proverbs 31:12–13, 16–20, 22, 30–31, *The Message*)[5]

Sometimes we get hung up on formal ceremonies that give what we call "legitimacy" to certain things. We all make our choices in life. I doubt not that some of us have made some bad ones, and I doubt not that some of us have made some good ones! Some are not good choices and some are. But yes, we find ourselves mothering others, whether it is we ourselves who have given physical birth to that child or that man, or another woman. Would it not be a sorry, sorry world without caring people like you—nurses, doctors, social workers, administrators, school principals, child-care workers, counselors and teachers, professors and wheelchair pushers, pastors and gardeners, quilters and knitters, cooks and salad makers, and on and on? That's what mothering is all about, caring for each other. And we've all been there!

I have a friend who is an engineer. He seems to think very differently than I do, but we have remained friends for a good fifteen years. His mom thanks me for looking out for him while she lives elsewhere. He told me recently that he hated children. I said to him, "But I thought you told me you wanted to get married." "Oh yes, I do, but not for children!" he said. "I want to get married to have a travel companion!" Even my "playfulness" sometimes irks him. But give him a problem with a machine and he is in his glory. There is not much he cannot figure out, with his good mind and his training as an engineer. . . . But that's with a machine. He has little patience with humans and their sometimes fickle relationships.

We who have been in human services of all kinds have done a lot of mothering along the way. Yes, this is indeed a home for unwed mothers!

Let us pray.

Gracious God, we thank you for the wonderful mothers among us here. Thank you for the many people in our world who care for others in all kinds of ways. Thank you for the opportunities we have to nurture others and care for them, for as long as we live. Help us to understand that you are a nurturing God, and that we are made in your image. Amen.

—*given at Brooks-Howell Home, June 27, 2003*

O World, I Cannot Hold Thee Close Enough

I must tell you how this brief meditation came about. It's been brewing for a while. A couple of weeks ago I went to lunch with a good friend, and we spoke of many things. Somehow, my work as a school social worker came up, and I spoke of my commuting twenty miles each way and needing all of that ride home just to unwind from the problems of each heavy day.

The next Sunday I heard a snatch of Edna St. Vincent Millay's poem "God's World." I got to thinking of that poem, not in its context of the beauties of our world in the fall, but in the context of the children of our world today, whom I should like to hug and comfort and bless and heal. I want to read the poem in its entirety, and then share my thinking for the children of God's good world, and their constant peril in the days in which we live.

> God's World
> O world, I cannot hold thee close enough!
>   Thy winds, thy wide grey skies!
>   Thy mists that roll and rise!
> Thy woods, this autumn day, that ache and sag
> And all but cry with colour! That gaunt crag
> To crush! To lift the lean of that black bluff!
> World, World, I cannot get thee close enough!
>
> Long have I known a glory in it all,
>   But never knew I this;
>   Here such a passion is
> As stretcheth me apart. Lord, I do fear
> Thou'st made the world too beautiful this year.
> My soul is all but out of me,—let fall
> No burning leaf; prithee, let no bird call.[6]

And here are some of the children who often float in my consciousness, in my prayers, and in my love.

Blond and curly-haired Marilyn, a fourth-grader whose family life was so unstable that she needed support for a year or so until she developed the inner strength to stand alone and be her own good person.

Joey, a first-grader whose mom preferred reading books to caring for her children's needs. On a trip with classmates he linked up with any adult he could find, for the assurance he needed that someone would care for him.

Melissa, whose family was so mixed up that it took us two full sessions to plot out the relationships of step-families, aunts, uncles, cousins, and in-laws so that Melissa finally understood where she belonged in this melee of people who were in and out of her daily life.

Carrie, at seven, as bitter as any cynical adult and much too knowledgeable about the world she lived in, seen too early and with too-young eyes.

Jimmy, a kindergartner who was well known about town. When he was hungry and unfed at home, he found his way into whatever place promised food, and stole what he needed.

Julie, who came to school really bonked out—enough to lead me to suspect drugs in her home. And, it turned out, it was because Mom never insisted that her children go to bed at a decent hour in order to be ready for school the next morning.

Patty could draw beautiful, happy pictures of nature scenes, with the warm sun shining on flowers and bushes here and there. But always above, she put in a very black cloud—for that's the way her life seemed. She wanted so badly to "settle down," but her mother moved every few months, and Patty would need to start all over trying to make friends and some stable way for herself.

John one day drew a picture of his school burning down, because that's what he really wanted! And then, belatedly, after his teacher had looked over his shoulder, he drew the fire engine with its help for such a disaster!

Patik, from India, spoke gravely but very calmly about the earthquake that damaged his home in February of this year and left him without a father. Then with a stutter that made it very difficult to understand him, he said, "My father died. He went to save a neighbor, and a wall fell on him."

Bhaveen, whose face registers nothing as he looks at photographs of his family lost in that same earthquake. He simply cannot yet comprehend the tragedy that overtook them.

In apology to Edna St. Vincent Millay, I offer my own thinking.

> O world, I cannot hold thee close enough!
> I love thy children—hurt and hungry, mean and lean,
> Tragedy upon tragedy blotting out their lives.
> O God, I love your children who cry for bread,
> And give of my small dimes that they may be fed.
>
> But more I must do—
> I want to hug each one and love her dearly,
> To dry her tears and sparkle her eyes,
> To fatten her body and help her to play,
> To forget the hurt, and grow in joy.
>
> Lord, I do fear
> Thou'st made the world too beautiful this year.
> Our spring days have been warm and fruitful,
> Bringing to life the pinks and blues
> And all the multicolored hues.
> I see your beauty and feel your joy.
> But turn to love a little boy.
>
> I want to hug each one, and draw him close;
> To dry his tears and bring some laughter
> To replace the blank sadness.
> To break open those tight shells of protection.
> To offer the nourishment each needs,
> and most of all, —to bring a clear understanding
> Of Godly worth and blessing.
>
> O world, I cannot hold thee close enough!
> There are scarcely enough years ahead
> To bless and cherish each hurting child.
>
> Do not let me die too soon, Lord.
> Let me do all that is possible
> to let each one know that she is yours,

A unique and beautiful child,
Newly created and greatly beloved.

My soul is all but out of me—let fall
No hurting child—not one more
Till love embraces each and all.

—Helene R. Hill

Amen.

—given at Brooks-Howell Home, May 5, 2001

Human Needs and Mission Projects

Recently I was away for six days. I am grateful that my flights were uneventful, except that when I left, I had decided I ought to wear my back brace—and of course it blew all the whistles as I went through security. It has two steel rods down its back. Two women took me off to a separate room to check it out before they let me fly!

Otherwise, the three different flights each way were uneventful, and I did a lot of good reading. Once in Grand Rapids, Michigan, they welcomed me with over 13½ inches of snow, a record this year! I went for the purpose of joining in the first celebration event commemorating the fact that the United Methodist Community House in that city—where I served as executive director for six years—has been serving needy communities since 1902. That is a hundred years now!

I used the plural on communities because the present location, in the southeast section of the city, is its third location. It moved to its present location in 1951. It was first a small house in a section that is now entirely warehouses and manufacturing. In 1902 that was the small area where people from other countries came to live. From there it moved to the southwest area of the city, and until that building was condemned, it shared facilities with a group called the Police Athletic League, or PAL, an after-school boys program that now operates in its own facilities.

Our community center, often called "The Methodist" by the neighborhood kids, now has a state-of-the-art building and a budget of $1.3 million for its multifaceted program. That kind of budget was not always the case. When I worked there in the 1960s, I remember sitting down frequently with the bookkeeper as we decided together what bills or parts of bills we could pay each month!

The Community House has the oldest day care in the city; it has a strong after-school program that gives help to children in all kinds of ways; and its third component is a strong program with senior citizens—again, with various kinds of services. Ours was the first agency in the city to have a meals program for older people.

The Community House is owned and supported by the women of our United Methodist Church in the West Michigan conference, and they do a tremendous job. They were there in force on Sunday to aid in the celebration and recognition. They are proud of their agency, and give it continual and loving support and care.

For those of you who are not familiar with this aspect of our mission work, there were once a hundred community centers around the country supported primarily by the women of our (then) Methodist Church. Some of you have worked in some of these. With the reorganization of our missions administrative structure it is more difficult, now, to find the centers that were once the administrative responsibility and privilege of the women's groups of our church. Many of them started very small, as in our case, when the women saw that people needed help. In Grand Rapids they started this so-called settlement work in an area of immigrants in our city in 1902. In 1904, they called their first deaconess, and Irene Cummings was appointed to settlement work. From that small beginning a vital social service agency, serving hundreds of people daily, has come about. I was the last deaconess to serve here.

I want to speak briefly about how much of our mission work gets started today, too, as we create new agencies and work on the cutting edge of our societal life. In the case of community centers, most were born with a combination of caring about human needs and the vision to forge an answer.

Human needs are what our vision in mission is all about. The women who started our center first saw the human need, and then found themselves saying, "This is not acceptable. What can we do? How can we solve this problem? We do not have the means to help, but we must help." And so they pleaded for money to help, and rounded up others who could help. And their vision brought about a community center with services. What a joy it was, last Sunday, to hear different people from the community telling us all what the Community House had meant to them through the years: how it had changed their lives from ones of despair and need to lives of joy, lives lived with an understanding of their own possible contributions to their neighborhoods and communities. From the beginning until now, the care and concern for human needs have been the key to our survival. That is surely true of the United Methodist Community House in Grand Rapids, Michigan.

And the care for human needs and the vision to bring about change are the keys to survival in other areas of life as well. Think with me for a moment about the needy situations that you know—the homeless men and women and children in our own city; the many people in our country on welfare; families struggling with minimum-wage jobs; adults and children with AIDS in Africa; Palestinian families with no possibilities of getting to work because of checkpoint after checkpoint and insurmountable barriers; Central American communities devastated by hurricanes; people in many countries where adequate health care does not exist; children caught in slave labor. ... Today there are so many human needs. These are just a few of them.

Our care for human needs, as understood through the prophets and the life of Jesus, and the vision to help and to change things are not only the basis of our mission enterprise. Today they are the keys to our very survival. This kind of caring and concern was expressed by Isaiah long ago in these words from 58:6–9: "Is not this the fast that I choose: to loose the bonds of injustice, to undo the thongs of the yoke, to let the oppressed go free, and to break every yoke? Is it not to share your bread with the hungry, and bring the homeless poor into your house; when you see the naked to cover them, and not to hide yourself from your own kin? Then your light shall break forth like the dawn, and your healing shall spring up quickly." (NRSV)

And in the only sermon that Jesus ever preached, he called attention to our common human needs as follows: "Blessed are the poor in spirit for theirs is the kingdom of heaven.

Blessed are those who mourn, for they will be comforted. Blessed are the meek, for they will inherit the earth. Blessed are those who hunger and thirst for righteousness for they will be filled. Blessed are the merciful, for they will be shown mercy. Blessed are the pure in heart, for they will see God." (Matthew 5:3–7 NIV)

Let us pray.

Gracious God, thank you for the vision and concern of many people in our past lives who have made possible our missions and social service programs today. Thank you for your movement in our own hearts to serve you and your children in need in the many ways that have presented themselves to us. It is good to know that you have made us to be concerned for each other and to care for the needs of others. In these days of greed and violence that present themselves daily before us, may we ever be mindful that you made us for yourself, and our hearts are restless until they rest in you. Amen.

—*given at Brooks-Howell Home, March 13 and October 16, 2002*

Hospital Visit

This morning I want to ask you to rejoice with me for my life and renewed energy and joy in living. Most of you know that I spent a few days in the hospital recently.

The diagnosis was congestive heart failure, and I hate to think how nearly gone I was. I thank you, God, for your being there through Helen Mandlebaum and Ruth Clark. It was they who called Emergency and made sure I got in to be where I needed to be.

When I arrived, there was much to do. They soon determined that three essential minerals that sustain our bodies were depleted from my body. These essentials were sodium, magnesium, and potassium. Thus the slowdown of functioning—I had been so tired for a week that I could hardly function. And thus the diagnosis, which was correct.

I was puzzled about the loss of so many essentials all at once. The key was the blood pressure medicine I had been taking, which had drained me of these minerals. I want to thank God for the emergency room staff and their help and diagnosis, for the three days of good care in St. Joseph's step-down program, and the care of all of you here at Brooks-Howell.

Yesterday I went to the doctor for some answers to the many questions I still had. She was very patient and straightforward with answers. The upshot of it is that the diagnosis, was correct. I am now much better, and in simple terms, I'm okay—as okay as any of us here are. That does not mean I can resume my helter-skelter pace with all of my former activities, but it does mean that in this difficult time, my heart was not basically harmed, and continues as strong as before. My blood pressure is normal, although I continue on a low dose of corrective medication. And so I hope to continue, with a sensible diet, exercise at the pool here at Brooks-Howell, and plenty of sleep and rest.

What did I learn from such an experience? First off, it scared me, as it would any of you. In my fright, I became much more aware of how dependent we are on each other—or how interdependent we are. We depend, sometimes, on beloved friends, such as you and the members of my good church, and sometimes on strangers. We trust strangers to know their business and to be the caring, concerned people we need, especially in our hospitals and nursing centers and our churches and schools and social services. Thank God for these good people who care about what happens to us!

I think of the technician who did the echocardiogram. I was talking and laughing with the two men who brought me down from the hospital room on a gurney, and she came to say, kindly, "Well, there's a lot of levity going on out here in the hall." Yes, there was. I had just learned that the name of one of those men was Niño, and he was relating how many people did not want him near them, equating him with the storms and heat and flooding of the weather phenomenon by that same name. The other man was from the West Indies. His accent betrayed him. I had met people from the Caribbean islands, and he was pleased that I immediately guessed he was from that area. So, in the quiet halls of the hospital, I found laughter in the company of strangers.

I also came to understand that God continues to be very near, in our panics and illnesses, as well as in our energetic activities and exercise. In our Sunday service, we sang together of God's love, modifying the words of a long-ago popular tune, to sing,

> You'll be loving us—always.
> With a love that's true—always.
> When the things we've planned need a helping hand,
> You will understand always—always.
> Days may not be fair—always
> That's when you'll be there—always.
> Not for just an hour, not for just a day,
> Not for just a year, but—always.

What a blessed assurance. Thank you, God.

And now we ask your blessing this day, our Gracious God, on all who serve us here at Brooks-Howell—our kitchen staff, our nursing staff, our housekeeping staff, our residents, our administrative staff—and all who love you and understand that it is your love that is manifest within us for one another. Thank you, God, for this food, and for all the gifts we know from your abundant hand. Amen.

—*given at Brooks-Howell Home, June 11, 1998*

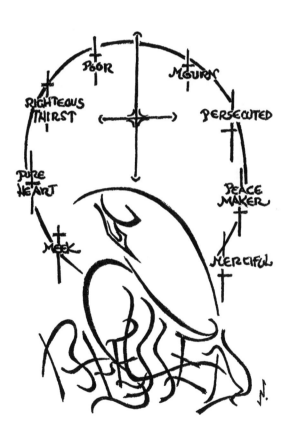

Neighborhood Center

Good morning, this is Helene. The other day I had the privilege of speaking with a group about one of our community centers where I worked in the mid to late 1950s and early 1960s as director. Neighborhood Center, in Harrisburg, Pennsylvania, is one of a hundred community centers that were once a group of such centers administered by the Women's Division. All are now administered by National Division.

My task in this center took place from 1954 through 1961, when I was appointed director of the center. The Methodist Mission, as it was then known, had been characterized in a letter as located in a "very crowded" area; my information said there were 108 children living in one block near the center. With visiting in the homes of the people, it took me three months to be sure to which block the information referred.

At that time, the Methodist Mission occupied an old-fashioned double row house, narrow and small, with three stories, such as the crowded row houses in Philadelphia. Before that time it had changed locations twice, and since that time it has changed locations twice more. It has always been in the same general neighborhood. It is now known as a good neighbor in a depressed inner-city neighborhood. Its present location seems to be permanent, with a state-of-the-art building, built in 1983, and well-suited for the mission of the agency.

With speaking about this, I was flooded with good memories of my time there. Then Tuesday, in the mail, came their latest quarterly newsletter. The center will soon be celebrating ninety years of service to inner-city people. I am expecting to be there in June to celebrate with them.

In the newsletter was an article titled "Neighborhood Center Memory," which was about Bessie Braxton, who was our kindergarten teacher when I was there. Joy of joys, Miss Bessie will be coming here with a couple who have adopted her, to my birthday celebration, so you too will have a chance to meet her! I quote her from the article.

> I have many memories of the days when I taught Kindergarten from 1940 to the 1960's at the Methodist Mission, as the Neighborhood Center was known in earlier years.
>
> In the early morning I would walk with some of the children to school at the Mission, picking up more of them as I went along.... I would end up with some eight children when we reached the Mission. (Because I was already losing my eyesight, I would have the boys and girls read the house numbers for me as we went along.)
>
> Two mothers would bring in six or seven of the other children, who often would go home at the end of the day with other mothers—ones who did not have babies at home at the time. The fathers often had to work long hours at the same job, but if a father had the day off, he might bring the children. And not only did parents walk children to school, they were also volunteers, helping to take the children on field trips, or to parties or the circus.
>
> In those days there were about 60 children in the school, which had a good PTA in which some 44 mothers participated. School began with free play, followed by devotions. There would be reading of the Bible verses, and stories and songs, and supervised play outside. Grace was said at meals, and the children were taught manners. We had our own holiday programs. The Christmas celebrations would first focus on the baby Jesus, and only later would Santa come with the presents. There were few discipline problems—a real feeling of community existed around the Mission, families were together, and everybody cared about each other and looked out for each other's children.[7]

As for me, there are many stories about specific children and adults from the time I was there, and I shall be writing some of these memories in my own biography. The center is often in my prayers and good remembrances.

I had not been there long when one of the families on that terribly crowded street needed my help. There were eight children in the family, and they came to our activities. The father of the family was electrocuted in his own home. There was a problem with the electricity and he went to the basement to see what was needed. The floor was dirt, which was often mud. When the electricity finally connected again, the contact with the water caused his death. I remember sitting with the family with the body for a part of the night before the funeral, as was the custom at that time.

Another story is from the days after we moved the center, when the entire area had been wiped out in urban renewal. It is about Louis. Louis was eleven years old and a vital part of the center. He often came after school, both for the activities for his own age group, or just to drop in and see if he could be of help to us. He often was. The center was a good place to "hang out" after school. For Christmas that year Louis had received, from the gifts of the women's groups who supported us, a pair of good warm mittens, much needed in a Pennsylvania winter. A few short weeks later Louis was talking with me, and I noted that he had only one mitten. In a chiding voice I said, "Louis, have you so quickly lost one of your mittens?" "Oh no," he answered. "I didn't lose it! I gave it away. There was a little kid who didn't have any, and it was cold, so I gave him one of mine. Now we each keep one hand in our pockets, and we both stay warm." Louis looked me straight in the eye as he said, "You taught me that, Miss Hill."

Another article in the newsletter is the following. I quote:

> Galatians 5:22-23. ". . . the fruit of the Spirit is love, joy, peace, patience, kindness, generosity, faithfulness, gentleness, and self-control. There is no law against such things." (NRSV)
>
> Since 1910 Neighborhood Center of the UMC has served God's children in Harrisburg. We have seen *love* expressed for and among the children of the inner city, *joy* on the faces of our families, *peace* among various groups coming together for a common purpose, *patience* in dealing with persons whose experiences are different from our own, *kindness* expressed in dozens of different ways, *goodness* of character that surpasses expectations for persons living on the margin of society, *gentleness* in dealing with the elderly, the young, and those with special needs, and *self-control* as those who would help stand back and guide people as they learn to help themselves.
>
> For ninety years the people of Harrisburg have known

God's love expressed through the mission and ministry of Neighborhood Center.[8]

Let us pray.

Giver of joyful life, we thank you that people with vision have established places of health and sanity in our crazy world. Thank you for the hard work and joyful sharing that have been a part of our mission work wherever we have found ourselves. Keep us always aware of your creativity within us and the fact that you have made us, too, to be life-givers. Amen.

—given at Brooks-Howell Home, March 30, 2000

Our Christian Faith Means Doing Justice

Based on Psalm 1, and Micah 6:6–8, NRSV.

I am probably one of several here at Brooks-Howell who subscribe to Working Assets, the long-distance telephone service. Occasionally, in justice issues, there are small victories, and we who are aware of issues are very grateful. In a recent case where I was involved, a letter sent through Working Assets to a big corporation has brought some justice.

Some of you have been aware of accusations against Nike shoes. Nike has been accused of employing teenagers, children under eighteen, in their large factories overseas. It has been accused of paying wages below the living minimum wage. In countries like Vietnam and Indonesia, living conditions are not like those in the United States, but there is an analysis and a strict accounting of the costs of living, and Nike's wages are below this level. Nike is also accused of using harmful chemicals without offering warnings or protection to workers who are exposed daily.

With all these issues, a letter was sent several months ago by customers of Working Assets. For those of you who are not familiar with this socially responsible long-distance service, each month there is an opportunity to be in touch with your own congresspeople on issues of justice concerns. A few such issues in recent months include:

> Funds for family planning services; a health plan for children (10 million children are without any health coverage); shutting down the School of Assassins (once known as the School of the Americas, at Fort Benning, Georgia, it is now called the Western Hemisphere Institute for Security Cooperation); protecting the northern Rockies wilderness; adult prisons are not for troubled youth; attention to the global warming issue; support for an international ban on land

mines; an end to insurance discrimination against women; stopping the Forest Service from logging the Tongass National Forest (it is in Alaska, and is the largest national forest in the States); a stop to the U.S. practice of exploding of nuclear weapons; enforcement of our civil rights laws; funding for quality child-care and after-school activities; and support for an appeal on the death sentence on sea turtles.

Each month, Working Assets briefly outlines two justice issues that are matters of concern, and offers, for a specified fee, to send letters to the congeresspersons from your state on this issue. Regarding Nike's unjust labor practices, 30,000 or more people sent letters to their congresspeople through the Working Assets network.

Those of us who did so recently received from Nike a very defensive letter, protesting that Working Assets had not been fair in their assessment and had not told them they were concerned, before issuing such a letter.

Just yesterday, I received a letter from Working Assets that refuted Nike's claims. Also enclosed was an article from the *New York Times,* in which Nike had agreed to change its labor practices in hiring children, and to use outside monitors in assessing conditions in its plants. It has not yet agreed to raising its wages to a living minimum.

This exchange of letters tells me very clearly that the company has become aware that we who are concerned citizens are watching, and are concerned about justice issues. This awareness is part of our Christian faith, inherited from Old Testament prophets and from the life and ministry of Jesus.

Why do I bring this to you as a part of worship? Because worship is not just rejoicing in the great abundance of God's good gifts, and our own good feelings about how our Gracious God loves us all always, always, always. Worship is also doing justice, and loving kindness, and walking humbly with our good God.

Let us pray.

Gracious God of justice and mercy, help us to be aware of the injustices of our world, both in our own country and in other parts of the world. Help us to see the people of other countries as our brothers and sisters, and teach us to be concerned about their welfare as well as our own. Thank you for a worldwide understanding of the righteousness of the prophets and the ways of Jesus. Amen.

—given at Brooks-Howell Home, July 7, 1998

Visit to Neighborhood Center

Yesterday I made note of the fact that fifty years ago, June 14th, I was commissioned a deaconess in New York City. I have lived and worked in various capacities in eleven cities and in one rural community, where I served as social worker with a rural consolidated public school for eleven years before retirement.

Over this past weekend I flew to Harrisburg, Pennsylvania, to help the community center there, now known as Neighborhood Center, celebrate ninety years of service and dialogue with their uptown community. The center was started by deaconesses in 1910 to give help to newly arrived immigrants from the Eastern European countries. One of the highlights of my experience was to hear two Orthodox Jewish sisters, who came to help us celebrate this past Friday, and some others who were a part of the center in its early days, lustily singing some of the old, old gospel songs that were sung at the mission in its early years.

Neighborhood Center's clients are now 75 percent black, and the neighborhood in which it sits is one of great deterioration. The purchase of the center's two vans (one brand-new!) was made possible by the arduous collection of labels from Campbell's products, and I was privileged to meet the woman who laboriously cut and counted, cut and counted, cut and counted, day after day, to make that happen.

I was also privileged to meet and talk with the present director, a Harrisburg resident who formerly taught in a business school. A hardheaded businesswoman, she has helped the center to stabilize its finances and look after the maintenance of the building in a very businesslike way. She is also responsible for a staff of 8 full-time people, 14–18 part-time workers, and 1,500 volunteers throughout the year.

This is a community center for which our church can rejoice. My seven years there, long ago, were years of challenging work in a double row house with inadequate space and facilities. Along with all the homes in our community, we were "urban renewed" to make way for an enlargement of the grounds surrounding the state capitol. We purchased a house and worked out a decentralized program using spaces in neighborhood churches and schools as these spaces were available. The present adequate building was built in 1983, and takes up an entire city block. I just cried with joy when I walked into the woodcraft shop, a beautiful room for boys and young men to learn skills that will benefit them throughout their lifetimes. It was a privilege to meet and talk with the staff person who helps these young people.

Yes, there is a preschool. There is also an after-school program, a chess club, a community choir, Cub Scouts and Girl Scouts, a project working on low-income homes for the neighborhood, a teen center, Suzuki piano lessons, a tutoring program, and a wonderful program for young mothers and mothers-to-be.

I was also impressed that the center incorporates a small chapel. The chapel seats not more than twenty people; its altar does not hold denominational symbols. It is very clear that it is open to any religious faith.

Long ago, when I was director of the agency, I was once asked if our purpose there was not to make more Methodists for the church. I think I answered the DS (district superintendent) who asked that question that perhaps that would happen. As I thought about it later, I was very clear in my own mind that our basic purpose in such centers is *not* to make more Methodists but to serve people *at their point of need*. Yes, it is partially supported by Methodist funds. But today, as in former years, it has embraced a wide variety of religious faiths. When we moved with the urban renewal program long ago, we moved into a house that had formerly housed Orthodox Jewish people, and there were mezuzahs on every doorpost. There were still Jewish people in the neighborhood, and they again became some of our members.

Especially today, such centers and other mission projects cannot survive on the support that Methodists give. In this case, about 20 percent of Neighborhood Center's $650,000 budget comes from Methodist giving. Other support comes from program fees, United Way, government grants for specific programs, and the generous support of various foundations. A quotation from 2 Corinthians 9:6–8 says,

> "The point is this: the one who sows sparingly, will also reap sparingly, and the one who sows bountifully will also reap bountifully. Each of you must give as you have made up your mind, not reluctantly or under compulsion, for God loves a cheerful giver. And God is able to provide you with every blessing in abundance, so that by always having enough of everything, you may share abundantly in every good work." (NRSV)

In speaking of this center's work, it is clear that the only way it has survived is to change, change, change, as the neighborhood and community have changed.

Let us pray.

Source of all the love we know, we thank you for the love that you have put within us for your children—our brothers and sisters, wherever and whoever they are. Amen.

—given at Brooks-Howell Home, June 15, 2000

God Bless!

The following brief account comes from a recent copy of *News and Views,* a monthly publication that reprints news articles related to peace and justice. It is published by the Atlanta Friends Meeting. The article is called "A Voice of Kindness in the Night," and was written by Stephanie Salter. It was published originally in a San Francisco newspaper.

Almost 10:30, and here I was shoving a frozen pizza into the toaster oven for a late-late dinner. Messages blinked from the answering machine; unopened mail lay in a formidable stack, and—damn—I still had to haul the garbage can and recycling bin to the curb for the next morning's pickup.

What a way to live.

Out on the sidewalk I heard him long before I saw him coming up the street in the cold, wind-swept darkness; the empty bottles he'd collected clinked against the sides of his supermarket shopping cart.

My blue plastic recycling bin would barely hit the concrete before this man swept by and pulled out aluminum cans, glass bottles, and clear plastic containers. After him, one or two others would roll through in the wee hours, salvaging the super-late deposits.

By dawn, well before official recyclers drove by, nothing would be left in the bins for blocks but bundled newspapers and cardboard—recyclables not worth the weight and precious cart-space for an independent "canner."

Clinking and rattling up the steep street, the man finally came into view a few houses away. He had two shopping carts tethered together and managed to steer the unwieldy pair with one hand. Each time he stopped to sort through a bin, he miraculously got the carts to pause—and stay—on the precarious slope.

He was taller than most canners I see and uncharacteristically erect. So many of them seem bent and shrunken—as much, I suspect, from the cold, wind and rain as from the wearing nature of their work.

Part of me (I blame it on a late-night mugging many years ago) was afraid of him. He wore a dark, hooded sweat-shirt and dark pants. His face, beard and eyes were as dark as the moonless night.

But he's pushing a load of empty bottles up a steep grade at 10:30 P.M., I reminded myself. The fear dissolved.

As he came closer, he hesitated. Instinct told me he was waiting for me to go back inside my house. He is probably accustomed to his mere existence scaring people.

I walked up my front steps through a bright pool of porch light. As I opened the door, I turned back around. He was headed toward my recycling bin. Seeing me, he paused again, then continued. Then his voice—so sweet and with such melody, I thought for a moment he was a 6-foot tall child—said, "Thank you."

My heart just broke.

Thank you, lady, for letting me take your empty wine and mineral water bottles. Thank you for the handful of empty aluminum cans. Thank you for not yelling at me because I'm shuffling along your street with a couple of stolen shopping carts the night before the recycling truck comes so I can drag all this crap to some guy who'll give me 2½ cents for some of the small bottles and 5 cents for containers larger than 2 liters.

With a forced lightness, I said, "Don't work too hard," and shut the door.

It was one of the dumbest, most inappropriate things I've ever uttered. Dumb, dumb, dumb. So I opened the door and stepped back out on my porch. The canner was on his way back to his carts. "Hey," I said. "That was a really stupid thing I just said. What I meant was, hang in there, and good luck."

From the street came the sound of the cans moving again up the steep hill. The tall man's voice called through the night: "God bless."[9]

Let us pray.

Gracious God, we thank you for the poor in our midst They keep us aware that they are your rich blessing to us; they have much to teach us. And help us all in our work for justice and a living wage for all of our brothers and sisters. Amen.

—*given at Brooks-Howell Home, September 9, 1999*

Be Grateful to Everyone

On this Thanksgiving morning, it is my privilege to share with you some thoughts about gratitude for *people.* This article showed up in Holy Ground's newsletter.

Holy Ground is an ecumenical women's retreat ministry here in Asheville, started by Dorri Sherrill and Sandra Smith. In the latest edition, they published an article by Debby Genz, who is the coordinator of Emma Family Resource Center, a wonderful nonprofit agency serving the Emma school district. When one travels in that area of West Asheville, the major impression is of many mobile home parks.

In the school, one finds an amazing mixture of very poor people from other countries, some Hispanic, some Eastern European or Russian, and others from other backgrounds. Some of the housing is what were once called projects—federal housing built for the poor in days gone by, and now turned over to private entrepreneurs and rented for inflated prices. West Asheville is the poorest section of our entire community. Emma Family Resource Center operates in a single-wide mobile home placed on the grounds of Emma Elementary School. It is always very crowded, because it is always doing a dozen projects at once. I worked there as a volunteer for almost two years. I recently went to visit again because I work on the Outreach Team at Jubilee!, and a request had come from Emma for additional funds for their community fund, which is used for all kinds of emergencies, including kerosene for heaters, overdue gas bills, sometimes rent, etc. This is a fund to which the community itself also contributes.

In her article Debby says,

> One of the most effective yet challenging practices my Buddhist teacher has given me to work with is the slogan "Be grateful to everyone in your everyday life." Everyone?! That

rude driver of the big SUV who cut me off on Charlotte Street this morning? That irritating colleague at work who is always critical and complaining? Should I be grateful to them?

Buddhist teachings point out that our mistaken belief in a fixed idea of self is the root of the pain and suffering underlying our human existence. We tend to measure everything according to "what is it to me?" We gravitate toward people who think like we do; we reject those who make us feel uncomfortable. We ignore those who appear to have nothing in common with us. Our chronic self-centeredness blinds us to the vivid dance of phenomena going on around us all the time and locks us into a cage of our own making.

The slogans of Lojong practice of which "Be grateful to everyone" is one, are an effective and radical tool to breaking our habit of self-clinging, for opening our heart and allowing us to expand into compassion. These slogans are taught once a student has done the groundwork of taming the mind through mindfulness meditation practice. Then the contemplation and daily application of these slogans is most useful in retraining our minds beyond their usual limited perspective. [*Lojong* is the Tibetan word for "transforming the mind" and is one of the Dalai Lama's main sources of inspiration. The central themes of Lojong include enhancing compassion, cultivating balanced attitudes toward oneself and others, developing positive ways of thinking, and transforming adverse situations into conditions favorable for spiritual development.]

The slogan "Be grateful to everyone" reminds us that our paths are not solo journeys. We learn, we open, we grow through our experiences and interactions. Without rubbing up against others, we'd have no feedback, no reflections to show us where we're stuck. Each time someone gets under our skin, this slogan suggests that instead of reacting with resentment or retaliation, we could appreciate the opportunity to see how attached we still are to our [own] storyline. We could soften rather than harden to our world. As Pema Chodron, author of *Start Where You Are*,[10] expresses it, this slogan means that all situations teach you, and often it is the tough ones that teach you the best. She says that these slogans help us to see that a separate, isolated sense of other is a painful misunderstanding that we could see through and let go.

Joanna Macy, author of *World as Lover, World as Self*, takes this practice a step further, suggesting the following.

> When you see the world as lover, every being, every phenomenon, can become, if you have an appreciative eye, an expression of that ongoing erotic impulse. It takes form right now in each one of us, and in everyone and everything we encounter, the bus driver, the clerk at the checkout counter, the leaping squirrel.[11]

I have long been amazed at how frequently Tibetan teachers express gratitude toward the Chinese who invaded their country, wreaked havoc, and forced their flight from their homeland. Despite the suffering they experienced as a result, they often comment that were it not for the Chinese, we would not now be receiving these wonderful teachings.

The outrageousness of the suggestion that we could be grateful to everyone invites an internal revolution to overthrow our imprisonment in our own egos! The next time you find yourself put off by someone, take a moment and see what lesson is presenting itself. I highly recommend it![12]

Let us pray.

Gracious God, help us to see you in the people we meet each day, and to understand that we can be grateful for each person and our contact with that image of you. Amen

—given at Brooks-Howell Home, November 23, 2000

Thank You, Deaconesses, For Your Good Work

Recently I have received a number of letters from UMW groups in various places, thanking me for my lifetime of service as a deaconess. At least two years ago someone wrote to ask for some material about my work, and I responded. I have found it a very heartwarming experience to receive thank-you's for my life and work. This meditation is dedicated to the deaconesses among us here. It is meant as a thank-you to all of you.

When I have the opportunity to talk with groups of women in our church, I always start with thanking them—because it was their gift to me, through scholarships available at National College that enabled me to go to college and thus become a deaconess. What is now the Women's Division has been, and still is, the strong support of what used to be called "deaconess work" from its beginning. The title of the program this year is "The Gift of a Lifetime." Certainly the women did not know what they were getting when they prepared me for work, nor did I know where life would lead me when I made the decision to be a deaconess. I can only hope that the women have been blessed by my work, as I have been blessed by their faith and trust in me.

The material in the program book speaks of two "buildings" that have resulted from my work. The first of these is in Harrisburg, Pennsylvania, which I discover is Lucy Rowe's hometown; Loise George lived in Harrisburg. Before I moved there, I received information that there were 108 children in one block near the Methodist Mission, as it was then called. This meant one block, two sides of the street, between two cross-streets. Now that's crowded!

Interestingly, the whole area was so crowded that it took

me three months of visiting to be sure which block that information referred to. Our entire area was being demolished in urban renewal, and our agency was relocated, by remodeling a former home/business on a busy street. This home was almost outgrown by the time it was ready, and we worked out a decentralized program, using empty rooms in churches and the public school.

When I left, I challenged the women in that conference with a letter, saying they had a wonderful program but it needed a place to be, and if they could not provide such a place, they needed to celebrate what they had done . . . and simply close up. Or, my letter emphasized, *build to enable the program.*

The letter sat around for some time, and then a good United Methodist woman took hold of it, and believed strongly in the program and knew it should be continued. She made an adequate building happen. That building takes a full city block now, and is the base for the wonderful program available to that neighborhood and community. In addition to twenty-five or so paid staff, the program uses 1,500 volunteers yearly. That, to me, is amazing. This agency celebrated its ninetieth year a few years ago.

In the second instance, in Grand Rapids, Michigan, the two day-care rooms, fairly new, were attached to a much older, small, three-room cottage, which provided space for kitchen/dining area, also used for many other meetings, and a small, former-sunporch office, where people entered. The agency had bought an empty house next door, but only one room was suitable for use as a meeting room. A decent building was badly needed, and plans were drawn and a building was built. It served its purpose and was very well used, until later, again, a United Methodist woman chaired the committee that made possible the larger building that now exists. This was the agency where I flew to Michigan twice last year, to participate in their celebration events, marking a hundred years of service to needy people. Interestingly, this agency was started in 1902 by the women of the church I later joined. They called an early deaconess, Irene Cummings, in 1904 to work with the Syrian people who were then new immigrants. Much later, I learned that some of these families are related to the Syrian people with whom I had worked much earlier in my career, in Toledo, Ohio, also in one of our United Methodist community centers.

Community centers, neighborhood centers, settlement houses, Wesley Houses, Bethlehem Centers, were all part of that earlier grouping of mission work—centers of life and health in the midst of some of the poorest of the poor, all God's children. Many were born as helps to the new immigrants in our country. All were/are located in inner cities, places where poverty and multiple problems of the poor still exist.

There are a number of residents here who have worked in various ways in such centers, and all, even as I, have been blessed immeasurably by knowing, loving, appreciating and partnering with the poor in our midst. Thank you to all of you.

In preparing a recent talk, I ran across a bookmark from some years ago, that speaks clearly of what a deaconess does. I should like to close with that.

> Why Be a Deaconess?
> To eradicate causes of injustice and all that robs life of dignity and worth;
> To alleviate suffering;
> To facilitate the development of full human potential;
> To share in building global community through the church universal;
> To identify with and participate in a fellowship biblical in origin, rich in historical significance, ecumenical and international in outreach, and supportive of present needs.
> —Author unknown[13]

Let us pray.

Good God, thank you for the work of deaconesses. Thank you for the selfless love of many unknown women who have worked in our mission agencies throughout the years, making possible the alleviation of suffering, the eradication of injustice, and the development of full human potential in many unknown places. Thank you for the deaconesses among us here. Help us to appreciate them and love them for who they are. Amen.

—given at Brooks-Howell Home, January 29, 2003

Housing Is Basic to Decent Life

Sometime ago a program at Jubilee! featured an actress who gave some readings. She based her readings on the houses where she had lived, and defined the periods of her own life by her moves into different houses. Our housing often defines who we are.

I came home and did some writing toward my own autobiography by defining and delineating the houses in which I had lived, and the differing places or cities in which these were located. I have slept in some very odd places at different times, mostly one-night stands here and there with speaking or traveling, sometimes camping, but I have never been homeless, nor have I ended up with no place to sleep. Even in Nicaragua, when Cristina was sleeping nine people at night in a place the size of a small two-car garage, or when I slept for several nights on an army cot, I was never without a place to sleep.

On Monday night I spoke to a UMW group. My hostess had told me that I would be staying with one of the women. I slept well in a king-size bed in a lovely big room. In the morning I commented to my overnight hostess that I was pleasantly surprised because I had been told I would be hosted by someone who lived in a mobile home. "You are in a mobile home," she said. "This is a double-wide without furniture." It resembled to me a lovely, rambling country home. It was comfortably furnished, and bore no resemblance to the mobile homes with which I have been familiar.

Eating in town with friends recently, on two separate occasions, I have become aware of condominiums being built in the center of town, in several places, here in Asheville. My thought both times was, "For whom are these being built?" I have been sharply aware of the need for affordable housing in this city, and also of the homeless people here, but instead of low-income housing, we are getting unaffordable condos.

And then I read an article in the recent issue of *The Other Side* that made me sharply aware of the homeless and their needs for housing. It is written by Ed Loring, a Presbyterian pastor who manages the Open Door Community in Atlanta, a place where the homeless are fed, provided the opportunity for showers and changes of clothing as needed, and, for some, employment in the agency. With a friend, I worked there one weekend, and my outstanding memory is that of carrying endless bowls of soup and refills to men who needed food. There we slept on the floor. The thrust of Ed's article is that housing is a most important aspect of changing the lives of the homeless for the better. He says, "We must build a social policy and culture that are rooted in housing for everyone." He notes that having a house or a place to call home needs to precede employment rather than the other way around. The way it is now, one must earn not only the rent for a place to sleep, but in these days, a stiff down payment, or deposit.

He tells the story of George, a homeless man who was able to land a decent job in a local factory. George was very happy, and worked on Monday, his first day, with dignity and renewed hope. That night he went to the shelter and could not sleep because of the rustling, the snoring, the coughing, and the occasional shout of someone saying, "Shut up! I can't sleep!" He rose the next morning at five A.M. and went out to the street, where he was caught in a downpour of rain. He sought shelter under the eaves of a nearby building and waited for the downpour to stop. He was late for work, and was reprimanded. That afternoon he got sleepy and had a hard time staying awake. He slept the next two nights at the shelter, and on Wednesday, at his work, he fell asleep on the job and was fired. He said, "If I just had a place to live, I could have gotten enough sleep and kept my job."

Thus Ed learned that the need is that *housing precedes employment,* instead of the other way around. *Housing also precedes education.* Homeless children have no quiet place in a shelter to study with the concentration they need. Adults who are homeless and are in rehabilitation or study programs face the same dilemma. And it is not easy to carry heavy books and notebooks around from shelter to street to soup kitchen to school, and have no place to put one's things. *Housing also precedes health.* How does one stay healthy sleeping outdoors in rain, sleet, or snow, and picking up germs from often having no toilets to use? Many people cannot take the medicines they need with the regularity that is needed, and they lack the stability needed to pay attention to something besides bare survival. *Housing also precedes evangelization.* Many evangelization programs of all kinds have been tried. The author says that "no church ought to call a person to accept Jesus Christ until it is ready to bring that person into a house and assist in the arduous task of making that house a home." I would add also, before offering a community to give support. We cannot expect the homeless to be sober. Drink and drugs, so easily available, dull the pain and the degradation of homelessness. This is certainly an article that provokes our thoughtfulness.[14]

Some of us have worked with Room in the Inn, here in Asheville, through our churches, and are aware of the homeless women who circulate among us. This is a program by which homeless women are housed for a week at a time in various churches. The program averages twelve or thirteen women per night, many of whom are working and need help until their dilemmas are solved. It has been a pleasure for me to meet and begin to know some of these women by name and face. It is a program that is only a stopgap measure to provide some semblance of routine and stability and decency for the women who come. Even so, the program has found that some women, with this support, have been able to move on to jobs and education and more stability in their lives. That is such a blessing. We can rejoice with that.

Homelessness is a phenomenon of our modern urban life. As our wealth has increased, there has been less thought given to those who are left out of the increasing wealth of some in our society. I recently learned that wealth creates poverty. I had not thought of that balance in that way before, but it makes sense. And so, instead of blaming these people for the circumstances in which they find themselves, we need to recognize that the maldistribution of the gifts of God really does cause problems. It seems to me that the answer is to recognize that the poor ones, too, are a part of our community and our society. They have their own gifts to share with us. The last time we had Room in the Inn at Jubilee!, on the night that I was there, we had the wonderful gift of a musical concert with several of these women singing for the rest of us for a good two hours. It was a great delight!

It is a fact; these are our brothers and sisters. We are all in the business of living on this planet together. May God be with us as we seek to make a decent life for all of us. Amen.

Let us pray.

Gracious God, thank you for our city's awareness of the homeless in our midst and the work that is being done to alleviate some of the suffering related to that problem. Thank you that our churches are aware and involved in this good work. Thank you for the understanding that the homeless, too, are our brothers and sisters. Amen.

—*given at Brooks-Howell Home, June 12, 20002*

Life-giving Center

From the spring 2002 issue of the Neighborhood Center's fund appeal.

March is Women's History Month, and Neighborhood Center has a wonderful history of providing services for women, children, and youth. The two of us—Jeanette Rehrig and Bessie Braxton—have been asked to co-chair Neighborhood Center's Spring Appeal. As two women with a lot of history, we are asking you to be generous in your support of the mission and ministry of Neighborhood Center.

from Mrs. Rehrig:

From the time I first learned about Neighborhood Center, as a volunteer at 610 Maclay Street, I was overjoyed at the many people whose lives were enriched by our programs. I watched children catch the joy of learning and progressing in school to a successful vocation. I saw students feel the love at Neighborhood Center, students who later joined the staff—passing on that love and ambition to others.

This is an organization that has continued to change its programs to meet the changing needs of the community and has shown integrity in its careful spending. Let's support it with our money and prayers.

from Miss Braxton:

The Center means a great deal to me and I am still able to help in a small way. It has always been interested in children, their education, activities, and spiritual life. There has always been someone available to discuss problems and to give guidance to those in need

It amazes me how much the Center has grown in programs, reaching out to people in many different ways. Whenever I go out, I see people that I have known in the past at the Center, and we reminisce about the good old days. There are some families who have sent their children to the Center for three or four generations, and they are glad and happy to tell me about their experiences. Many of these Center alumni have gone to college and with others, are in good jobs.

Neighborhood Center's programs change to meet the changing needs of the community—what doesn't change is the need for Neighborhood Center itself. It is a place where people can come for food, parenting advice, childcare, tutoring, access to healthcare, recreational programs, cultural events, scouting, a cold drink of water, or whatever they need.

Let us pray.

Gracious and Generous God, Our Mother-Father God, you are indeed a generous and giving God. You send the sun and the rain each day, and these come to all no matter who they are. You ask no questions about age or color or sexual preference. You put no restrictions on your gifts—the graceful trees, the blooms of spring, the quiet streams, and the noisy ocean. You give them generously. Teach us so to give—not asking why or when or how much. Teach us, too, to say thank you—for delightful children, for the wonders of spring, and most of all for you, the most Gracious Giver we can ever know. Amen.

—*given at Brooks-Howell Home, April 17, 2002*

A Place to Live

Recently, when I was here, I spoke about homelessness, and what it does to our living. I spoke of how health and education and psychological health are not possible without the first basic—a place to live. This past week, across my desk came a copy of Habitat for Humanity's international newsmagazine, *Habitat World*. The same difficult aspects of life were also talked about in this issue regarding poverty housing. Here are a few statistics from that magazine. The figures come from a number of sources.

-1.1 billion people live worldwide in inadequate conditions in urban areas.
—(United Nations Center for Human Settlements)
-1.3 billion people lack access to clean water.
—(*Global Issues*)
-2.4 billion lack access to sanitation.
-11 million children die each year from preventable diseases like pneumonia, diarrhea, malaria, and measles.
-Nearly 1 billion people are illiterate.
-More than 110 million school-age children are not in school.
-If the world were to invest an extra 30 cents of every $100, all children could be healthy, well-nourished, and in primary school.
—UNICEF
-24 percent of homeless people in the United States have full- or part-time jobs.
—Ohio State University
-There are 35.1 million internally displaced people and refugees worldwide.
—U.S. Committee for Refugees
-There are 100 million homeless people worldwide.
—United Nations

-Homeless people in the United States increased by 24 percent in 2001.

— US Conference of Mayors

-There are 12 million American children living in poverty (5 million live in extreme poverty!) Annual income for a family of three living in poverty is $13,861; annual income for a family living in extreme poverty is $6,930.

—National Center for Children in Poverty

-Of the world's 6 billion people, 2.8 billion (almost half) live on less than $2. a day, and 1.2 billion of them live on less than $1. a day.

—World Bank

The same issues discussed earlier apply also to poverty housing: that is, issues of health, education, mental stability and psychological health, and issues of daily survival.

I worked to get my master's degree in social work at Boston University during the time of the public housing boom. Ed Logue, in Boston, was one of our nationally known figures at that time, widely known for his work with public housing, and particularly for the creation, in Boston, of Columbia Point, a giant housing project—then one of the largest in the nation. It was built to accommodate 2,500 people—2,500 people is a city! When this housing project was built and families moved in, the big fiasco was that it was built on a point of land separated from the remainder of the city, and no one thought to put up one grocery store, Laundromat, drugstore, and any other kind of service accommodation. That was soon remedied, of course, as many enterprises moved in to take advantage of such a large group of citizens.

One of my social work student assignments in Boston was to organize services for the elderly in the Roxbury housing project. This was the project where, a few years later, riots occurred. When I read about the riots there, I thought back about this project, and it was clear to me that the way it was built simply fanned the flames of the riot. I have worked in housing projects in Wilmington, Delaware, and in Nashville, Tennessee. In Boston, in summer work, I visited our elderly clients in housing projects that were seven stories high. The residents all rejoiced when the elevators were working; they were often not working. When the elevators did not work, some residents climbed seven floors to their small apartments. During the year when I was unemployed, I landed a job as a housing project manager in Battle Creek, Michigan—a job I was unable to take because of interesting circumstances, but that is a story for another time. Later, I was very grateful not to have the job.

The testimony of an elderly woman in Nashville, where I worked in a housing project as part of my work in a community center, was something I shall never forget. The housing that she had previously known in a rural area meant broken windows, bitter cold weather in the winter, an outdoor toilet, and no running water or electricity in the house. The house was literally falling down around her. In one of our meetings when there was an opportunity for sharing, she lifted high praise to God for her small three-room apartment, warm and snug and equipped with electricity and running water, and nearby neighbors whom she could enjoy. What a blessing it was to her.

Let us pray.

Gracious God, thank you for groups like Habitat for Humanity, who help to provide homes for families who need them. Thank you for this home in which to live. Thank you for comfortable rooms, for good food, for available toilets and bathing facilities, and for comfortable beds for sleeping and resting. Thank you, God, for friends who are near and health care people to look after us as needed. Thank you for those who care for us, and make this home possible. Thank you for alerting us to brothers and sisters who need places to live, and food to eat. Amen

—*given at Brooks-Howell Home, June 26, 2002*

Elderly Irish in Boston

On Saturday morning, on WCQS-FM, there was a bit about the remembrance held of late to commemorate the Irish famine, years ago, and its influence on the immigration of Irish people to our country. When they sang the famine song, it rang a resounding note in my heart, and tears came to my eyes as I recalled its melody. It took me back in memory to Boston.

My second-year social work field assignment at Boston University was to organize services for the elderly in the Roxbury housing project, which was quite close to Roxbury Neighborhood Center, and was seen as a part of their responsibility. The Roxbury housing project was a very large complex, and I started with visiting some of the elderly in their small apartments. A good-size group was soon on solid ground, well-organized, and moving along, despite people on the edge who were not quite sure they wanted to be a part of the group.

As the group grew, it created a wide variety of activities that spoke to most of the interests represented. This group garnered honorable mention a few years later, on a national level, for their monitoring, at the nearby Massachusetts State House, any legislation pertaining to the elderly. We sometimes sent delegations to speak on legislative issues of concern to our elderly people. Also, in my year's work there, we always had reports to share from home visiting, reports of individuals who were ill, or of people who needed reassurance from others to remain involved in the group.

One day I found myself at the home of a dignified elderly woman. I quickly learned she was Irish—no surprise in Boston!—and she was one of the many who had come to the United States during the great potato famine. As I sat in her small living room, she began to reminisce about her early life. Even now I can recall how, as she told me of her early years, she was engulfed by her experiences from so long ago and far away. It seemed to me a very holy moment, and I sat quietly and listened.

She had been an unwanted child. In those days of the famine, no one wanted one more mouth to feed. As a small child, she was shifted from one relative to another, and because she was the extra one in each family, there was no place for her to sleep. She slept on the cold, damp sod floor. Her storytelling of her sad childhood drew me in. When she told of sometimes hearing the eerie wails of the elfin life of Ireland, I too could hear the eerie wails of the wee ones on the open Irish fields. Even as I remember this event so many years later, it gives me goose bumps as I tell it. It was a very sacred moment.

As a young woman, she had come to America and had found a good life here. The woman was never a regular part of the housing project group itself, but her neighbors kept an eye on her, and made sure she was not forgotten in her small apartment. I have often silently thanked her for giving me this wonderful experience of hearing the wails of the spirit-folk.

In that Boston complex, there was another incident with an older woman that I have never forgotten. When I visited her one day, I found her steaming with anger. She was simply sputtering and somewhat incoherent. When I finally got her story, I did not blame her for being angry. I found myself angry, too!

She had just been moved from one apartment to another. She did not question the necessity of the move. What made her so angry was that, with the move, they had literally taken away her life. She was not well enough to get out much, and her former apartment had faced the main street. From her window, she could watch the life of the city. The public bus system was there, the cars and trucks were there, the walking and talking people were there, and there were often happenings on the street that made her feel that she, too, was still a part of that life. Her new apartment was back on a quiet courtyard, with no such life at all. It was silent and dark and quiet all day long. There was nothing to watch, nothing to see, and nothing to keep her mind stimulated and active. Enough said!

In a way, that is the story of some of our lives here at Brooks-Howell. As we get older, we find ourselves moved further and further toward a quiet life with less going on. We find it a real contrast to our former lives with many people. It is not easy to keep our balance as we make the needed changes to a different life style.

Let us pray.

Gracious God, we thank you for the abundance of life that we have known. Thank you for our experiences with your amazing children—people of different ages who have helped us, each in his or her own way, to know more of you and your compassion. They have helped us to understand your abundant love, shown to us often as they accepted us as workers and those who ministered to them. We thank you for the experiences we have had that have helped us to love you more, and for the delights of the people we have known in the past, as well as those we know here and now.

And now we give you thanks for the food we are about to eat, and for this new good day. Amen.

—*given at Brooks-Howell Home, July 24, 2002*

Missions in Nepal

When I opened the *Prayer Calendar* the other day, I found the following paragraph from our missionaries in Nepal. Our missionaries are Les and Deborah Dornan, who work in Tansen Hospital, a hospital supported through the Presbyterian Church (USA)'s International Health Ministries Office. It is in Kathmandu, Nepal. Deborah's birthday was July 2.

> Once a week Les sleeps at the hospital to cover emergencies. One midnight, a large truck pulled up to the ER and wounded people were unloaded from the back. There had been a bad bus accident several hours from Tansen, so injured passengers were loaded into the truck for transport to the hospital. It was found upon arrival that five people had died in transit. Les spent most of the night dealing with the others. Thank you for your prayers that allow this hospital to function in a country where emergency services are still mostly a dream.[15]

When I read the paragraph, I was reminded of Dr. Bethel Fleming, the first missionary I knew in Nepal. Her husband, Bob, was an ornithologist, and while his wife worked as a doctor, Bob studied the birds of Nepal and wrote a wonderful book about them. I should like to tell you this morning about Bal Kumari, one of the young people whom Dr. Fleming helped. Bal's birthday is July 12.

Several years ago, Barb and I took into our home a young woman named Bal Kumari Rajkarnikar. Bal is from Nepal. She lived with Barbara Crounse and me for almost two years as she studied to be a nurse. We had a great time together. She often called us her crazy sisters!

In Nepal, Dr. Bethel Fleming was a medical doctor in the large hospital, which she helped to start in Kathmandu. One day there came a young girl into the hospital, and she very much needed medical help. This was Bal, who was then fourteen years old. Her family had abandoned her because she was ill and they had no way of getting medical help for her. Furthermore, Bal had "ticked them off," if you will, because twice they had arranged a marriage for her, and Bal had frustrated their attempts. At the last arrangement, she managed to burn her birth certificate, which is a vital—and necessary—part of the wedding ceremony. This caused her great trouble, of course, when she later prepared to come to the States. She was able to manage, however.

When she had become ill, her parents felt they had had enough, and simply abandoned her. I do not know how she found herself in the hospital, but that was her salvation. Dr. Bethel Fleming, at the hospital, gave her the attention she needed, and brought her again to sound health. Bal had not learned to read or write in her own language. The Flemings—Dr. Bethel with her husband, Bob—in effect, adopted her. They taught her reading and writing in Nepalese. Bal wanted to be a nurse, and Dr. Fleming made it possible for her to come to the United States to study.

Bal had a very difficult time with American English, which she had primarily learned before coming here. She was determined to become a nurse, however, and she persisted and worked hard. After living with us and studying at our junior college for two years, she went on to complete her nursing degree at Goshen College, in Indiana. Of course, Barb and I drove down for her graduation.

Bal returned to Nepal twenty years ago. Missionaries who are there today will tell you that Nepal is still a very difficult place for Christian missionaries, and for Christians. Bal worked in the hospital where Dr. Bethel Fleming had worked, and she found it very hard going. Her coworkers were not kind to Christians, and she was that as well as a young woman who had gone to the United States to study, who knew so much more than they did. They did not like it one bit!

Bal finally found her working relationships so difficult that she sought some way out. Years before, a medical doctor had come from England to work as a missionary at the hospital, and he and Bal had become good friends. The doctor had then moved to Australia, where he again worked in a hospital. Bal wrote to him, and finally was able to move to Australia to work there as a nurse. She has worked for some time in Hobart Hospital, in Tasmania. This is the last address I have for her.

I wish I could tell you that I know what has happened to Bal. I cannot tell you that. I have written her several times, but receive no answer from her. My letters have not been returned, however, and so I want to believe that she is still living, although she may be unable to write, for some reason. In her hospital work, she had strained her back and was not able any longer to work with lifting patients and doing the heavy work that is sometimes necessary for a nurse.

I should like to close with the brief glimpse of life in Nepal from Norma Kehrberg, who has just retired from mission work in Nepal. This, too, is from the *Prayer Calendar*.

> Amidst expectant hopes of the advent of democracy in Nepal, there is growing despair, as Nepal is becoming mired in a civil war. There were few material comforts 20 years ago, but at least there was peace. Now, with some marginally increased physical comforts and the freedom of democracy, there is no peace. Pray for the people of this rugged mountainous country who expected and deserve so much more from their elected leadership. Pray for the leaders of the government and of the struggle. Help them to see that without negotiation, there will be no peace. Amazingly, in the midst of a deteriorating situation, the Christian Church continues to grow. Pray for the leaders of the church so that they can lead the indigenous Nepalese church in continued spiritual growth and discipline.[16]

—given at Brooks-Howell Home, July 10, 2002

Nicaragua

Matthew 5:13-16, from *The Message*:

"Let me tell you why you are here. You're here to be salt-seasoning that brings out the God-flavors of this earth. If you lose your saltiness, how will people taste godliness? You've lost your usefulness and will end up in the garbage.

"Here's another way to put it: You're here to be light, bringing out the God-colors in the world. God is not a secret to be kept. We're going public with this, as public as a city on a hill. If I make you light-bearers, you don't think I'm going to hide you under a bucket, do you? I'm putting you on a light stand. Now that I've put you there on a hilltop, on a light stand—shine! Keep open house; be generous with your lives. By opening up to others, you'll prompt people to open up with God, this generous Father in heaven."[17]

Most of you have by now heard that I shall be leaving for Nicaragua next Wednesday morning, for two months. God willing, I will then fly back to Miami, and out to Cancun, and on to Havana, Cuba, for the International Women's Solidarity Conference taking place there, from April 11 through April 21. Hopefully, I'll be at home again on April 22.

I have wondered what I should share with you about Nicaragua. While I am going primarily to rekindle friendships and to give supportive help to our missionaries and others there who are working to help the poor, I will also be rejoicing with the families with whom I lived, and many Nicaraguan friends —many of whom feel they have been forgotten by the outside world.

In 1994, I wrote a free-verse poem about what I would remember about Nicaragua, and I will share that with you, to give you some word-pictures of some of the people I shall be seeing again.

Nicaragua

What shall I remember of Nicaragua?
Perhaps that the word itself is a tongue twister for those who neither know nor care.
Perhaps nothing as the media portrays just now.

No! I'll remember that it was a brief time of hope for those whose dreams touched reality,
And that now it is a dream deferred for all who know the love of God.

What shall I remember of Nicaragua?
The ambush and killing of Ben Linder.
The weekly protest demonstrations at the US embassy against our murderous policies.
The beautiful dance of Roger when our gift bus came rolling in.
The warmth of Cristina's love for her family of six.
The open smile of Carmen as she made tortillas at an open fire.
The joy on the face of Leticia when she greeted me.
The calls of "Abuela" as I walked down the street.
Hearing and reading children's rhymes with Ana Luz.
The healing hands and warm embrace of Peggy our missionary.
The rich blessing of Daysi as she ministered to my needs.
Maria and Ramon and their delightful busy family.
Yami, chattering all the way to the market.
The People s Mass at Batahola Norte.
Hermes and Daysi and their politically split family.
The friendship of Josefina as she practiced her English.
The delight of Rosanna, my godchild.
The five-minute greeting chant of a church when Daniel came.

What shall I remember of Nicaragua?
The devastating shock of the 1990 election.
The tears of Maria, the confusion and deprivation of my families.
The frustration of Ramon with no employment.
Small children working at the traffic lights for a few cordobas.
Mothers begging for food for handicapped little ones.
Distended bellies and children dying.

Thieves on the street.
The myopia of our US foreign policy as it destroys these
  people.
The deep pain and sorrow of watching a friend dying.

What shall I remember of Nicaragua?
Hope resurgent in new beginnings.
Small businesses started in churches, their base of hope and
  faith.
> a sewing cooperative, a bakery,
> a fruit-drying business, a soybean farm,
> a medical clinic, a typing class.

The strong faith that keeps people ever watchful for new
  openings of freedom.
And for aye unto aye, the warm love of God extended to others.

Oh, Nicaragua, I shall remember you!
—Helene R. Hill, March 24, 1994

Shall we pray?

Gracious God, thank you for the experience so many of us have had of knowing faraway people—beloved ones whom we are not now privileged to see but continue to love very deeply. Help us to understand how we ourselves are your light and breath of life for some of your other children. Thank you that you have put yourself within each of us, to be light and life for others, even as they are for us. We know that you are there, ever present, to help and encourage and rejoice with us. And now we give you thanks for this food, and your joy with us. Amen.

—given at Brooks-Howell Home, February 4, 1998

Nicaragua Experiences

I should like to share this morning a bit about Nicaragua and my understandings from that recent trip. I will start with the entrance song of the *Missa Campesina*.

You are the God of the poor,
  The human and simple God,
The God who sweats in the street,
  The God with the weatherbeaten face.
That's why I can talk with you
  The way I talk with my people,
Because you are God the worker,
      And Christ was a worker, too.

You go hand in hand with my people,
  You struggle in countryside and town,
You line up in the work camp
  To get your daily wage.
You eat snow cones there in the park
  With Eusebio, Pancho, and Juan José.
And you even complain about the syrup
  When they don't give you much honey.

I've seen you in the grocery store,
  Eating in the snack bar,
I've seen you selling lottery tickets
  Without being embarrassed by that job.
I've seen you in the gas stations
  Checking the tires of a truck,
And even filling holes along the highway
  In old leather gloves and overalls.

You are the God of the poor,
  The human and simple God,
The God who sweats in the street,
  The God with the weatherbeaten face.

> That's why I can talk to you,
>   The way I talk with my people,
> Because you are God the worker
>   And Christ is a worker, too.[18]

In Nicaragua, I learned more than I wanted to know about this small country now.

In eight short years, it has come to exceed Haiti in its indices of poverty. Everywhere one looks, there are indications of this. The infrastructure has deteriorated badly. People seek any means possible by which to make enough money to put food on the table.

Unemployment is now 70 percent. The systems of education, health care, and social services are in shambles. Education has been privatized, which means that students pay for every expense, and they pay to attend the schools. When the new government came in 1990, the first things eliminated were the preschools and adult education. There was a quick and thorough revision of textbooks at every level to eliminate references to the *campesinos* and/or the Sandinista revolution of 1979.

In the small village of seventy families where our Witness for Peace group spent five nights, we held several meetings in the small school. It broke my heart to become acquainted with Lisette and her cousin, who are already beyond third grade, which is as far as their school goes. These intelligent girls will have no further education because they cannot afford the transportation to attend school in another village.

The health system, too, has been privatized. Government doctors receive fifty-six dollars a month. For the last three months, doctors have been on strike, and many communities are left with no health care beyond that of the nurses. A woman doctor, covering five small villages because she was the only one who served while on strike, talked with us. When one of our group asked if they could initiate such and such a procedure, the doctor said, "We cannot make the decisions that would benefit our people. We are at the mercy of our national debt, and the structural adjustment policies of the World Bank and the International Monetary Fund." These structural adjustment policies, the second round, will now privatize both water and electricity.

Some of you are aware that I came home exhausted—really wiped out. A part of this was the depression which envelops one, when you live day after day with the awareness of such a difficult situation.

In the midst of this stands the Christian Base Community where I was privileged to teach English again, and to attend the "People's Mass" (*Missa Campesina*), when I was in town on Sunday night. I will close with the Credo of that mass, which is a part of every service.

> *Chorus:* I believe in you,
>   Architect, Engineer,
> Artisan, Carpenter
>   Mason and Assembler,
> I believe in you,
>   Constructor of thought,
> Of music and the wind,
> Of peace and love.
>
> I firmly believe, God,
>   That from your generous mind
> All of this world was born;
>   That from your artist's hand
> As a primitivist painter,
>   Beauty flourished;
> The stars and the moon
> , The little homes, the lagoons,
> The small ships navigating
>   Down the river toward the sea,
> The immense coffee plantations,
>   The white cotton fields,
> And the forest that has been mutilated
>   By the criminal hatchet.
>
> I believe in you, worker Christ,
>   Light of light and the true,
> Only begotten Son of God;
>   Who in order to save the world
> Became incarnate in the humble and pure
>   Womb of Mary.

I believe you were beaten,
    Tortured with jeers,
Martyred on the cross
    During the time of Pilate,
The Roman imperialist,
    Shameless and inhuman,
Who by washing his hands
    Wanted to erase the mistake.

I believe in you, companion,
    Human Christ, Worker Christ,
Conqueror of death;
    With your immense sacrifice
You begat the new person
    For freedom.
You are resurrected
    In every arm that is raised
To defend the people
    From the dominating exploiter;
Because you are alive on the ranch,
    In the factory, in the school,
I believe in your struggle
    without surrender,
I believe in your resurrection.[19]

—given at Brooks-Howell Home, May 28, 1998

Hurricane Mitch

I had done some research on another issue for this worship, but that was upstaged by the hurricane named Mitch. Mitch hit the western coast of Nicaragua, the coast it shares with Honduras, and went inland to many other places.

This western part is the area of the country I visited on my first trip to Nicaragua, in 1988. We went through León and Chinandega on our way to a small village called Santo Thomas del Norte on the Honduran border, which, at the time, had been recently attacked by Contra forces. Both of the larger cities, León and Chinandega, are near the Pacific coast and were badly damaged by Mitch. Flooding has also taken place in Managua as well. Jim Brown, from Jubilee! Community Church, has shared with me information from the Center for Development in Central America (CDCA). This newsletter carries the sad story that Cuba immediately sent a planeload of Cuban doctors to help in the emergency, as Cuba often does to countries in need. The government of Nicaragua, now headed by Arnoldo Alemán, sent them home, rather than letting them come into the country to give help. Alemán wants to tightly control all NGOs (nongovernmental organizations) operating in Nicaragua, and has not included any NGOs in discussions regarding disaster response.

Just this past week, I have answered another alert that came through from Nicaragua Network, indicating that Alemán is not permitting any outside aid to Nicaragua unless he can control that aid. From my being there this spring, I knew that this was a big and gritty issue. Alemán wants the NGOs out of the country unless he can control them. One of the ways he is doing that is to heavily tax outside aid. The example given was that of a shipment of rice, valued at $8,100, which Alemán is not permitting to move from the warehouse until a tax of $10,000. is paid for its entrance. There are an estimated twenty to fifty truckloads of help from various groups in the United States and elsewhere that have been sitting in the warehouse until some release is secured for their distribution to the people who need help.

The letter from the CDCA indicates that the best way to send money for the physical help needed now is through the International Red Cross. The alternative is to send it by personal check to people you trust. I would send it directly to our missionaries, or missionaries who work with CEPAD, the Council of Evangelical Churches of Nicaragua.

There are an estimated 13,000 people either stranded and/or made homeless or unaccounted for, so far. There is no doubt that that figure will rise as rescue and search efforts get under way. Many are stranded by flooding, and unable to be rescued. Nicaragua owns only six helicopters.

It is difficult to know what to say, or how to pray, in such a situation. Let me read sections of the letter.

> The island of Ometepe is a mudslide area . . . and we don't have details yet. One farmer arrived yesterday saying that he had lost six people in his family that he knows of, so far. Magdalena has just found out from family in the Chinandega area that she has lost four nieces and nephews . . . all of her brother's children were swept away in the mud. And the information is just beginning to come in. . . . Meanwhile, local prices of basic staples that are now in limited supply (beans, rice, etc.) are skyrocketing in price, adding to the distress.
>
> Please continue to keep the people of Nicaragua in your thoughts and prayers. The folks that we know had no margin of safety, and they are in need, not only of your concrete support, but in need of your bond of strength and friendship as you have expressed it and continue to express it. As they bury their dead, rebuild their homes, and seek food for their families, knowing of your love, prayer, and support will be of immeasurable value. Thank you.

Let us pray.

Gracious God, we sometimes do not know how to pray. We know, however, that you are a loving and gracious God, caring for your children, no matter who they are, and no matter what difficulties they face. We know that your love is always over all. We pray that your presence will be with these our brothers and sisters who are experiencing deep waters. Surround them with the understanding of your love in the midst of their grief and worry. And help us all to begin to understand how to work with your way and will in our lives. Amen.

—given at Brooks-Howell Home, November 5, 1998

Who Remembers the Poor?

I recently received the latest copy of the newsletter of the Center for Development in Central America, or the CDCA, as it is commonly called. Yes, I support it. This group started as a community in North Carolina, and later moved lock, stock, and barrel to work together in Nicaragua. I had learned about them long years ago, in Nicaragua, and when I was there last, in 1998, my friend Neill and I had the opportunity to visit with them at their own location. Their house and now their large community is on the edge of Ciudad Sandino, a city of 100,000 people on the edge of Managua, which has no city services—no water, no electricity, no sewage service. The citizens who live there have made astounding progress in provision for these necessities.

We learned that the central house of their community was formerly owned by the sister of the dictator Somoza, who was overthrown by the Sandinista revolution of 1979. Next door to the house at that time (1998), was a very large open field which was owned by a cooperative, a group of 2,000 farm workers, who produced sesame seed for their living. The people of CDCA supported their work. They also made self-contained, above-ground toilets, and did various kinds of experimental farming.

During Hurricane Mitch, in 1998, the government relocated 1,000 families from the flooded areas near Lake Managua to this open field—a master stroke, indeed. In addition to providing for people who needed to move, it was an effective way to remove one more cooperative from the economy of Nicaragua. Again there was no water, no food, no electricity, no sewage services, and no apparent ways of making a living to support themselves, provided by the government.

Since then, the work of CDCA has centered on the help it can gather for these families. They have helped with toilets, started a sewing co-op, a woodworking co-op, an agricultural co-op, a medical clinic, and other services. Yes, it gladly accepts and houses work teams of all kinds.

From this basis, I should like to read several paragraphs, called "Reflection," in this latest newsletter.

> September 11 - the one year anniversary is coming up. We heard on the news that New York is planning a very fitting remembrance of the day. Ex-mayor Giuliani will read the names at Ground Zero of those who died in the attack.
>
> During the war here in Nicaragua, when people died in battle, their names were called and people responded with *"Presente," "Presente," "Presente"* [How often have I thus responded!] Thus, the people would not let their names be forgotten.
>
> The Vietnam Memorial Wall powerfully carries the names of the U.S. soldiers who died violently in the Vietnam War— so that their names will not be forgotten.
>
> But who remembers the names of the poor? Losing a parent, spouse, sibling, or child in a towering inferno is no more painful than losing a loved one to poverty. Losing a loved one in battle is no more painful than losing one to poverty. All are needless deaths.
>
> And to add insult to injury—many who die in poverty die with no visible means of remembrance—children with no toys for a mother to hold, or no photos for loved ones to frame or to see. We have been asked many times to go to a wake and take pictures of the dead baby or child or father so the family has *something* [Yes, I, too was asked to do that in Nicaragua! And the first time I did it, it really shook me!] We think of all the photos and flowers at Ground Zero and realize that there are often no pictures (of the poor). They are forgotten.
>
> Gandhi said, "Poverty is the worst form of violence." Why? Poverty, like violence, can be prevented. It is crippling. It is destructive and it causes death. But, unlike violence, it is slow, it is usually hidden, and it is accepted.
>
> Poverty is an accepted form of terrorism. The threat of poverty terrorizes people. It is a powerful tool to get the populace to do what you want them to do—Nazi Germany is an excellent case in point.

So poverty is violence, as war is violence. Poverty is terrorism, but in an "acceptable" form.

The question is—who remembers the names of the poor? When will their names be recalled?[20]

I recall the words of Jesus, "Blessed are the poor."

Let us pray from this lovely hymn by Sy Miller and Jill Jackson.

> Let there be peace on earth, and let it begin with me;
> Let there be peace on earth, the peace that was meant to be.
> With God our creator, children all are we.
> Let us walk with each other in perfect harmony.
> Let peace begin with me; let this be the moment now.
> With every step I take, let this be my solemn vow.
> To take each moment, and live each moment
> In peace eternally.
> Let there be peace on earth, and let it begin with me.[21]

Amen.

—given at Brooks-Howell Home, September 14, 2002

Missionary Letter

I should like to express my gratitude for the last two contributions to our morning worship. On Tuesday, LeGrand Smith told us about the march of 200,000 people this past weekend in Washington to protest the possibility of war with Iraq. Yesterday, Ruth Clark told us about the letter that the Deaconess Convocation group, in our recent meeting, sent to Bishop Sharon Brown Christopher, commending her for her strong stand with the Council of Bishops against this proposed war. I should like to share with you this morning, a recent missionary letter from Nicaragua, from Nan and Miguel Mariena, two of our missionaries.

First, a bit about Nicaragua. One of the pieces of news that we have never known from our own country's media is that Nicaragua's revolution in 1979 came directly out of the people's understanding of our common Bible. In 1963, Pope John XXIII instigated a number of reforms in the Catholic Church. One of these was the importance of reading the Bible in one's own language. In Nicaragua, primarily Catholic from the Spanish conquest, the Bible had been read to people in Latin, a language not understood by them. When Bibles became available in Spanish, they were read and studied and began to be understood. There were discussions together, as the people absorbed the stories and began to understand that God is always on the side of the poor. The Exodus story was particularly meaningful. They realized that they must get rid of their own dictator, Somoza, who, with his family, had ruled their country for almost fifty years, to the detriment of the poor. This is how the Sandinista revolution of 1979 came about. This is a shortened version, but it is the true story of what happened in Nicaragua.

The United States knew that they must displace that revolution because Nicaragua was such a good example of what could happen to its neighbors, and our country set about to do so. Thus came the Contra war, with strong monetary support from the United States. It is shameful that our own country interfered in the Nicaraguan election of 1990, which displaced the Sandinistas, and also with the more recent election, in 2001, when Daniel Ortega, the leader in the revolution's government, was again ahead in the polls for election.

In these intervening years, our country has strongly supported the International Monetary Fund, the World Bank, and other corporate impositions in that small country, and now Nicaragua is utterly devastated. With that background, let me read from Nan's recent letter. You should know that Nan and her husband, Phil Mitchell, had gone to Nicaragua as missionaries in 1988, with their two small children, just before I went there later that same year. Phil died in Nicaragua, of natural causes. Nan went through a difficult time while she decided what was best for her family. She then married a Nicaraguan doctor, Miguel Mariena, who was commissioned a missionary by our Board of Global Ministries at the second Global Gathering. This letter is the first after Nan returned to Nicaragua after a recent time in the States. It says, in part:

We are flying over rolling hills covered with frothy snow. We break through the clouds into the late afternoon sky of Nicaragua in rainy season, green, gray and surreal. We're looking at Lake Xolatlan (Managua Lake), the same lake that rose more than twenty feet during Hurricane Mitch four years ago, taking lives and land. I see that the lake is high and is emptying its excess water through a narrow river into vast Lake Cocibolca (or Nicaragua), called the "Sweet Sea" by the conquistadors. From the sky, the tenuous nature of the thin strip of land separating the two lakes reveals that at any time circumstances may restore the historic large single body of water. . . .

We're back in Nicaragua.

On our second afternoon, I'm accosted by the horror of two girls—perhaps a little older than my almost twelve-year-old Nora—in tatters, dirty, with their Gerber jars of glue, going through the trash on our street. Hundreds of homeless children, all victims of multiple forms of abuse, sleep precariously on cardboard at night on the sidewalks, and sniff glue to dull the unbearable pain of their existence.

The newspapers are full of pictures of starving children and chilling headlines like MORE CHILDREN DIE. This is not Biafra; it is Matagalpa [a city in Nicaragua[. Carlos Emilio Lopez, the Ombudsman for Child and Adolescent Rights, describes the 4,000-plus children with severe malnutrition in Matagalpa, where the coffee crisis has fattened the unemployment rate to 75 percent. He begs the Minister of the Family to protect the human rights of these starving children. A peasant organization has been proposing for three years that $25 million dollars be used to bring the 100,000 poorest families (nearly a million people) out of their at-risk status. The proposal would provide them with a milk cow, a pig, chickens, and seed. Where would this truly small amount of money come from? It seems that when governments and international financial institutions provide funding, it is always for things like paying the interest on the external debt (paying themselves) or for projects, supposedly to help the poor, that mainly benefit U.S. commercial interests.

Our first Saturday we walk to Managua's vast Eastern Market, together with thousands of others who make their weekly shopping sojourn. As we walk past one of hundreds of tiny slipshod sheds that serve as little stores, I'm touched by two boys working diligently, preparing hope for the day's sales. About the ages of fourteen and five, their neat and starched appearance is one mark of their mother's hard work to escape poverty. We pass by six or seven old women and men asking for a *limosna* (handout). Usually propped up against a wall, these are fragile souls who have worked and suffered many humiliations their entire lives only to end up begging, alone and scared, struggling to survive to see another dawn.

On our way home we see a little girl about seven in her thin, faded dress, squatting down, spoon-feeding her one-year-old sister at the edge of the road with the most incredible tenderness and care. As our walk ends, I savor the many reminders of why I feel such a profound respect for the poor . . . and the barely existing people around me. Most of them labor tirelessly and honestly, usually in simple, mundane, or degrading tasks to make ends meet, feed hungry children or just survive themselves. . . .

Tomorrow we're making our first trip to the countryside. I

find myself tensing up, preparing myself psychologically for the jolts I'm likely to encounter—unemployment, lack of rain for the crops, and the accompanying desperation of the people. Accompaniment is often the best I can offer.[22]

Nan goes on to make sure that all of us know how to give support to her and Miguel and to our other missionaries in their amazing and often heartbreaking work in the name of Jesus Christ and our wide-flung church.

Let us pray.

Gracious God, we thank you for these courageous people who take your good news to people throughout our world who need to know your love and care. Amen.

—*given at Brooks-Howell Home, October 31, 2002*

Child Labor in Southeast Asia

"God is love." "Jesus loves the little children." "Jesus loves me, this I know." We learned these early in our Christian experience, and even as older adults we continue to hold them sacred and cherish their truth.

We think of childhood as a happy time, a time when children play games and learn to read and write and count their numbers and dream about their futures, and absorb the love and care that are given generously by parents and caring adults.

This past Sunday I gave a book review to the teens at Jubilee! There were a good two dozen of them, ranging from thirteen up. Some of you are aware of the book that has shown up on the UMW reading list this year called *Free the Children*, by Craig Kielburger, with Kevin Major.[23] This past summer I was privileged to meet the author of this book at Chautauqua, where, at eighteen, he was the youngest person ever to speak for the religion department in the Hall of Philosophy. Craig Kielburger, a Canadian who finishes high school this year, was the outstanding experience of my time in Chautauqua last summer.

Craig was twelve years old and in the seventh grade when he read a brief paragraph in the *Toronto Star* that told him about a boy his age, Iqbal Masih, from Pakistan, who had been shot and killed because he had become an outspoken critic of child labor. Iqbal's story was that when he was four years old, he had been sold by his parents for less than sixteen dollars, with the promise that he could go to school, would learn carpet weaving in his spare time, and would receive payment for his work. Instead of schooling or money, he was often chained to the carpet loom, where he tied small knots all day long. He was beaten for mistakes he made, and given watery lentils once a day. There was no schooling, of course. At ten, he was able to escape.

That story started Craig on a long journey himself, as he learned all he could about this and other aspects of child labor, found other young people to join him, and founded a group that has become a worldwide movement to free children from child labor. *Free the Children* is in our library, here at Brooks-Howell. He wrote it at age thirteen, with the help of a competent adult. It traces the beginnings of the movement, to his seven-week journey to South Asia when he was twelve and thirteen, and to what he saw there, firsthand: the conditions and wide-ranging scope of child labor. With notes he took, he documented what the child laborers from various places in Bangladesh, India, Thailand, and Pakistan had to tell him. His companion on the journey was an adult, Alam Rahman, who preserved images with a camera and a camcorder. Alam, a Canadian human rights worker whose parents were from Bangladesh, was Craig's chaperone and friend throughout the trip. The overall coordinator of his trip was UNICEF, known worldwide for its work with children's health and well-being.

Normally, I do not use book reviews for worship, but circumstances alter cases, as they say. I have now read this book twice, and I listened on Monday to a tape from Chautauqua that contained one of Craig's lectures. I've not yet put the book and its vivid pictures of suffering children out of my mind.

One of the most poignant images is that of a pretty eight-year old girl in India, who spent her days pulling apart used medical syringes that had been gathered from hospitals, the streets, and the garbage. She pulled them into three parts and sorted them into three separate bins, where some parts were resold. She wore no protective coverings on her hands; her feet were bare on the soiled floor. If she cut herself, as she sometimes did, there was a bucket of water nearby, and she rinsed off the blood and continued her work. As Craig and his friend talked with her, an older woman came into the room. She said they needed to leave because if the girl's boss found her talking with others, he would beat her.

At the end of the book, Craig asks, "What is a normal childhood?" He contrasts the harsh and difficult life of many children with the pampered life of the children of affluence, and states that both are exploited. *Free the Children* seeks to bring a better balance to both groups of children.

Let us pray.

Gracious God, forgive our lack of caring that our world is one. Forgive us that we have so little understanding of the pain in which so many of our sisters and brothers live. Thank you for these glimpses we have of your children in other parts of our world. Help us to understand that it is only fate by which we have been born into wealth and health and plenty, and others have been born to a life of struggle and hunger. Help us to respect others, no matter who they are, knowing that they, as well as we, are your children. Help us to do what we can to ease their pain and suffering. And now we thank you for our daily bread, and for all of the sustenance we receive from your generous hand. Amen.

—*given at Brooks-Howell Home, May 29, 2002*

Arise, Shine, for Your Light Has Come

A Scripture verse with which we are familiar is one from Isaiah: 60:1. "Arise, shine; for your light has come...." (NRSV)

This is the last day before the new year. On this day it is good to remember that God is eternal and everlasting, and that God dwells within us. Isaiah says, "Arise, shine, for your light has come." God is here, in our everyday lives, not only to comfort and confront us in our living, but also to help us to be light to others. "Arise, shine; for your light has come!"

I have been reading and rereading the account of a woman on trial for murder, for whom the state of Georgia wants the death penalty. It is a moving account. There are those who sanction the killing of people because they see these people as evil. They do not see these convicted people as capable of being redeemed and perhaps rehabilitated for productive and useful lives. It is very clear that our physical lives are not eternal, even though Christians believe in a heaven that belies the deterioration and recycling of the body, that new life may be born from the old. And yet we believe that in our psyches and personalities, very clearly there can be new life from the old.

I should like to share this with you. I found myself moved by it and I hope you will too. It is written by Pam Stevenson, a Mennonite volunteer from Canada, working with her husband Bill at New Hope House, in Georgia. New Hope House is a place where people on death row are nourished, and their families are provided counsel and comfort.

I quote:

> The past month at New Hope House has been a time of 'firsts" for us; being in Georgia, observing a death penalty trial, encountering death row prisoners, meeting families who have lost or may someday lose their loved one by a state killing. The most important lesson we have learned at New Hope

House is that prisoners on death row are real people, not "bogeymen" or "bad guys." Being in their presence has dispelled a lot of our misconceptions concerning who find themselves on the row and why. Discovering that the man or woman on death row is somebody with beliefs, feelings, dreams, disappointments and needs like the rest of us has been somewhat disconcerting because it implies that anyone could be in their position. We have had the chilling experience of seeing the prosecutor point his finger at the defendant and call her "evil itself." It is much easier to justify electrocuting monsters than real and troubled people!

Their families are also real people whose suffering is unimaginable. During the trial Bill and I attended, we came to know and care for the mother of a thirty-year-old female defendant. We quickly learned that in a real sense this mother was on trial too. It is an experience which we will never forget.
. . .

> Jury selection lasts eight days. On breaks and during lunches we huddle together in a protective cocoon in hallways and a cafeteria with the defendant's mother and other relatives. The lack of windows in the tiny courtroom contributes to the sense of alienation from the outside world. Beyond these walls life goes on as usual but for those who await the trial's outcome, the world stands utterly, deathly still.
>
> The trial lasts six days. I toss and turn at night. Bill tells me I am talking in my sleep. The days and nights begin to blur together. A giant weight lies upon my soul. The tension in the court is palpable. The enforced silence of the two striving families screams in pain, horror, anger, confusion, fear. . . . Each day the evidence accumulates, testimony builds upon testimony, arguments escalate, legal wrangling rises to a pitch. Our faces take on a drawn, haggard expression. I feel my heart ache each time I watch the tall, dignified woman ahead of me take her place in the seat directly behind her daughter. I think of my own daughters and stepdaughter and can't begin to imagine how I would manage.
>
> At last the trial comes to a close. The final arguments are

compelling. Both for the defense and the prosecution. How the jury decides its verdict depends solely upon its perception of the truth. But how does one determine the truth? Both the defense and the prosecution use the same facts to arrive at totally opposite conclusions. One version of the truth will set the defendant free. The other will lead to the electric chair.

The verdict is reached in just two hours. I notice the quiet desperation in the mother's demeanor as she glances toward the jury box. I know how hard she has worked at being strong for her daughter's sake. But from my perch on the bench behind her, I have seen her anxiously wringing her hands to keep them from trembling. The vulnerability of the gesture touches me, and I reach out to give her a reassuring hug. When I slip into the wooden pew, she clasps my hands in hers. They are icy cold and trembling uncontrollably. Suddenly I feel my hand being squeezed with amazing force. The verdict is guilty on all counts. As her daughter is led from the courtroom, the mother begins to sob quietly, her breath coming in short, choking gasps. There is nothing any of us can do to stop the tide of mourning.

Within twenty-four hours we return to the hallways outside Courtroom G for the jury sentencing. The small courtroom is packed with spectators, cameras and reporters. Reporters follow the defendant's family to the restroom. Curious bystanders stare and eavesdrop on whispered conversations. There is a feeling of doom that we all try valiantly to shake but can't seem to. . . .

We enter the courtroom. As the jurors take their places in the bar, I fight to quell the bile rising in my throat. I know their decision. It is written on their faces. Yet, hearing the words, "death," "electrocution," and watching the woman ahead of us crumbling under the merciless blow; seeing her daughter mouth the words, "I love you," none of that has helped me grasp the devastating reality that someday she may be executed by the state of Georgia.

In the weeks following the trial, Bill and I have met many families and loved ones of the prisoners on Georgia's death row. Each guest at New Hope House has been a special blessing to us. We have been deeply moved by our trust and appreciation for even the simplest kindness. At times they speak of their loved one, of the event that brought their lives to this terrible predicament, of their shame, their fears, sorrow, hurt, anger and of the bone weariness of the waiting and waiting and waiting. . . . [24]

Some of you will remember that I was moved and shaken by the story of Assata Shakur, a black woman from New York City whom I met in Havana, Cuba, in April. Hearing her story of being convicted for a murder that she could not possibly have committed, and being sentenced to life imprisonment in solitary confinement was a horror I hoped never to hear again. This spiritually beautiful and caring woman has found refuge in Cuba, and has been reunited there with her daughter. And yet I am hearing the same story again in this recent account: a black woman sentenced to be executed for a murder to which her former friend has already been convicted and sentenced! This, to me, is outrageous and demands our concern. Assata helped us to understand that our inner-city areas have been targeted in recent years to "prove," if you will, that black people are evil criminals, and should be imprisoned. And so, our prison population has expanded in recent years, and primarily with black folks. We who are white live our lives in fear because our society has made monsters of others, and dehumanized them by keeping them in poverty and many now in chains.

In closing, I should like to share a litany about the death penalty, using the Scripture with which we started. Please say with me:

Leader: *Arise, shine, for your light has come.*

All: *Arise, shine, for your light has come.*

Leader: *In the second week of December our country executed for the five hundredth time since 1976. Five hundred human beings dead to satisfy the desire for vengeance.*

All: *Arise, shine, for your light has come.*

Leader: *Five hundred families grieve, many in silence, at the death of their loved one.*

All: *Arise, shine, for your light has come.*

Leader: *Over 3,000 men and women wait on death row. Will notice of their execution date come today?*
All: *Arise, shine, for your light has come.*
Leader: *Why do I vigil with a handful of folks outside the prison whenever there is an execution? If I don't protest this barbarity, then my silence condones it.*
All: *Arise, shine, for your light has come.*
Leader: *A petition for a moratorium on the death penalty has come in the mail. Would you like an opportunity to sign it?*
All: *Arise, shine, for your light has come.*

Let us pray.

Gracious God, we thank you for helping us to become aware of the sufferings of our brothers and sisters. Thank you that your light has come. Help us to understand that we are your light in the world in which we live. Amen.

—*given at Brooks-Howell Home, December 31, 1998*

We're All God's Children

Last night, returning from a solidarity meeting of the School of the Americas Watch, l decided to bring you a few excerpts from that meeting, and from an earlier meeting this past week.

Let me start with last night. There was a gathering of probably seventy-five people in the small space of International Link, a community center for people from other countries, in the center of Asheville. The center offers various kinds of help to those seeking to make their way in these United States and in this city. It is often not easy. There are times set for Spanish conversation, for learning English, for tutoring in English for people from other countries, and there are often sale items available from other countries, such as dresses, blouses, and other clothing items.

The gathering last night was a fund-raiser for the two young women from Asheville who have been arrested, and will be tried for what is called crossing the line," at Fort Benning, Georgia, where the School of the Americas still exists, in spite of the massive protests that have taken place against it in recent years. The School of the Americas is also known in Central and South America as the School of Assassins. It has recently been renamed by the Defense Department because of the protests, but the same school, with its same curriculum, remains. It is the place where the military of Central and South American countries are trained in insurgency warfare. The term *insurgency warfare* is the official military (Department of Defense) term for what is known in Central and South American warfare as torture and intimidation and the putting down by any means possible of any protest against the horrible conditions of poverty in which the native people live.

On display last night were the drawings and three-dimensional creations of Katherine Temple, who for her art project in her recent university experience, depicted in this manner the massacre that took place in El Mazote, El Salvador. They are not "pretty" paintings or depictions.

The two young women, Katherine and Clare Hanrahan were on WCQS-FM last week answering questions regarding why they would involve themselves in such a protest, and they defended themselves well. These are two very sharp young women. Their trial will start Tuesday, May 22, and both need our prayers and wholehearted support.

The group sang several songs. Some lines were, "I will never rest until all oppression is ended!" "People like you help people like me go on, go on!"

Fact: People arrested at SOA Watch have served altogether a total of thirty years!

Toward the end of the meeting, a young woman of Hispanic heritage, possibly Mexican, told of her own trial coming up on Monday of this next week, May 21. The situation is this. She was in her apartment, and two policemen came in without knocking. She said to them, "You should knock before you come in." They arrested her for contempt and impertinence. She said they gave no indication of why they were there in the first place. She also said that people who do not speak English are often harassed in this town.

The night before last, I attended a meeting of Women's International League for Peace and Freedom, of which I have been a part from shortly after my move to Asheville. The topic of the meeting was a follow-up to the conference that we had sponsored, along with UNCA, on March 31, called Race Wave, a thorough discussion of the racism that permeates Asheville. At that meeting, we heard a number of stories regarding discrimination against African Americans who live here. We had earlier heard from a former high school student who had told us about how African-American young people are tracked into certain subjects, with little recourse. This young woman told of how she and her mother both had to fight the system to get her into advanced classes, so that she could move on to college. The other night we heard that there are a number of African-American women in the school system, working as aides in classrooms. There are very few black teachers, however, because they are carefully screened out. A number of these aides already have degrees in various disciplines, such as psychology and other areas related to education, but they are employed in our city and county school systems only as classroom aides.

My good friends, this racism has got to go! I am always heartened by reading the Gospels and understanding that Jesus related to all kinds of people. It is very clear that he did not relate only to those who were like him, but he made connections with women, with children, with fishermen and shepherds, with tax collectors and with prostitutes. One of my bumper stickers says RESPECT KNOWS NO COLOR. Respect also knows no gender, no status, no economic class, no age, and no stylish clothing. We are all in this boat together. Life would be much simpler, and also much more fun, if we could appreciate people for the wonderful beings that God made them, rather than looking at things that simply don't matter. When I was quite young, sometime in my teens, I learned a fact of life, and that is that God has spread good intelligence and good sunshine all over the world and among all of God's children—be they of Native American heritage, from Africa or Australia, in prison or out, Pygmies or six feet tall. It is a fact of life—we are all God's children!

Let us pray.

Gracious and abundant God, we love you, not because you are like us, but because your heart is big enough to embrace differences and to love all of your children equally. You constantly challenge us to understand that you are the parent of each and all, no matter who they are. Amen.

—*given at Brooks-Howell Home, May 17, 2001*

Prison Visit

Good morning. This is Helene Hill, with worship. I should like to share with you a bit about my experience of a weekend in November when a friend and I drove to Alderson, West Virginia, to visit a mutual friend in prison.

Geri Solomon, who is director of International Link, a community center in the middle of town and I went together. We went to visit Clare Hanrahan, who is serving a six-month sentence in a federal prison camp for protesting against the School of the Americas a year ago in November. Clare has been given a six-month sentence for trespassing on government property.

The School of the Americas is located at Fort Benning, Georgia, and is the training camp for the military of Central and South America. The school is now called the Western Hemisphere Institute of Security Cooperation. The name has been changed but, as the protesters say, the shame is the same. Here the militaries of Latin American countries are trained in torture and repression, to support the dictators that exist in their countries. Here in Asheville, as in many parts of our country, groups have formed to protest the existence of the school. This year, there were 10,000 protesters at the school. Last year Clare was one of twenty-six who were arrested.

Geri and I left about 5:40 P.M., after her workday was finished. We had good directions, and good roads, and made good time. We had called the Hospitality House ahead of time to let them know to expect us late, and we arrived about 11:30 P.M.

The next morning, after a good breakfast, we drove to the prison, about a mile away. We met Clare, and were privileged to visit with her for approximately four hours. She was delighted to see us. Our noon break was with foods from vending machines. We survived with fruit drinks, preferring to wait to eat a decent meal. Clare was delighted with our company, and briefed us on procedures and rules, which were plentiful. The visiting room was a good size, with six rows of ten chairs each, with rows too far apart for visiting easily. In another section, there were steel picnic tables in a kind of outside shelter with a roof. Down the steps from this was a large playground area, with benches scattered over the grounds, and playground equipment and a space big enough for playing ball. All of this area was surrounded with a high fence.

Saturday is a busy day for visitors, and by late afternoon the outdoor playground area resembled nothing more than a large neighborhood playground, busy with families pursuing their delights in small groups—children swinging, a ball game going, people playing games at the tables and busy in conversation, as each group relished the pleasures of seeing loved ones for such a brief time.

Our impression of Clare was that she was "nervous and fearful," and rightly so! The least infraction can put more time or more severe punishment on any prisoner. Clare is strong mentally and spiritually, but the prison life had "got to her." She told tales that were unreal: like her visiting with someone, and putting her hand across the back of her visitor's chair, and being called to account for that. She was told that her space was the chair and nowhere else. When I asked about the lack of touching, she said that hugs were permitted when the prisoner comes and goes, but not while visiting. No other body touch is permitted because it could involve visitors passing drugs to the prisoners.

In the afternoon time, the two of us were standing at a railing, and I reached out to give Clare a spontaneous hug. She said immediately, "I may pay for that." She made it clear that she could get punishment for that if the guard wanted to "pick it up." So much depends on which guard is on duty, and how that person is feeling that day—his or her mood. She discreetly pointed out one guard who "threw his weight around"; she was not happy with his being on duty. When prisoners come and go to the visiting area, they can be strip-searched before and after.

There is little concern for any health problems that prisoners may have. She spoke of women with cancer and with diabetes who got no attention to their dietary or other needs. Each prisoner is assigned work. Clare's work at first was in the building in which her cell was located, and it was cleaning the toilets and other bathroom facilities. For a while she had the job of picking up cigarette butts outside the building. She had asked for and was fortunate to be assigned to her current job—what was called horticulture, caring for plants. Actually, this was a kind of coursework, with learning experiences. For new prisoners, a small plant is provided, and she had planted many of these in small pots.

Clare spoke of the shoes she was wearing. They were clunky black shoes. She noted that they were the prison issue, and made big blisters on her feet until they were broken in. The alternative shoes cost fifty dollars a pair, and she could not afford them. Clare is part of the War Resisters League, and keeps her income low so that she does not pay taxes, which, as you know, go primarily to fund the military of our country. She noted that her one salvation was the walking she was able to do daily. The prison is in a beautiful setting, and the out-of-doors area is great for restoring one's spirit. Clare had the days counted until she would be free. Her release date, barring any further infractions or changes is January 15. One of the things she looks forward to on coming out is a good vegetarian meal at the Laughing Seed. In normal life, she watches her food intake and eats healthful foods, but in the prison, healthful foods do not exist. There is only white bread, and iceberg lettuce, and vegetables from cans and meats; there is no attention to a healthful diet.

I found myself appalled at the put-downs on every side. A prison beats down one's spirit. Its purpose seems to be to make people docile slaves, existing at the whims of their guards. It is almost impossible to abide happily by the rules and regulations that exist. I was very glad for the experience of visiting, but will carry with me for a long time, the feeling of repression and the beating down of the human spirit.

Let us pray.

Gracious God, help us to value the freedoms we know: the blue skies, the warm sun, the gentle breezes, and the ability to go where we will with joy and a lack of restrictions. Help us to give our respect and encouragement to those who, like Clare, serve prison terms for their beliefs and convictions. Put within us the courage to live by what we believe even though it may bring us persecution and possibly jail terms and heavy fines. Thank you for your strength within us. Amen.

—given at Brooks-Howell Home, December 12, 2001

The Death Penalty

In the last week or so, several items have come across my desk regarding the prison system and the death penalty, and it seemed important to bring these items to your attention. And why not in morning devotions? It is in our devotional life that we express our love for God and all of God's children.

First I will quote parts of an article written by Sister Helen Prejean, whom many of you will remember as the author of *Dead Man Walking*,[25] the account of prisoners on death row in Louisiana. Sister Helen is a good friend of my good friend, Sister Margarita Navarro, in Nicaragua, and is a current nominee for the Nobel Peace Prize. This article appeared in the July 1998 issue of *Holy Ground Newsletter*.

> I have already accompanied three men to their deaths in Louisiana's electric chair and I have "seen with my eyes and touched with my hands" the suffering face of Christ in these "least of these" as they went to their deaths. I have seen the death penalty close up and have no doubt that it is the practice of torture. Conscious human beings anticipate death and die a thousand times before they die. . . .
>
> The death penalty is very much a poor person's issue (90 percent of the 3,200 souls on death row in the United States are poor), and I have found that as a general rule those involved with justice for poor people readily oppose the death penalty whereas those separated from poor people and their struggles readily support it. They are more prone to see poor people as the "enemy." . . .
>
> . . . One of the first acts of the constitutional courts of South Africa (under Nelson Mandela's leadership) was to unconditionally forbid state execution. The leaders of South Africa understand all too well that when governments are given the right to execute their citizens, invariably the deepest prejudices of the society exact full sway in the punishment of those

considered the "dangerous criminal element." How can any government . . . have the purity and integrity to select certain of its citizens for punishment by death? . . .

"I just pray that God holds up my legs," each of the condemned said to me as they were about to walk to their deaths, and from the depths of my soul, from Christ burning within me, I found myself saying, "Look at me. Look at my face. I will be the face of Christ for you." In such an instance the Gospel of Jesus is very distilled: life, not death; mercy and compassion, not vengeance. Surely, our [Gracious God], it is not the will of Christ for us ever to sanction governments to torture and kill in such fashion, even those guilty of terrible crimes.[26]

Then, a few notes from Assata Shakur, a beautiful black woman, now a Cuban citizen, who talked with us in Cuba on my recent trip. This woman has been a political activist since the 1960s, with the Vietnam war and Black Liberation movements. She was targeted by the FBI from college days, as a member of the Black Panthers. In 1973 she was captured and shot in the shoulder. Even though hospitalized, she was chained to her bed and tortured. On trial on false charges, she was accused of murdering a New Jersey state trooper, even though the evidence was clear that she could not possibly have done it. She was given life plus 30 years plus 30 days for contempt of court. She said she could understand the 30 days because the trial was such a farce. The rest of her life was to be spent in solitary. In 1979 she was liberated by friends. After hiding out for a long time, she went to Cuba and became a citizen.

She noted that in New Jersey, 80 percent of the population is white but 80 percent of male prisoners are black; 80 percent of women prisoners are black. In New York, 12 percent of the population is black, but 90 percent of the prisoners are black. "Prisons are the reincarnation of slavery," she said. There are factories in prisons using slave labor. She noted that, since 1979, the female population in prisons has tripled. She said, "Prison is like living permanently in a slave ship." She referred to Jonathan Kozol's book, *Savage Inequalities*.[27] (This is a book that I have just ordered for the library, and would recommend it for your reading if you are interested in children and particularly in racism.)

Our closing prayer comes from a publication called *Take Action, Not Lives*, published by the People of Faith Against the Death Penalty, an Interfaith Program of the North Carolina Council of Churches. The prayer is adapted from a prayer by Sister Helen Prejean.

> *God of Compassion,*
> *You let your rain fall on the just and the unjust.*
>   *Expand and deepen our hearts*
>   *so that we may love as you love,*
>   *even those among us*
> *who have caused the greatest pain by taking life.*
> *For there is in our land a great cry for vengeance*
>   *as we fill up death rows and kill the killers*
>   *in the name of justice, in the name of peace.*
>   *Help us to reach out to victims of violence*
>   *so that our enduring love may help them heal.*
> *God, you strengthen us in the struggle for justice.*
>   *Help us to work tirelessly*
> *For the abolition of state-sanctioned death*
> *and to renew our society in its very heart*
>   *So that violence will be no more.*[28]

Amen.

—given at Brooks-Howell Home, July 30, 1998

NOTES

1. Peterson, *The Message*.

2. Peterson, *The Message*.

3. Title article on compassion, *Holy Ground Newsletter*, IX:3 (March 2003).

4. This statistic was given in a mid-2003 issue of *The Washington Spectator*.

5. Peterson, *The Message*.

6. This poem was accessed from http://www.bartleby.com/104/130.html, October 2003.

7. Bessie Braxton, "Neighborhood Center Memory," *Neighborhood Center Newsletter* (Harrisburg, Pennsylvania, Neighborhood Center, date unknown).

8. Ibid.

9. More publication data than that given in text not available.

10. Pema Chodron, *Start Where You Are* (New York: Random House, 2001).

11. Joanna Macy, *World as Lover, World as* Self (Berkeley, CA: Parallax Press, 1990)

12. Debby Genz, "Be Grateful to Everyone: A Buddhist View of Gratitude," *Holy Ground Newsletter* (Asheville, NC: Holy Ground, late 2003). Used with permission of Deb Genz and of Sandra Smith.

13. This poem was first published in the 1976 edition of the *Book of Discipline* of the UMC. Authorship is not attributed.

14. Ed Loring, "Housing Comes First," *The Other Side* (May-June 2002).

15. Susan Thomas, ed. *Prayer Calendar: A Guide to Prayer for United Methodist Mission, Missionaries, and Deaconesses Around the Globe* (General Board of Global Ministries, United Methodist Church, 2002).

16. Ibid.

17. Peterson, *The Message.*

18. Ernesto Cardenal and Carlos Mejía Godoy, *Missa Campesina* (Publication data and permission sought but not found.).

19. Ernesto Cardenal and Carlos Mejía Godoy, *Missa Campesina* (Publication data and permission sought but not found.).

20. "Reflections" article in newsletter of CDCA, fall 2002.

21. "Let There Be Peace on Earth," by Sy Miller and Jill Jackson. Copyright © 1955, Renewed 1983, by Jan-Lee Music (ASCAP). International Copyright Secured. All Rights Reserved. Reprinted by Permission.

22. Nan Mariena, missionary letter to Helene Hill, September 10, 2002.

23. Craig Kielburger with Kevin Major, *Free the Children* New York: HarperCollins, 2000).

24. This story is taken from a 1998 appeal from New Hope House.

25. Sister Helen Prejean, *Dead Man Walking* (New York: Random House, 1994)

26. Sister Helen Prejean, Letter to Pope John Paul II, reprinted in *Holy Ground Newsletter* (July 1998). Used with permission.

27. Jonathan Kozol, *Savage Inequalities* (New York: HarperCollins, 1992).

28. Sister Helen Prejean, prayer, in People of Faith Against the Death Penalty, *Take Action, Not Lives* (North Carolina: 2003).

About Getting Older

Gratefully Aging

As part of a prayer chain in my church, I was struck a week or so ago when a person showed up on the prayer chain who had broken her ankle. The young woman who called me to prayer described Dori as "an older woman." So, last Sunday, I greeted Dori as she came in, and asked her that personal question, "Dori, do you mind if I ask how old you are?" "Not at all," she replied. "I'm fifty-eight." "Well," I thought to myself, " 'older' depends on the perspective."

There are stages and changes in growing older. Anyone who thinks the changes in our lives stop as we grow older, is simply not very bright. The one thing about life that is steady and sure and unchangeable is that there continue to be changes.

One hears young people bewailing the fact that they've turned thirty, thinking life is over. Well, they've not even begun to live! And some think age forty is a dividing line. Ah, yes! And age fifty is known as "the big 5-0"! Well, most of us are a bit older than any of these young squirts, and we, too, are still changing and growing and understanding that there is much more to come. I surely hope so!

Now for the aches and pains. All of us know from personal experience that aches and pains go with getting older. Our bodies begin to show the wear and tear of our busy useful lives, and show up with things wrong that we never knew existed. In my younger days I talked about my car, which could have 5,297,656 things that could go wrong with it! Well, a car is only a mechanical body, but *our* bodies are physical and psychological and spiritual—and some of us do have some mechanical parts besides! So, as we get older, we begin to understand that many things can go wrong.

Cleo Barber, in her preparations for the "Extravaganza" tomorrow afternoon, has made clear the fact *that there is life after age ninety*! I'm very glad to know that! Several of these 90-pluses will be performing in one way or another tomorrow afternoon. I, for one, find myself looking forward to hearing and seeing them all!! I think that here, we are in a very special place, because we are with others who serve as our mentors and guides as we move through our younger years.

Attitudes toward aging are another matter. I think there is not one of us who has not had some anger inside them because we simply cannot do what we used to enjoy doing! Of course we find substitutes, and you and I both show up with smiles on our faces because we have found satisfactions in life. Instead of climbing the hills and mountains around us, we watch videos of mountain climbers and those who frolic with skis and bobsleds. Instead of playing basketball, now we keep score. And in my case, instead of standing in the heat for hours in Fort Benning, Georgia, (which I can no longer do!) to swell the number of protesters who know the School of Americas must be closed, I quietly host those who are making plans for transportation and housing. Here, in my own home, I will help in any way I can, to spread the word and make their ability to protest an easier accomplishment.

It is not easy to accept the limitations that come with growing older. From a cane to a walker to a wheelchair is simply not a prospect that anyone enjoys contemplating. The loss of our physical abilities is a terrible loss to each of us. In the process of losing our physical abilities, most of us keep our good minds so that we *know* and *understand* and *feel*, to the very end, what is happening to us. The saddest of situations is the one in which we do *not* know, as with those who have Alzheimer's.

What is always good is to know that God is in our midst, in the midst of all of the changes that come to our lives, and that here at Brooks-Howell Home, we are among friends who support us and care about what is happening.

Some of us have been greatly concerned about our Cummings Health Unit. We feel a sense of dread when we think that we, too, may be there someday soon. What if we worked to change all that? What if we make the Cummings Unit a place where we *want* to go, knowing that we will be surrounded by love and cared for by friends here in this community? What if we saw each person in Cummings as a valued child of God, even as we know we are? How would it change your day, if daily, you visited a person in Cummings, and just sat with that person to show that you care?

God is in our midst, and I am very grateful.

In closing, I should like to read again a part of 1 Thessalonians 5:13–18, from the Peterson translation. I am reading only portions.

> Get along among yourselves, each of you doing your part.... Gently encourage the stragglers, and reach out for the exhausted, pulling them to their feet. Be patient with each person, attentive to individual needs.... Look for the best in each other, and always do your best to bring it out..... pray all the time; thank God no matter what happens.[1]

—given at Brooks-Howell Home, September 23, 1999

Getting Old

I have heard several lately say, "Oh, I'm getting so old!" Old age! In the Old Testament old age was much respected and longed for. God told Abraham he would be buried in a "good old age." (Genesis 15:15) Job says, "Wisdom is with the aged and understanding in the length of days." (Proverbs 16:31) The Psalms tell us, "The righteous flourish like the palm tree and grow like a tree in Lebanon. . . . They still bring forth fruit in old age." (Psalms 92:12–14) The men who grow the date palm prize the trees that are a hundred years old because they give the sweetest dates.

Do you know that the Caucasus Mountain region in the former Soviet Union is home to the world's largest well-documented number of people above a hundred years old? A 1970 census placed the region's centenarians at nearly 5,000. Every day on television and/or radio we hear of people who are a hundred or more. So the number is increasing. In the Old Testament, twenty-one individuals over a hundred years of age are listed.

There is plenty of advice urging us to save for our declining years, but most of it is about saving *money*. If we want serenity and security, we ought to save friendships and make new ones, save memories, dreams, books, music. We should give our time and our talent as well as share our worldly goods, so that we have a sense of making a contribution to life.

"I'll soon be dead," the candle said. "I inch by inch decline, but I make light of my sad plight for while I live I shine."[2]

Although the years bring aches and pains that render our muscles inert, one consolation still remains—thank goodness our wrinkles don't hurt!

Think of what old age bestows upon a tree—beauty, strength, and majesty.

You Tell Me I Am Getting Old

You tell me I am getting old. I tell you this is not so!
   The house I live in is worn out, and that, of course, I know.
   It's been in use a long, long time; it's weathered many a gale.
   I'm really not surprised that you think I'm getting frail.

The color is changing in the roof, the windows are getting dim.
   The wall is a bit transparent and I'm looking rather thin.
   The foundation is not so steady as once it used to be.
   My house is rather shaky, but my *house* is not *me*!

My few short years can't make me old. I feel I'm in my youth!
   Eternity lies ahead—a life of joy and truth.
   I'm going to live forever there. Life will go on—it's grand.
   There will be so many friends there—a true and glorious band.

The dweller in my house is young and spry –
   Just starting on a life to last through endless day!
   You see the outside, which is all that most folk see.
   I say you don't understand—you've mixed my *house* with *me*.

—Source unknown

'Tis said and 'Tis true. . . .
The best is yet to come.

This devotion was written and shared by Leola Greene when she was ninety-seven years young. Ms. Greene was a missionary who lived at Brooks-Howell from October 1961, until her death on June 26, 1988. She was a missionary to India, and worked in education. Sarah Margaret Watson shared that when she died, she left a hundred dollars so that residents could have a party in her memory. Her biography can be found in Book I, page ten of the *Life Stories* in the archives room.

   —devotion given sometime ago at Brooks-Howell by Leola Greene
   —given at Brooks-Howell Home, January 8, 1998, by Helene Hill

Facing Death

Some of us find it difficult to deal with death. When Jane Curran, a United Methodist pastor who works with Hospice and is a good friend to Brooks-Howell residents, does sessions with us on helping us deal with facing death, her sessions are always very well attended. Part of the reason, of course, is that Jane is a very well-trained hospice worker and a very good counselor. She is a person who serves us well in that capacity, and we have come to appreciate her sensitive and caring approach in this area of our lives. The basic reason, however, is that death is an unknown to us, and we want to know more about how to meet it.

Over the weekend, I came home from church to find a message on my answering machine from my niece, who asked that I phone her as soon as possible. It was midafternoon before we were able to connect, and I learned then that one of her nieces, a great-niece to me, had been killed the night before in an auto accident. Sagana was in her mid-twenties, and was divorced, and leaves a little girl who is seven.

Shock and grief were the order of the day, and with the facing of other deaths, I have found myself grateful for the small tasks that need doing. They are helpful for working through the grief and sorrow that are a part of facing another's death. I phoned several relatives and friends and ordered flowers and wrote notes to loved ones, especially to two cousins of hers, also great nieces, who had been very close to her.

Death is sometimes unexpected and sudden, as was this. Surely she did not anticipate that her trip home that night would be the last trip she would take. The shock is felt by many people, of course, who must now deal with the loss of an employee, the fact that a wonderful friend is gone, that her bright face will no longer grace her cousins' home, that the fun of being with her will no longer be a part of their lives. It is not easy to adjust to death.

Facing our own death is a different matter, of course. Death will come to all of us, whether suddenly or slowly, whether we anticipate the change or receive it in shock at the suddenness of it. It is not a change that most of us anticipate joyfully. It means change as we move into another phase of life. Our experience with moves on this earth tell us that major moves and changes in our living are not easy. I think I would liken facing our own deaths to our jumping off a very high cliff, and finding it difficult and scary to trust that God will give us the wings we need to reach the next area of life. Sometimes we are able to prepare for the transition, and accept it with joy.

At Jubilee! there are always meditation readings, and a few Sundays ago, there were several regarding death. I recommend reading and contemplating a poem by Mary Oliver, "When death comes." In part, it says the following.

> When it's over, I want to say: all my life
> I was a bride married to amazement.
> I was the bridegroom, taking the world into my arms.
>
> When it's over, I don't want to wonder
> if I have made of my life something particular, and real,
> I don't want to find myself sighing and frightened,
> or full of argument.
>
> I don't want to end up simply having visited this world.[3]

In addition, yesterday, as LeGrand Smith shared with us several pieces of delightful and wonderful music, he used one of my favorites. I suggest you also review the words of that lovely hymn by Anne Warner and R. Lowry, "How Can I Keep from Singing?"

—*given at Brooks-Howell Home, February 6, 2002*

NOTES

1. Peterson, *The Message*.
2. Source unknown.
3. Mary Oliver, "When Death Comes," *New and Selected Poems* (Boston: Beacon Press, 1993).

Praise and Thank You

Praise God

I'd like to start with reading Psalm 98 from the Peterson translation.

> Sing to GOD a brand-new song.
> He's made a world of wonders.
> He rolled up sleeves,
>   He set things right.
> GOD made history with salvation,
>   He showed the world what he could do.
> He remembered to love us, a bonus
>   To his dear family, Israel—indefatigable love.
> The whole earth comes to attention.
>   Look—God's work of salvation!
> Shout your praises to GOD, everybody!
>   Let loose and sing! Strike up the band!
> Round up an orchestra to play for GOD!
>   Add on a hundred-voice choir!
> Feature trumpets and big trombones,
>   Fill the air with praises to GOD!
> Let the sea and its fish give a round of applause,
>   With everything living on earth joining in.
> Let ocean breakers call out, "Encore!"
>   And mountains harmonize the finale—
> A tribute to GOD when he comes,
>   When he comes to set the earth right.
> He'll straighten out the whole world,
>   He'll put the world right, and everyone in it.[1]

Yesterday I read the brief meditation on this psalm in the *Upper Room Disciplines*[2] for today. The author writes that she is not much for shouting her praise, and swinging and swaying and clapping in praise to God, as she sometimes sees on TV. She refers to those who shout and sing loudly and clap their hands in praise, as "showy." I tend to agree with her. That is not the way I usually praise God. I would not feel comfortable praising God in that way. She goes on to make an astute remark. She notes that when she thinks of how much praise she herself seems to need, for even the smallest things that she feels she does well, she wonders how she can withhold her praise of God!

Oh yes, me too! I need to acknowledge my own need for praise, for thank-you's, for appreciation from others in my life. I enjoy getting thank-you notes, and I count on birthday cards and Christmas notes to give me joy. It makes my day when someone notes s/he has seen my letter to the editor, or my article in our own Brooks-Howell newsletter, *Serendipitor.*

And so, I want praise from others; my heart yearns for it and thrives on it. It makes me feel good when someone notices that I've put on a skirt for such and such an occasion, and they express their feeling of being honored. We all like praise, and some of us seem to need more of it than others. Praise gives us a glow deep inside.

What the author is saying is that if we need that much praise, why do we withhold it from God, who has done so much for us?

It is God who has made our amazingly complex and delightful world. It is God who loves us unconditionally, always and at all times and in all places. It is God who has put love in our hearts, and has enabled us to love others and to do good and not harm. It is God who deserves our unceasing praise and acclaim.

Because we are different people, we praise God in many different ways. Not all of us are comfortable with shouts and noisy clapping. Some of us like rock music, and some of us like classical. They are both ways to praise God. We each praise God in our own ways. For some of us it is a quiet praise, and for others it is a more open and noisy praise. The important thing is that we praise God—the God who has made us and keeps us always in good care. The important thing is that we do offer our praise. I often think of the phrase I learned from Doris Armes's father, who, when he said grace on Sunday noons always said, "Thank you, God, for your kind care and keeping." It seemed to me such a gentle, sincere word of praise.

The important thing is not how we praise God, but that we do praise God and return our thanks for the wonderful world and the wonderful life that are ours each day we live.

Let us pray.

Gracious God, we praise you for yourself, beyond our fondest dreams of love, and beyond the best that we can imagine. Thank you that you have put your love within us, and that you have taught us how to love. Amen.

—given at Brooks-Howell Home, May 21, 2003

Several Prayers

A number of us have been meeting on Sunday afternoons to take a new look, in our discussions, at various aspects of our faith and its expressions in the here and now of today. In that process, Ann Janzen and I will be bringing some materials this Sunday afternoon on the Trinity and how we name God. In that connection, I went through the bulletins from Jubilee! for names for God. In the process, I found several prayers that I should like to share with you. All our prayers are in the context of the entire service of worship. There is no Amen, since we move immediately into silent prayer.

The first is dated February 2, 1997.

Goodness is a word that confuses us sometimes, O Holy Kindness. Like the name we call you: *God*, . . . the word *goodness* carries so much cultural baggage that we're not sure what it really means.

Our mothers say, "Be good" and take your medicine because it's "good for you." Our schoolteachers say, "Do your homework, for goodness sake." Our friends say, "Don't be a Goody Two-shoes." Charlie Brown says, "Good Grief!" And our health-nut friends say, "Ben and Jerry's tastes good, but it's not good for you."

We have been told that you, God, are pure goodness, yet ugly and terrible things happen in this life . . . things that don't seem "good" in any way, shape, or form. We have been told that good people are rewarded, but it doesn't seem to always play out that way. What does it mean to be good? What does it mean to be God?

Open our eyes, our hearts, our bodies to a creative awareness of goodness: the goodness of full moons and snowy woods . . . the goodness of howling wolves and suckling babies . . . the goodness of shared grief and released anger . . . the goodness of passionate kisses and compassionate hands . . .

the goodness of breath and silence . . . of silliness and forgiveness . . . the goodness of being alive . . . the goodness of this moment. And maybe when we wake up to the "good" news that we are immersed in goodness, then perhaps we will see that we are also up to our eyeballs in you.[3]

The second is from May 16, 1999.
> How did we forget that we are partners with the plankton and the sparrow?
> How did we forget that we are partners with the ocean and the oak?
> How did we forget that we are partners with the full moon and the howling wind?
> How did we forget that we are partners with the Serbs and Albanians?
>> The Russians and the Nigerians? The atheist and the right-wing fundamentalist?
>
> How did we forget that we are all created by your heart and hand? By your love?
> No wonder we sometimes feel lonely and abandoned . . . or feel we're going it alone . . . or that no one cares . . . or that the world is out to get us.
>
> May we lay down our human arrogance,
>> our religious arrogance,
>> our national arrogance,
>> our racial arrogance,
>> our economic arrogance.
>
> May we lay it all down long enough to remember who we are . . . whose we are . . .
> and what a grand and amazing world we're partners with.

And the last one comes from Mother's Day, 1999.
> When we were being knit together in our mother's womb,
>> *You were there.*
> When we came slipping and sliding into this world,
>> *You were there.*
> When we suckled at our mother's breast,
>> *You were there.*

When we took our first stumbling steps into our mother's arms,
   You were there.
When we fell down and had our boo-boo's kissed,
   You were there.
When we went off to school,
   You were there.
When we were happy and glad,
   You were there.
When we cried and felt lost,
   You were there.

Holy Mother God,
You are there with us
   through birth and death,
   through joy and sorrow . . .
   in our wise and stupid choices
   in our hopes and our fears,
You are there.
Knitting us together, giving us birth,
suckling us, catching us when we fall,
and kissing our boo-boos.

Grant us the great and good sense to do the same . . .
to be the same . . .
for some other part of your great family of creation.[4]

Amen and Amen.

—given at Brooks-Howell Home, May 11, 2000

Saying Thank You

At Jubilee! a banner hangs. My guess is that it was the first one made with the beginning of this community church thirteen years ago. It features the quotation from Meister Eckhart, the early mystic, and it says, "If the only prayer you ever pray is 'Thank you,' that would suffice."

In a recent copy of *The Other Side*, I found a brief meditation that I should like to share. This is a summary of that article. It was titled "The Alchemy of Gratefulness," and was written by Patricia Pearce.

People who are happy tend to be those who are grateful. Often, it is the wealthy who lack gratitude, and it is the poor who express it and/or live it. Sometimes the losses and disappointments in life can strip us of the nonessentials. As one person said, "Now that my house has burned down, I can see the moon rise." From personal experiences in working with the poor, I found a great sense of gratitude for the fun of life. And it is in countries like Haiti and Cuba and Nicaragua that we often find people rejoicing with dance and fun, even though their circumstances are so often desperate.

Learning to give thanks is a spiritual discipline worth cultivating. The gift of thanksgiving enables us to see beauty and hope even in very difficult times. I am reminded of one of our residents in Cummings, our health unit—Linda Frost. Although she finds herself laid out almost flat, day after day, she always has a smile and a positive word about her. It is we who make the choice to sing in the rain.

Usually we have to cultivate such an attitude through practice. It does not come naturally. The author of the *Other Side* article says that, sometimes, at the end of a very difficult day, "I fall into bed in a funk." She notes that she recognizes her need for spiritual discipline, and so she starts, often reluctantly, naming the things for which she is grateful—her warm bed, a place to sleep safely, an indoor toilet. As she moves on, she finds, "my recitation has a snowball effect." She says, "Soon the hardness in my chest has dissipated, and I become more aware of how good it feels when the air fills my lungs as I breathe." She finds her attitude transformed. And so she says, "I discover anew that thanks is not something we give. It is something that gives to us. It is the alchemy that can transform the dross of our mundane lives into shimmering gold that reflects something holy."[5]

Let us pray.

Gracious God, sometimes it is so difficult to say, "Thank you." When days are full of pain and difficulty, we find ourselves complaining rather than praising. It is good to recognize that you are the source of all of our blessings, Thank you for the faith we have in you, and the joy that brings us daily. Amen.

—given at Brooks-Howell Home, January 21, 2003

Thank You, God!

There are many wonderful experiences and understandings coming from our daily lives for which to be thankful to God. I am sure we all remember the early gospel song that said, "Count your blessings, name them one by one." There are many times when we do not feel like saying "Thank you, God," but when we stop to do just that, and to be specific about what we are grateful for, we are amazed at the comfort and joy we find in life. I'd like to recall with you this morning a few of the blessings of my life.

> Thank you, God
>> For the people who live here, and their amazing array of talents and gifts.
>> For your presence and joy within us.
>> For sisters and brothers, cousins and children, grandchildren, and nieces and nephews.
>> For the beauty of our earth, for the sun and rain, the mountains and trees.
>> For hobbies and trips and activities that keep our minds alert.
>> For friends who phone us, and those who come to take us to meetings.
>> For lives well lived and work well done.
>> For books and magazines to read and sunsets to see, for music to hear and a soft cat to feel.
>> For compassionate minds and spirits that heal and bless our days.
>> For the skills of maintenance people who mend our TV's and bring our flowers to bloom.
>
> Thank you for yourself in the midst of our days and in the midst of our lives. How poor our daily rounds would be were it not for the joy you bring to us.

Thank you for pain—we all live with it. No one wants it, but it seems that it mellows us, and gives us gracious spirits.

Thank you for your strong and sure discipline, bringing us up short at times, but also bringing us to a better understanding of your life in our midst.

Thank you for our opportunities to be together and to appreciate each other's company.

Thank you for warm beds and tasty food and legs with which to walk and tongues with which to talk.

Thank you for the constancy and reality of your love in the midst of our common life.

Thank you for yourself—always gracious, always caring, always beyond us, always present, always loving us no matter who we are, or who we think we are. Amen.

—given at Brooks-Howell Home, September 24, 1998

Thank You, Thank You, Thank You!

I should like to start with a few verses from Psalm 138: 1–3, as translated by Eugene Peterson. I quote:

> Thank you! Everything in me says "Thank you!"
> > Angels listen as I sing my thanks.
>
> I kneel in worship facing your holy temple
> > and say it again: "Thank you!"
>
> Thank you for your love
> > Thank you for your faithfulness;
>
> Most holy is your name;
> > Most holy is your Word.
>
> The moment I called you, You stepped in;
> > You made my life large with strength. . . .[6]

"Thank you, God." I find myself saying those simple, yet profound words often during the day. Recently I read a brief meditation about a person who thanked God for the rain on her face as she walked home in the rain—because she had forgotten her umbrella! I remember thinking, I'm not sure I would have thanked God for that!

But it's so good when we can turn the happenings of our days into opportunities to give thanks. So often it seems they are not occasions for thanks. Just as I was ready to walk out the door this morning, the phone rang. And as soon as I hung up, it rang again—and so I was a half hour late to my destination. Yes, I thanked God that I had had both phone calls. They were both important. But I also had a lingering sense of guilt—a feeling of being very sorry to be late.

Sometimes it is difficult to give thanks. Or to be thankful for the everyday things that happen to us. How does one thank God for a knee replacement surgery that doesn't work, that only results in unbearable pain—and more pain? But yes, it could be worse! As someone said the other day when I was complaining, "But you're still alive and you can get around, and you seem quite active." Oh yes! I had forgotten to say, "Thank you, God!"

I am reminded frequently of Meister Eckhart's saying, which hangs on our church wall: IF THE ONLY PRAYER YOU EVER PRAY IS "THANK YOU," THAT WILL SUFFICE.

The words *thank you* do something very special for our souls. They signify an attitude of gratitude. It has struck me that we, who are sometimes Pygmies among the wholesome beings of our universe, often seem to have an overblown sense of our own importance. Perhaps that is how our mission program was born. We feel we have something to give to others who do not believe as we believe. There are untold stories of missionaries who have gone off to other lands to give the people living there the faith that our lives and culture have taught us—and who have become frustrated and sometimes even overbearing because the people living there want to give us their understandings too, and the faith they have found in life. Yes, that is legitimate and good.

We find ourselves frustrated that there are so few "converts" to our way of life. I shall never forget the comment of the African man who could not believe in a God who would be so cruel as to send his son to earth to die Sometimes our faith is so intertwined with our lifestyle and culture that one can hardly see the difference, and the imposition of our faith becomes the imposition of our culture and lifestyle. Thus we have lost the wonderful earth-understandings of the early Native Americans, and the love and appreciation for the land that permeated all of our continent before it was "discovered" long ago. A simple thank-you might have helped us to appreciate that others, too, have understandings of life to offer, and that these are worth listening to.

Thank you carries an attitude that is very different. It implies an appreciation of the other person and his or her gifts to our common life, an understanding that all of us have gifts to share, and that we are interdependent in our life on this planet. We can learn from each other when we learn to say thank you.

Let us pray.

Thank you, God.
Thank you! Everything in me says "Thank you!"
*   Angels listen as I sing my thanks.*
I kneel in worship facing your holy temple
*   And say it again: "Thank you!"*
Thank you for your love
*   Thank you for your faithfulness;*
Most holy is your name;
*   Most holy is your Word.*
The moment I called you, You stepped in;
*   You made my life large with strength. . . .*
Thank you, God. Amen.

Postscript:

Just as I finished writing this, my friend phoned. I told her I had just finished a piece for morning worship and she asked what it was about. When I told her it was about saying thank-you, she said, "I remember when you wrote about that before." Then I too recalled that, yes, I had written an article, long years ago, when I was writing for the African-American newspaper in our city. I wrote regularly about the children and groups in our Community House. One night, I had taken the group of girls who were our "community singers" out to a church, where I told the group about our work and the girls sang several numbers. After the program, the women came up to the girls to thank them for their lovely music. The girls did not know how to receive their thanks, and seemed quite embarrassed. I wrote the article to say that it was often a foreign thought for inner-city girls to think they had something to give that was worth the thanks of other people. And that was exactly why our agency was there—to help them to understand that everyone has gifts to share. And so I continue to pray, "God help us to understand that each one has gifts to share. Help us to say thank you." Amen.

—given at Brooks-Howell Home, July 9, 2003

Thank you, God for wintry days,
    For love that helps us know
Your care in spite of icy blasts
    And dangers wrought by snow.

Our gracious Maker and our God,
    Assist us now to praise,
And give you thanks for health and peace,
    And joys of all our days. Amen.
              —Helene R. Hill, probably 1997
              May be sung to Azmon, CM, #57

When summer comes our thoughts are turned
    To You who cradle all our earth
With food for all, abundant life,
    And gracious gifts beyond all worth.

Forgive us now for careless ease
    With which we waste the gifts you give.
Grant us a care for friend and foe
    That in your love, we all may live. Amen.
              —Helene R. Hill, probably 1997
             May be sung to Old Hundredth, #57

NOTES

1. Peterson, *The Message*.

2. Garlinda Burton, Marjorie Suchocki, and Hyeon Sik Hong, *Upper Room Disciplines 2003: A Book of Daily Devotions* (Nashville, TN: Upper Room Books, 2002).

3. Patricia Pearce, "The Alchemy of Gratefulness," *The Other Side* (November-December 2002).

4. Above prayers from Jubilee! Community bulletins. Used with permission of Rev. Howard Hanger, pastor.

5. Patricia Pearce, "The Alchemy of Gratefulness" *The Other Side* (spring 2003).

6. Peterson, *The Message*.

Bibliography
and
Recommended Reading

Bibliography

Scripture

Peterson, Eugene H. *The Message: The New Testament, Psalms and Proverbs.* Navapress, Colorado Springs, CO, 1993, 1994, 1995.

———. *The Message, Psalms.* Navapress, Colorado Springs, CO, 1994.

———. *The Message.* Navapress. Colorado Springs, CO, 1993.

Metzger, Bruce M., and Roland F. Murphy, editors. *The New Oxford Annotated Bible, with the Apocryphal/Deuteronomical Books*, New Revised Standard Version. New York: Oxford University Press, 1991.

non-Scripture

Albom, Mitch. *Tuesdays with Morrie: An Old Man, a Young Man, and Life's Greatest Lesson.* New York: Broadway Books, 1997.

Armstrong, Karen. *A History of God: the 400-year Quest for Judaism, Christianity and Islam.* New York: Random House, 1994.

Auel, Jean. *The Shelters of Stone.* New York: Bantam Books, 2003.

Blindell, Grace. *What is Creation-Centered Spirituality?* London: Association for Creation Spirituality, Centre for Creation Spirituality, 2001.

Buechner, Frederick. *Telling Secrets: A Memoir.* San Francisco: Harper/San Francisco, 1991.

Camara, Dom Helder. *Hoping Against All Hope.* Translated by Matthew J. O'Connell. Maryknoll, New York: Orbis Books, 1987.

Chittister, Joan D. *Fragments of the Face of God.* With icons by Robert Lentz. Maryknoll, New York: Orbis Books, 1996.

Condren, Mary. The *Serpent and the Goddess: Women, Religion, and Power in Celtic Ireland.* New York: Harper-Collins, 1989.

Daly, Mary. *Beyond God the Father: Toward a Philosophy of Women's Liberation.* Boston: Beacon Press, 1985.

———. Gyn/Ecology: The Metaethics of Radical Feminism. Boston: Beacon Press, 1978.

———. *Pure Lust: Elemental Feminist Philosophy.* London: The Women's Press, 2001.

Eisler, Riane. *The Chalice and the Blade: Our History, Our Future.* San Francisco: Harper / San Francisco, 1987.

Fiorenza, Elizabeth Schüssler. *Bread Not Stone The Challenge of Feminist Biblical Interpretation.* Boston: Beacon Press, 1984.

Forbes, James. *The Holy Spirit and Preaching.* Nashville: The Abingdon Press, 1989.

Fox, Matthew. *Original Blessing.* Santa Fe: Bear and Company, 1983.

Hall, Douglas John, and Rosemary Radford Ruether. *God and the Nations.* Minneapolis: Fortress Press, 1995.

Hanrahan, Clare. *Jailed for Justice.* Asheville, NC: Brave Ulysses Books, 2002.

Hayner, Vance H. *By the Still Waters.* Fleming H. Revell Co., 1934.

Hobe, Phyllis, ed. *Faithful Guardians: Listening to Animals.* Trans. by Edmund Colledge, SJ, and James Walsh, SJ. Boston: Paulist Press, 2001.

Julian of Norwich. *The Life of the Soul: The Wisdom of Julian of Norwich.* Translated by Edmund Colledge, OSA, and James Walsh, SJ. Boston: Paulist Press, 1996.

Kielburger, Craig, and Kevin Major. *Free the Children.* New York: Harper Collins, 2000.

King, Martin Luther, Jr. *Strength to Love.* Minneapolis: Augsburg Press, 1989.

Kozol, Jonathon. *Savage Inequalities.* New York: Harper Collins, 1992.

McFague, Sallie. *Models of God: Theology for an Ecumenical, Nuclear Age.* Philadelphia: Fortress Press, 1987.

Prejean, Sister Helen. *Dead Man Walking.* New York: Random House, 1994.

Ruether, Rosemary Radford, *Sexism and God-Talk: Toward a Feminist Theology.* Boston: Beacon Press, 1983.

———, *Women and Redemption: A Theological History.* Minneapolis: Fortress Press, 1998.

———. *Women-Church: Theology and Practice.* San Francisco: Harper and Row, 1960.

———. *Womanguides: Readings Toward a Feminist Theology.* Boston: Beacon Press, 1985.

Ruether, Rosemary Radford, ed. *Gender, Ethnicity, and Religion: Views from the Other Side.* Minneapolis: Fortress Press, 2002.

———, ed. *Women, Healing Earth: Third World Women on Ecology, Feminism, and Religion.* Maryknoll, NY: Orbis Books, 2003. Copyright 1996 by Orbis Books for the individual authors.

Ruether, Rosemary, and Eleanor McLaughlin. *Women of Spirit: Female Leadership in the Jewish and Christian Traditions.* New York: Simon and Schuster, 1979.

Schaef, Anne Wilson. *Meditations for Women Who Do Too Much.* New York: Harper and Row, 1990.

Solle, Dorothee. *Revolutionary Forgiveness: Feminist Reflections on Nicaragua.* Maryknoll, NY: Orbis Books, 1987.

Suchocki, Marjorie Hewitt. *God, Christ, Church: A Practical Guide to Process Theology.* rev. ed. New York: Crossroad, 1989.

Thistlethwaite, Susan Brooks. *Sex, Race and God: Christian Feminism in Black and White.* New York: Crossroad Publishing Co, 1989.

Tillman, Elizabeth Brockwell, and Earl Wolf. *Discovering Great Lakes Dunes.* Michigan State University Extension Service, Michigan Sea Grant and Gillette Natural History Association, 1998.

Upper Room Disciplines: A Book of Daily Devotions. Nashville: Upper Room Books, 2002, 2003, 2004.

Walker, Alice. *Anything We Love Can Be Saved.* New York: Random House, 1997.

Walker, Barbara G. *The Crone.* San Francisco: Harper Collins, 1988.

Warren, Ina W. *Care and Feeding of the Natural Rituals of our Lives: An Earthy Almanac Guide for Greening Worship Services.* Year C, vol. 1 of 3, 1998. Unpublished.

West, Cornel, and Kelvin Shawn Sealey. *Restoring Hope: Conversations on the Future of Black America.* Boston: Beacon Press, 1997.

Other Recommended Readings

Fletcher, Geace Nies. *The Fabulous Flemings of Kathmandu*. New York: E. P. Dutton, 1964.

Take Action—Not Lives, Newsletter of People of Faith Against the Death Penalty, 110 W. Main Street, Suite 2-G, Carrboro, NC, 27510.

Susan Thomas, ed. *Prayer Calendar, 2002: A Guide to Prayer for United Methodist Mission, Missionaries, and Deaconesses Around the Globe*. New York: General Board of Global Ministries, The United Methodist Church, 475 Riverside Drive, New York, NY, 10115.

About the Author

HELENE HILL grew up in Toledo. Ohio, a strong workmen's town, in a working-class family. In college, she made the decision to be a social worker. Her training as a deaconess of the United Methodist Church gave her the spiritual and educational background to express her work in terms of her faith. Thus, as she formulated her pieces for morning worship , it is not surprising that these pieces, orally given, became an expression of that faith.

The author is the fifth child and first girl in a family of six. As a child she was often teased by those big brothers. They were precious anyway! When she was twelve years old, their mother died, and the family split apart, with brothers going to relatives, and the two daughters staying with Dad, who soon remarried. After many changes, Helene found herself attending a small deaconess training college, in the context of what is now the United Methodist Church. This was National College, in Kansas City, Missouri, which has now become St. Paul's Theological Seminary. It was far away from her home in Toledo, Ohio, where she had grown up.

Here she began to get her feet on the ground with the possibilities of work in what is now the United Methodist Church. One might say she just "slipped into it," but it fit, and she stayed with it. She worked with the Department of Community Centers of what is now the Board of Global Ministries of the United Methodist Church for thirty years, in several states. One might say that she learned about urban poverty by working in the midst of it.

The last eleven years of her work-life were spent as school social worker in a large public, rural consolidated school in Michigan. Here she learned, again from the inside, about rural poverty. Along the way, in and out, she has continued to be interested in theology and "the God-business." She became a commissioned deaconess in the church in 1950, and that relationship shaped and formed her life. When diaconal ministry became an option, she became commissioned with that designation in the West Michigan Conference of the UM Church. She is still close to the United Methodist Church.

Later education meant an undergraduate degree in education from Northwestern, a master's in social welfare from Boston University, and six months as the Georgia Harkness Scholar in Residence at Garrett Theological Seminary, where she studied liberation theology and feminist theology.

Along the way, she began to travel the world, at first with worldwide deaconess meetings, and later with the boldness of a person at ease in the world. As retirement approached, she began to read about what might be possible in her later years, and made the decision to help Nicaragua with its revolution. She went briefly to explore, with a Witness for Peace delegation, in 1987, came back to learn the language, and then returned to live there and give what help she could. She went as a volunteer, but felt that this was the most significant part of her working life! The experience gave her life a new direction, as she returned to the United States, to help educate the entire church about the poor of our world, and the connections between our ways of wealthy life, and the poverty-stricken "Third World."

Today Helene continues "exploring" our faith and what it means in our everyday lives. The context of her faith has always been the everyday work she does—teaching a child, helping adults to understand the mission work they support, stopping to visit a sick neighbor, picking up a mess of paper on the street, writing letters to prisoners and to legislators, teaching English as a second language. She has always been a "doer," and is convinced that faith does not mean much until it is related to the "every-dayness" of life. To her, faith is the solid base and frame of life—and makes all else possible.

Here in *A Faith Expressed*, Helene offers a simple expression in the every-dayness of some Morning Devotions from Brooks-Howell Home, her retirement home in Asheville, North Carolina, hoping that it may help others to see a larger and more tolerant, loving God than many of us seem to know.

About the Illustrator

NAOMI RUTH GLEASON WRAY was raised in Detroit, where she and her family was active in St. James Methodist Church. During her growing-up years, Naomi also took art classes and used her artistic abilities in a variety of ways. She earned her BFA in studio art and an art teaching certificate at Wayne State University in Detroit.

After beginning graduate studies, she became a short-term (I-3) missionary of the Methodist Church with the Woman's Division of the Board of Missions. Under the three-year program Naomi taught art and related subjects for teacher education in India. While there, she established a library at Hawa Bagh Women's Training College in Jabalpur, India.

In 1956 she married Fred Wray, a fellow I-3 who had served in India as pastor. Together they attended Boston University for a year of graduate study, where Naomi finished a degree in fine arts (art history). They then returned to India.

Until 1993, Fred and Naomi served in India in several different locations and positions, while also rasing their family. On both the undergraduate and graduate levels, Naomi has taught history of art and architecture, archaeological methods, and how the arts integrate with church needs in education and creative worship. Wherever possible, she emphasized Indian Christian art and integrated her curricula with other departmental disciplines, like music.

In 1999, six years after the couple retired to Virginia to be close to their seven grandchildren, Fred died of cancer. Three years later Naomi moved to Brooks-Howell Home.

She is currently acting as agent for Frank Wesley, India's foremost Christian artist, about whom she published a book (now out of print). Besides her own artwork, Naomi's current projects include writing a new book about the Christian art of India, and arranging exhibitions of Indian Christian art in seminaries, colleges, and churches throughout the USA.